THE FAITHFUL SCRIBE

THE
faithful
SCRIBE

A STORY OF ISLAM,
PAKISTAN, FAMILY, AND WAR

Shahan Mufti

OTHER PRESS
NEW YORK

Production Editor: Yvonne E. Cárdenas
Book design: Jennifer Daddio/Bookmark Design & Media, Inc.
This book was set in 13.4 pt Mrs. Eaves by Alpha Design & Composition of Pittsfield, NH.

Maps on page x by Valerie M. Sebestyen.

1 3 5 7 9 10 8 6 4 2

Library of Congress Cataloging-in-Publication Data

Mufti, Shahan, 1981–
The faithful scribe : a story of Islam, Pakistan, family, and war / by Shahan Mufti.
pages cm.
ISBN 978-1-59051-505-1 (hardcover) — ISBN 978-1-59051-506-8 (ebook)
1. Mufti, Shahan, 1981– 2. Mufti, Shahan, 1981–Family. 3. Islam and
culture—Pakistan. 4. Islam and politics—Pakistan. 5. India-Pakistan Conflict, 1971.
6. Pakistan—History. 7. Pakistan—Biography. I. Title.
DS385.M83A3 2013
929.2095491—dc23
2013000897

Author's Note: This book is entirely a work of nonfiction based on real events. I have drawn
facts from my own memory, my reporting of events, which occasionally relied on memories of
others about events in their own lives, or their memory of the memories relayed by others.
I have also used works of written history that have been recorded, over many eras,
by recognized historians from around the world. In all cases, I have strived to be as
accurate as possible in portraying events and characters of the past and present.

FOR AMMA AND ABBU

If all the trees on earth were pens and all the seas,

with seven more seas besides, were ink,

still God's words would not run out.

—THE QURAN 31:27

Mufti–Qazi Family Tree

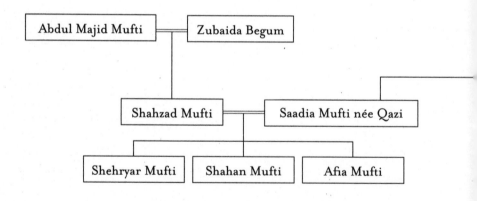

* This family tree includes only names mentioned in this book.

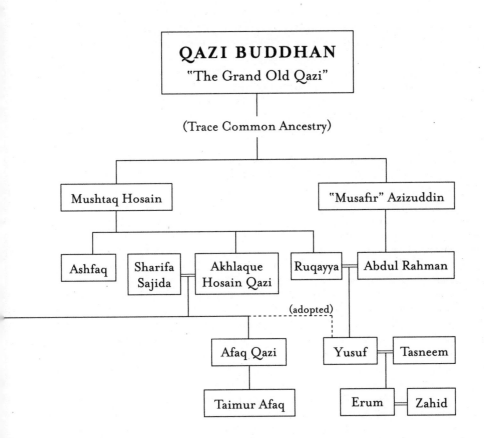

QAZI BUDDHAN
"The Grand Old Qazi"

(Trace Common Ancestry)

Mushtaq Hosain

"Musafir" Azizuddin

Ashfaq

Sharifa Sajida

Akhlaque Hosain Qazi

Ruqayya

Abdul Rahman

(adopted)

Afaq Qazi

Yusuf

Tasneem

Taimur Afaq

Erum

Zahid

Pakistan and Surrounding Region

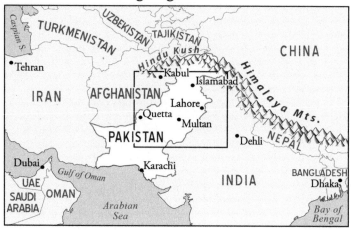

The Land of Five Rivers

Region of Kashmir
Administered by Pakistan;
Claimed by India

Region of Kashmir
Administered by India;
Claimed by Pakistan

Home

IF WE MEET at a party in New York you might ask me where I'm from. People usually end up asking me that. It's not that I'm very exotic looking. I am average height, slim, and I have ambiguously brown skin. I wear those dark-framed glasses that are pervasive in the legions of writers and journalists who find their way into this city, and I have plentiful facial hair that swells and recedes depending on the number of deadlines I am juggling. None of this makes me stand out terribly in New York. This is a city where the trains are filled with people from all countries of the world, each person with his own surprising story. That's one of the things I love most about being here. What might make you wonder about me is my language, specifically, the way in which I use and pronounce words. At first my American-accented English sounds perfectly natural. You will likely assume that I am American, and you will be right. I am American, and so you might judge it impertinent to explore my ethnic background. But in the flow of conversation, I might use a word—"supper" instead of "dinner" maybe—that pricks your ears as unusual. Or I might just launch, with passion, into a monologue about the sport of cricket. Then, spotting the lull in conversation, you may finally lean in and, over the pleasing din of courteous conversation, ask, "So, where are you from?"

"Pakistan," I will reply. "Well, my parents were both born in Pakistan." I was born in the American Midwest, but I have shuttled back and forth between America and Pakistan for my entire life. A year here, four years there, five months here, two weeks there; if I sit down to count it all, I might discover that I have split my time equally in the two countries down to the exact number of months. I'll tell you, "I'm 100 percent American and 100 percent Pakistani." It's true. Both countries and cultures are equally home to me. You might ask me where in Pakistan my family is from. I would tell you Lahore, and explain that it is the heart of the region in Pakistan known as the Punjab. I speak Urdu and Punjabi just as well as I speak English. For this reason, working as a reporter in Pakistan has been easier for me than it is for most other American journalists. And no, no one in Pakistan would think I'm from anywhere other than Pakistan.

I know that in your mind you linger on that word: Pakistan. No matter where you've been for the past decade, you've probably heard of this place, and often. You probably recognize the word well. It's a pop of a gunshot in the room. "Pakistan!" During the past few years you have been bombarded with information, images, ideas about this country, much more than you can recollect at this moment. But there are basic impressions: it is next to Afghanistan; it is next to India; it's Muslim; it has nuclear bombs, many nuclear bombs; it's the place where a man named Osama bin Laden was finally found. Whatever specific details you can recall are probably more or less accurate. So while I speak, you will be thinking of that Pakistan. But I also am thinking, as I speak to you, about the place that you picture in your mind—and to me it looks like a caricature, a dark parody.

Later in the evening, we might find ourselves together again, a group of common friends sitting around a coffee table loaded with empty glasses and half-eaten hors d'oeuvres. More comfortable and familiar, the conversation might flow more freely now and more honestly. Why is Pakistan such a mess? It's a fair question, but unless you have a few days to talk about this, I will try to point to the kernel of the problem. Pakistan is a unique country, and so it has unique problems. In August 1947, months before the state of Israel was created as a refuge for a nation of Jewish people, Pakistan came on the map as a home for all the Muslims scattered over South Asia. These Muslims were from dozens of different races and ethnicities and they spoke dozens of different languages and dialects. The one hundred million Muslims living in South Asia in 1947 made up more than a quarter of the world's Muslim population. Millions of Muslims packed up the stuff of their lives and migrated to this new state that hot summer, and Pakistan became the world's largest Muslim country at the time.

It was a remarkable new state. Most other Muslim countries that had won independence from European colonial rule during the twentieth century came to be ruled by kings or emperors or emirs. But Pakistan, emulating countries in Europe and America, aspired to become a constitutional democracy. Turkey was another Muslim-majority country that was formed as a constitutional republic after the First World War, and it self-consciously modeled itself after European countries as a staunchly secular state. But in Pakistan's case there was an important and fateful twist: Pakistan strove to incorporate Islam into its constitutional democracy.

The first Pakistani constitution declared the country a "democratic state" that would be guided by "principles of democracy, freedom, equality, tolerance and social justice as enunciated by Islam." While in one passage it stated that "the Muslims of Pakistan should be enabled individually and collectively to order their lives in accordance with the teachings and requirements of Islam," in the next it promised "adequate provision" for minorities "freely to profess and practice their religion and develop their culture." The first article of the constitution gave the country a name: "Islamic Republic of Pakistan." It was the world's first Islamic democracy. President Harry Truman of the United States wrote a letter to Muhammad Ali Jinnah, Pakistan's founding father, to tell him that the new country "embarks on its course with the firm friendship and good will of the United States of America." There had never been a constitution quite like Pakistan's before, and there has never really been a state like it ever since. This unique birth, I will suggest to you, is really when Pakistan's troubles began.

It had to be this way. The country was to be home to millions of people who did not share one language or ethnicity and sometimes engaged in vastly different cultural practices. The people of Pakistan did share a common religious identity; they were nearly all Muslim. And so it was hoped that despite all differences, this common Islamic identity would seal the nation. From the very beginning, people doubted that such a nation could ever work, and it was always going to be a tough challenge for a young state. Pakistan's experiment in Islam has been afflicted from the very beginning; the country's military has consistently disrupted democratic evolution, and the people's chosen representatives have failed, again and again, to live up to their promises. But the truth is that conditions outside the country never really helped, either. Pakistan sits right at the crossroads of the Middle East and South, Central, and East Asia. Just consider Pakistan's neighbors: China is to the northeast; India lines the eastern border; Afghanistan and Iran are to the west; the Persian Gulf nibbles on the southern coastline. It's a tough and volatile neighborhood.

And then, of course, there's America. It's very far away, but for better or for worse, America has been there at every tortuous twist and turn in Pakistan's modern history. Other countries in the world might be able to draw an imaginary line in time between the end of the Cold War and the beginning of the War on Terror, but for Pakistan, America's first global war bled fluidly into the next. The Cold War finished in Afghanistan and the War on Terror began there, and both times America chose to fight its war through Pakistan. America and Pakistan, my two countries, have been locked in a tormented embrace for my entire life and ever since Pakistan became an independent state. This nearly perpetual state of international war has taken its toll on Pakistan, but it's not all America's fault. To blame America would be a lazy explanation for the deep problems of a complex country.

I am a journalist and I have covered this latest global war from the front lines in Pakistan, and people sometimes ask me about the violence I have witnessed. Many thousands of people have died in Pakistan. Many have died by the bombs dropped from the robotic airplanes, called drones, which the CIA flies remotely over villages and towns in Pakistan's northwest. But the great majority of Pakistanis have violently died at the hands of other Pakistanis. Why are Americans bombing Pakistani villages? Why are Pakistanis murdering each other in extraordinary numbers? This violence is difficult to explain. All violence, I find, is difficult to explain. To be honest, I do not fully understand the reasons why people take each other's lives, but I have seen plenty of violence and so I know that there cannot be a singular, easy reason to explain every life lost.

I could try to describe the violence to you. I could try my best to explain how sizzling slabs of human flesh tend to cling to the walls or hang limply and quietly from tree branches after a bomb has ripped through a bustling marketplace with deadly ease. I could describe the trajectory along which a suicide bomber's limbs tend to scatter and what that might tell us about the kinds of explosives he is using. But you probably don't want to hear all this right now, and I don't like talking about this much either. So I will sanitize this talk of violence.

I might speak abstractly about "military offensives" and "tactical leverage" and "political motives" and "instability."

Still, conversation about violence always becomes too morbid and too gloomy to continue. Exhausted by our collective curiosity about the world faraway, we might just drift back closer to home, back to the lighter experiences of being. We might chat about the richness and poorness of life in our shared city, New York. Maybe someone has discovered the best food-truck selling fish tacos deep in Queens. And as people begin shuffling out the door I would call after you. Clasping your hand, I would bid you a fond farewell. I would tell you that I sincerely hope we meet again at "one of these things."

The truth is, I would feel good about our encounter. I am caught in a war between two places I inhabit simultaneously. Pakistanis frequently kill American soldiers in Afghanistan. Pakistanis have tried to attack and kill civilians in many cities around the world. The American military and the CIA, meanwhile, will likely kill many more Pakistanis in any given week. The militaries of the two countries, all handshakes and stiff smiles for the cameras, seem to extract special satisfaction from terrorizing each other. The two countries are entangled in a secretive war that is unlike any other in the world. And that is why I would feel especially good about our meeting, because amid all the lying and cheating and killing and all the cloak-and-dagger diplomacy, I would have been able to tell you at least some of my story. I live for these moments of storytelling.

But I must be honest: I also know that I failed once again to explain the real story about a country that you really were hoping to learn more about. You see, it all goes back much further than six decades of history. In some ways the country's story goes back more than fourteen hundred years, to the birth of Islam, or even before that to the creation of language, or maybe even to the rise of mountains and the carving of rivers in the land millions of years ago. When I told you that I speak Urdu, the national language of Pakistan, I could have also explained that the word "Urdu" was used to describe a mélange of different ethnicities that settled in military encampments in the shadows of the Himalayas centuries ago. "Pakistan" is actually an Urdu phrase, I might have added, made of two words: *pak* which means "pure," and *stan* which, like the English word "stand," describes a state of being. The country is literally called the "Space of Pure." Since you don't speak Punjabi, you would not have realized that when I said that my family is from the Punjab region, I was actually saying that they are from a "land of five rivers." I never got to tell you that there is a seven-hundred-year-old grave on the banks of one of those rivers that, I am told, belongs to one of my ancestors. I never got to explain that the city of Lahore is named after *Loh*, the son of the mythical Hindu god Rama. There were so many avenues we could have taken to travel to the heart of the matter, but they mostly went unexplored.

It's not your fault or mine. How could you even begin to understand the story of a whole nation in one brief encounter? How could we even expect to understand each other's life stories in all their perfect contours? It would be impossible even if we lived down the street from each other. And stories of nations are convoluted and distinct, just like the stories of our own lives. Nations, like people, use stories to construct a particular place for themselves in this world. Nations have memories too—while you might remember that pep talk on that long drive home, the nation recalls the speech by the great leader atop the hill. You have that especially painful schoolyard fight, and the nation has that bad war on the border. You survived the terrible accident, and the nation lived through the great civil war. There was that move during middle school to a new city, which changed you forever, and the nation recalls the great migration, which changed everything.

Nations, like people, collect these stories as they grow. They line up words and they cement them together to build sentences, and these sentences join together to form concrete stories. These stories are stacked one upon the other with each passing day. And then one day, the special place in the world is built. From inside this palace of stories, we look out at the sprawling space around us and at the other palaces of stories built by other people and nations, some near and others far in the distance. From inside this space, we can explain to the world our existence and answer those questions that seem so tough when asked by an outsider, like "Where are you from?"

The words that make up a nation's history are vivid and colorful to that nation, because they choose those words carefully. Your stories are familiar and stirring because they are your special stories. And each story builds perfectly on the last one, because it is nations, like people, who decide the architecture of their existence in this world. When you pick one story from this edifice and share it with a stranger, it doesn't always translate. A word that you might have learned from your grandfather or from your founding father, which so clearly evokes a warm feeling in you, might sound like garbled noise to a person who speaks another language. And since others don't know how a particular story fits into the larger structure, they can never understand its full value or its meaning. At the end of it all, only you understand the grand scheme of your palace of stories.

HERE IS ONE of my stories. When the airplanes struck on September 11, 2001, I was in a leafy college campus in rural Vermont a few hours' drive north of what would become known as Ground Zero. The air was crisp. The trees had not yet burst into the fiery yellow, orange, and red fall foliage that I had learned to anticipate eagerly. I was on my way to my morning class when a classmate stopped me in my path, and with cold concern beaming through her wide-open blue eyes, she told me about the attack on America. The towers were on the periphery of my consciousness. I had seen them passing through New York City a handful of times, but I had never really stood still to admire their splendor. On the morning of September 11, they were seared into my memory forever.

I changed course and turned toward the nearest television set. The cafeteria lounge was overflowing with people watching the events live. I saw the two towers billowing smoke from gaping dark craters near the top floors. The camera did not move for a long time, and it seemed like nothing was really happening. Then, with a most awesome fluidity, one tower began to sink in on itself. I heard gasps and a girl burst into tears, bawling and screaming loudly as her friends tried to lead her away from it all. A few minutes later the second tower crumbled to the bottom of the screen. I stood there watching. Where, a few moments earlier, there had been two of the tallest structures built by man, there was now only dreadful black smoke.

The next morning, the editorial in the *New York Times* described the day before as "one of those moments in which history splits, and we define the world as 'before' and 'after.'" It was one of those days for me too. I woke up that morning to a double ring of my phone: an off-campus call. The serious-sounding man on the line introduced himself as an agent from the Bureau of Alcohol, Tobacco, and Firearms. I don't recall his name. I don't remember much of the conversation either, but I do remember two things: he made no reference to the events of the day before, and he asked me whether I felt safe where I was. I was in Vermont, one of the most serene places I had ever lived, so naturally I said yes, I did feel perfectly safe. And as his cold silence settled in, I felt more deeply imperiled than I had ever felt before.

Before he hung up abruptly, the man had said that he would call me back, and for many weeks my heart jumped every time my phone would double-ring. But he never called back. And I was left with only the eerie and bare knowledge that someone had sought me out in my dorm room in Vermont the day after the attack on America. As time passed I began to wonder whether the man really was a federal agent. Maybe it was a prank by some lonely person who, in search of his own answers, had decided to reach out that morning? Was it someone I had once met in passing? Maybe even someone in my own small college town? Was he watching? Why?

Everyone trudged the campus grounds quietly in the days that followed, as if we were all processing what had happened in New York and were writing the story in our minds to fit into the architecture of our own lives. I tried to make sense of the number: three thousand dead. I wondered about the girl who had started to weep in the cafeteria. I heard her father worked in one of those towers. But then my thoughts would always return to the phone call, and it made my blood chill every time. Eventually I decided that I would never find out who had called me, and so I decided to leave that question behind. But I did understand why he had called. After eliminating every other reason, I recognized that I had received that phone call because of my family name: Mufti.

My surname is one of those words that I must explain for you to see how it fits into the disturbed architecture of my life. The word "mufti" has the same root as the Arabic word "*fatwa*." A fatwa is any opinion based on the law of Islam given by a recognized authority, or a mufti. It doesn't have to be a death sentence; it could simply be an opinion on what health insurance plan to choose. And it's a nonbinding opinion, so different muftis might, for example, choose different insurance plans. So my last name literally means "One who gives a legal opinion." Somewhere in my ancestry someone had once worked as a jurist in an Islamic court, and the name, I was told, had stuck. I had always known what my name meant to myself, but while Ground Zero was still fuming, I considered—perhaps for the first time—what it meant to others. It was this name that landed me on the wrong end of a cold phone line.

"This is a clash of civilizations," a student spat out in class one day. He was upset when he said it, and the words sounded dirty to me. I began to hear others using this phrase to explain all that rumbled in my world, just as the gears of another global war machine were beginning to turn over hungrily. "The clash of civilizations" was a phrase first used by the British-American professor Bernard Lewis, who taught history at Princeton University. Lewis wrote an article in 1990, as the Berlin Wall was falling, for the *Atlantic* in which he claimed that "the roots of Muslim rage" were in the religion of Islam, which had "inspired in some of its followers a mood of hatred and violence." The rage drew "its strength from ancient beliefs and loyalties," and it was a continuation of "the struggle between these rival systems" of Islam on the one hand and the West, rooted in Christendom, on the other. It was a rivalry that Lewis believed "has now lasted for some fourteen centuries." The real crux of the conflict between these two competing civilizations, Lewis said, was this: while Western civilization had evolved to separate church and state, the Islamic civilization had not. Since Western civilization was now triumphant and dominant in the world, "fundamentalist leaders" of Muslims were threatened by the idea of religion being separated from state in Muslim countries as well.

Lewis lamented that "Muslims experienced no such need and evolved no such doctrine" to separate church from state. But it was a cynical view. There had been no real separation of church and state because, as Lewis had noted elsewhere, there is no church in Islam. "The very notion of something that is separate or even separable from religious authority, expressed in Christian languages by such terms as *lay*, *temporal*, or *secular*, is totally alien to Islamic thought and practice." Lewis wrote this as an indictment but it was just reality, and while his claim that church and state could never be separate in Islam was technically true, so was the opposite: religious authority has always been diffuse, contested, and decentralized in Islam. There has never been an entity in Islam comparable to the Catholic Church. Islamic religious authority never coalesced around any central authority like the Pope. Since no central church ever existed in Islam there was also never an institution that tried to exert power over the state in the same way. So how do you even separate two units, when one of the units doesn't even exist? That is what was most depressing about Lewis's worldview: he identified a feature of Islamic tradition as the main cause for a supposed historic conflict with the West, and then pointed out that it was an intrinsic feature of the Islamic tradition. He pointed to an ailment in the relationship and also pressed that there was no cure for it. Violence between Islam and the West, he seemed to be suggesting, was natural, inevitable. The entire thesis reveled in hopelessness.

There is something about Islam that allows for "an explosive mixture of rage and hatred," Lewis wrote toward the end of his magazine article. To illustrate this, he pointed to two examples of undue anger and violence against the United States in the Muslim world, and both of them were from Pakistan. The first event was the burning of the American embassy in the Pakistani capital, Islamabad, in 1979, and the other was the uprising, a decade later, against the publication of *Satanic Verses*, by Salman Rushdie, before a fatwa of a death sentence was passed against him. Pointing to these two instances in Pakistan, Lewis argued, "It should by now be clear that we are facing a mood and a movement far transcending the levels of issues and policies and the governments pursuing them. This is no less than a clash of civilizations."

It was painful to read Lewis lead into the phrase "a clash of civilizations" with two examples from Pakistan. Yes, it was the world's only country founded for people bound together by their shared Islamic identity, but upon its independence from British rule, Pakistan had also purposely chosen to express its Islamic identity through a constitutional democracy inspired by the West. It was a country founded on the principles of "democracy, freedom, equality, tolerance, and social justice as enunciated by Islam." Pakistan was a product of the mixing of two civilizations. But where would the world's original democratic Islamic republic stand in Lewis's clash? How would it stand?

A contemporary of Lewis's at Harvard, Samuel P. Huntington, picked up on Lewis's idea and made it the central thesis of his own article, published in the popular monthly magazine *Foreign Affairs* in 1993. Huntington predicted that after the end of the Cold War, conflict would be mainly about cultural issues and that a "clash of civilizations will dominate global politics." Huntington defined a civilization as the broadest cultural entity, and he counted "seven or eight" civilizations in the world. It was all a bit arbitrary. The island of Japan got its very own civilization in his thesis, while there was only "possibly" an African civilization. Then there was a Confucian, a Christian Orthodox, a Hindu, and a Latin American civilization. And of course there existed a Western civilization and an Islamic civilization, which, as Huntington described in great detail, were already locked in an emerging global conflict. "The fault lines between civilizations will be the battle lines of the future," he wrote. "The centuries-old military interaction between the West and Islam is unlikely to decline." Instead, he predicted, "It could become more virulent."

These ideas about a civilization clash had sprouted among the dank rubble of the demolished Berlin Wall at a time when everyone scrambled to make sense of the post–Cold War world. But they waned and wilted over a decade and all but died off. Then from the wreckage of the twin towers in New York they rose once again, growing abundantly as they knotted through the global imagination with ease. The words of these professors were read as the prophecies of sages. Huntington cultivated his magazine article into a book, and *The Clash of Civilizations* became an international best seller after the attacks. Bernard Lewis, meanwhile, sat down to advise the administration of President George W. Bush on its new war policy. And so there it was: a clash between an Islamic and a Western civilization was made real by a swift terrorist attack and the sheer force of a well-told story.

Weeks after the attack, American forces invaded Afghanistan, Pakistan's neighbor along its long western border. It was a cruel joke of history that the first battle in this new era of war landed on the doorstep of Pakistan, the only country in the world whose founders and whose written constitution had made a real effort to enmesh the political values and norms of the Islamic civilization with the Western civilization. America began paying billions of dollars in military and economic aid to Pakistan in order to win its loyalties in this war and to use its seaports and network of highways to supply American forces that landed in the tens of thousands into landlocked Afghanistan.

At first only a few stray American missiles landed on Pakistani soil, but over the decade that followed, the violence from the American war in Afghanistan would bleed deep into Pakistan. A few years in, the Pakistani military began mowing down its own people along the Afghan border, and soon guerrilla fighters from that region started a campaign of beheading Pakistanis in the outlying regions. Then suicide bombers started sneaking into Pakistani cities and slaughtering people by the dozens in mosques and restaurants and playgrounds. America began to send in robotic airplanes to bomb Pakistani villages, leaving heaps of dead bodies. Soon America and Pakistan became rivals, engaged in their own shadowy and bloody conflict for control over the region. There was misery in Afghanistan, and thousands of Pakistanis and thousands of Americans would die over a decade.

People like Huntington had thought that the clash of civilizations would unfold on a global and continental scale. But that never happened. Some of the most important Muslim countries sided with America and the West in its wars. Global politics marched on to its standard beat. Instead, the clash of civilizations tore open inside Pakistan. As the violence consumed the country more every day, the nation of Muslims in the Islamic republic began searching desperately for a path that would deliver them from the bloodshed and misery. Some said the only way left was to erase all traces of Western ideals from the Pakistani state and to remove any symbols and institutions that represented Western civilizations in the country. Others argued that unless Islam was carved out from the soul of the nation, it would consume it like a cancer. They said an Islamic democracy was a mirage. Most Pakistanis simply yearned for a just, peaceful, and prosperous life. They did not care whether it came in a secular or an Islamic guise. Through the decade of violence, those who continued to hold fast to the founding ideal of the country grew fewer and fewer, and quieter. But they did not disappear. A peaceful existence, some continued to believe, was in line with Islamic as well as Western values. There was no need for one to be annihilated by the other. The promise of Pakistan was becoming endangered.

Was it hopeless? Or was there some way Pakistan could survive and deliver to the world an example of a state that could bridge civilizations, a place that could feel 100 percent Islamic and 100 percent Western? The answers mattered to me. I began reporting from Pakistan as a journalist. I revisited the stories of a nation. I traveled through space and time over thousands of miles and thousands of years, examining each tier of the palace of stories Pakistan had built, sentence by sentence, layer by layer, subjecting it all to cold historical analysis. In New York, London, New Delhi, Islamabad, Mecca, and many points in between, I revisited the character and places that made up Pakistan's history. I traveled through the country, meeting people and touching gravestones, navigating a landscape mangled by violence. I read many volumes of history during the long travels up and down the Indus River that runs the length of Pakistan, from the Himalayas to the Arabian Sea.

And there is something else you must know: as I unraveled the history of Pakistan and Islam, I found my family tales embedded within it. I soon realized that it was much more than my last name, Mufti, that tied me close to an Islamic past and a national story. There were columns in my own palace of stories that stood in the story of the nation. And so I began studying my own family's past too, and it all began to fit together seamlessly. I have an old yellowing scroll that ties my bloodline to the tribe of Muhammad. In my office are the spiral-bound notepads from the hours of interviews with religious scholars, politicians, and military commanders and my own father and mother. Among the scholarly detritus in my room is an old tattered diary with a fading pink flowered cover that belonged to my maternal grandmother in her teenage years when she lived in Afghanistan after World War I. The biography of the Prophet Muhammad, originally written more than a thousand years ago, sits on my shelf. The travelogue of a Chinese traveler who passed through the Punjab is even older than that. This leather-bound notebook with a broken string tie is the one that I kept by my hospital bed in India after I got into a terrible accident. All around me is a papery palace of stories. These letters with runny and patchy ink are addressed to my great-grandfather; these old British military documents tied together with a white handkerchief describe the war heroics of a great-uncle. A news clipping announces my birth in a local Ohio newspaper; my paternal grandfather's expense diary charts his fluctuating fortunes. Among these heaps are different renditions of the holy book of Islam, the Quran. It's all here in stacks and rows around me. I am surrounded by towering columns of words, my own grand palace of stories.

I am forever tied to these stories. But what about you? Will you really be able to forget about Pakistan when this war ends? You will probably not. I know that after the war in Afghanistan ends, the violence in Pakistan will continue, and you will not be able to look away from the world's sixth largest country, which also has nuclear weapons. Iran is right there too, neighboring Pakistan. And much later, when all the tangles in the Middle East are straightened, the world will turn its attention to Asia, charting a future course with two rising powers, China and India. And once again, Pakistan will be there, bordering both of these countries. You, like me, will not escape Pakistan anytime soon. You, like me, are tied to it in geography and history. And maybe that's a good thing. If you have come this far, why not stay to see how it all builds to a climax? If you're anything like me, you might even believe that this will all end well.

I could not extricate myself from this story even if I wanted to. My own story is part of Pakistan and Islam. It is tangled with America's and with the rest of the world's. Family, religion, nation, and war are all cemented into the structure. So it is a pleasant twist of fate that I speak your language. I am no historian, but I am a journalist, and what I do best is tell stories. And I believe I have a key to the door that leads into this palace of stories. So let me be your dragoman. Allow me to invite you into this house and see how it looks from the inside. I want you to be able to see each word in its perfect relief and I want you to see how each story fits together. I want you to peer out the windows and see how the world looks from here. You might leave this palace of stories and still not fully understand its architecture and design, but at least you will have seen where I come from. And then, perhaps, you will even help me see where we are going.

Now all that is left for me to do is to pick the moment where it could all have started and then, as people have been doing for generations and generations wherever humans have built homes and civilizations, begin telling the story.

One

WAR CAME TO LAHORE on the evening of December 3, 1971. The sun had melted into bloody orange on the western horizon when the *azaan* crackled out from the bullhorns that clung to the minarets nettling the dusky landscape, calling the faithful to prayer. Saadia, my mother, who was twenty-two years old at the time, laid out her prayer mat on the cold hard floor of her room and began the rhythmical motion of *namaz,* facing in the direction of the holy mosque in Mecca. When she finished, she neatly folded over one corner of the mat and, as she had been doing for many weeks, turned on the black-and-white TV set in time for the evening news telecast. That is when Saadia first learned, along with millions of others, that the Indian army had attacked her country, Pakistan. Lahore was Pakistan's largest city near the Indian border, and when the air-raid sirens began wailing in the distance, Saadia's hands and feet began tingling with anxiety.

India was always Pakistan's most dangerous enemy. The two countries had appeared on the map, as two of the most populous countries in the world, when they were split from a single British colony in South Asia twenty-four years earlier. They had already fought two wars; one began months after their independence in 1947, and the other, only six years previously in 1965. But this one beginning in 1971 looked to be the most dangerous of all. Pakistan had two distinct wings, West Pakistan and East Pakistan, which were separated by a thousand miles of India, which hung between them like a hornets' nest in the Indian Ocean. The two wings of Pakistan had been caught in a civil war for months as the eastern wing was trying to break free from the west. Caught, quite literally, in the middle of the civil war between Pakistan's two wings, India had lately become fully involved supporting East Pakistan's armed struggle.

The Indian attack on the western wing came as no surprise to Saadia. For weeks, India had been gathering forces on its border near Lahore, and the drums of a full-scale battle were beating loudly in Islamabad and Delhi. The Pakistani government had expected an Indian attack for days and had ordered brownouts in Lahore. This meant that Saadia's family had to dull all lights in the house by wrapping dark paper around the lightbulbs. But no matter the warning and preparation, you can never be ready for war. And for Saadia, all this could not have come at a worse time. She was supposed to get married the next day.

For two days the house had been packed with nearly two dozen guests who had arrived from different parts of the country for the wedding. The night before, at around sunset, the house had been bustling with activity, but now it was eerily silent. The entire wedding party was attending a prewedding *mehndi* celebration at the groom's house a few miles down the river. They had all dressed up nicely before they left, and the women from both sides would be singing their favorite wedding songs, delicately painting each other's hands in henna, and the men would be gathered around the coal heaters nibbling on sweets. Saadia might have gone too, but the elders decided that the bride should give this prewedding bash a miss. She had never visited the groom's family home, never as much as spoken to the groom in her life, and it seemed improper to disturb that delicate dynamic hours before the wedding. Saadia, never eager for the limelight, was happy to miss out on the fun.

She was left alone at home with an old and frail aunt who was in no physical shape to grapple with such extravagant festivities, and a younger cousin, nine months pregnant, due any day, whose husband was a soldier in the Pakistani army. The family maid had stayed back home as well, and she was the one who broke the news of the war to the pregnant woman, suggesting tactlessly that the Indians had in all likelihood already attacked her husband's border post, which was some fifty miles south of Lahore. The cousin began wailing loudly and my mother and the aunt frantically tried to compose her, but she was hysterical. It was very unusual for women to be home alone after dark on an ordinary day, and so it all was getting increasingly nerve-racking for Saadia. Then there was a thunderous explosion in the sky, followed by the sounds of jets roaring eastward toward the border. The pregnant cousin fainted and the other women fell very quiet as it became darker and darker.

After what must have felt like eternity, Saadia's father, Akhlaque Qazi, and her mother, Sharifa Sajida, returned home leading a herd of panicky guests. Many of them had arrived in Lahore only days before, and they now huddled like frightened refugees in my grandfather Akhlaque's house. Saadia rushed to her father's side and stood close by, waiting to hear words of comfort. He was distracted as he told her grimly that the air-raid sirens had gone off while they were still on the road, on their way back home, and that they had to park and wait for the jets to pass. He rushed off to the bedroom and pulled out a charpoy bed by its light wood-framed post and let it drop under the roofed part of a veranda lining the façade of the single-story house. He switched on a dim light and stepped onto the taut jute ropes of the bed and called everyone's attention. The crowd gathered around in a hush under the awning.

My grandfather was a small claims court judge at that time. The sight of frightened faces looking to him for relief would have not been all that unusual for him. It was mostly women at home, as the men were either off to war or had rushed out to scrounge for emergency supplies before the bombing started. "The Indians have attacked," Akhlaque began, opting to state the obvious first. He spoke loudly in Punjabi, the family's native language, over the sirens that were now wailing wildly, signaling the destruction about to descend. Jet fighters were now slicing the sky above with their shrill engines. "I spoke with the elders in the groom's family," he continued "and we have decided the wedding will go on as planned tomorrow."

Akhlaque's hair was still dark black at that time, and his skin was plump and fresh. He wore thick-rimmed glasses. He was not yet fifty, marrying off his firstborn, but he had long commanded the authority of an elder in the extended Qazi clan. "If any of you wish to leave now and return to your homes, be sure that I will not hold that against you. If any of you have no place to go, this is your home for as long as you like." As Akhlaque stepped off the charpoy, there were loud whispers in the crowd but not a single person moved. They would all stay the night in my grandfather's humble three-bedroom house.

With this sudden and strange turn of events, Saadia became a silent spectator to the drama of her own wedding. It was as if the war had made her suddenly invisible, a peripheral prop in a much larger scheme of history. Strangely, she felt relieved. As people began settling on their mats laid out on the cold floor and burrowing into the wool-stuffed quilts for the night, my mother slipped back to the corner of the living room with the radio. It was quieter inside. Radio Pakistan was playing songs by Noor Jahan, the sensational film actress and singer best known for her chirpy and playful *filmi* numbers, but now the radio played the anthems she had recorded during an earlier war against India. "The brave boys of the nation," Noor Jahan crooned, "my songs are for you." Then came on the more somber, "You won't find these sons sold on street carts." In it, a pleading Noor Jahan, in her nasally perfect high pitch, implores a mad, grieving mother to stop visiting the bazaars in search of a replacement. Saadia swayed gently to the morose tunes in the dark, as tears finally began streaming from her eyes down the sharp angles of her pale face. The songs took her back to the time when she had first heard them as a young teenager. That previous war was only six years ago, but it seemed so much longer. Saadia was never the same after that war. The song ended and a voice on the radio announced that Indian ground forces had reached Battapur. The calmness of the announcer troubled Saadia. That was only twenty miles away from Lahore.

Six years earlier, in 1965, my mother was a sixteen-year-old and had recently started her undergraduate degree at the Lahore College for Women when she first experienced war. It was a warm morning in early September when two thunderous ear-splitting claps in the sky sent the entire neighborhood into frenzy. What was that unearthly sound? Neighbors started yelling over walls consoling each other, finding meager solace in their collective confusion. Saadia's first instinct was to rush out the door to find her younger brother, who was only nine years old at the time and alone at school. When she returned home with him, a messenger from her father's office at the local court arrived with a brief note: "Don't worry. It was our own war planes that broke the sound barrier." My mother knew from skimming the newspapers that India and Pakistan had both been blustering for weeks, and she turned on the radio hoping for some more clarity. After a short wait, the voice of Ayub Khan crackled from the speakers. He was the former military general who had come to power in a coup years before and who now ruled Pakistan as president:

My dear countrymen, Asalamu'alaykum. The time has arrived when a hundred million Pakistanis are tested. Today early in the morning Indian forces launched a ground attack on Pakistan in the direction of Lahore. Like cowards, an Indian aircraft made a target out of a passenger train waiting at the Wazirabad station. From the very beginning Indian leaders have hated the very existence of Pakistan. And they have never truly accepted in their hearts this separate free state for Muslims. For the last eighteen years they have been preparing for war against Pakistan. The hearts of a hundred million Pakistanis that echo the call of "La ilaha ilallah, Muhammad al Rasul-allah" *[There is no god but God, and Muhammad is the Messenger of God] will not rest easy until the enemy is forever silenced. Perhaps, the Indian leaders don't yet fully appreciate what nation they have roused. In our hearts there is faith, and a belief ever strong and we know we battle for truth. A state of emergency has been announced in the country. War has begun. Our brave soldiers are advancing to decimate the enemy. Allah has provided the armed forces of Pakistan with an opportunity to demonstrate their valor. My countrymen: step forward and battle the enemy. May God be with you. Amen. Long live Pakistan.*

President Ayub spoke for no more than two minutes, but when the speech ended Saadia felt as if she had been shaken by an unearthly force. She truly believed in that moment that President Ayub was speaking to her, asking for her help in protecting the nation. He was Pakistan's first military president and a popular leader and an internationally recognized statesman. He had asked Saadia to battle the enemy alongside the men in the army, and she decided that was exactly what she would do. As was tradition in the Qazi family, Saadia had started wearing the *niqab* a few months earlier when she had finished high school. Before stepping out of the house, she now covered herself from head to toe in a loose black cloth with only her eyes visible. But this did not stop her from doing her part. She merged into the stream of people that spilled onto the streets of Lahore in the days that followed the declaration of war. She knocked on doors, collecting in a basket food donations from neighbors for the soldiers fighting on the front. The government officers' community, where Grandfather Akhlaque's family lived, organized "civil defense" classes where Saadia learned the basics of first aid. The boys in the family, while they were not given arms, learned how to fire rifles.

This war was fought mainly between India and Pakistan's western wing. It began in the region of Kashmir, a few hundred miles north of Lahore, among some of the highest mountains in the world. Kashmir was caught on the border between India and Pakistan, and the two countries had battled for possession of Kashmir ever since they became independent states in 1947. The two armies withdrew to a cease-fire line brokered by the United Nations in 1948, but in August 1965, under the orders of President Ayub Khan, the Pakistani army furtively crossed the cease-fire line in an attempt to take all of Kashmir. India had responded by attacking Lahore. The battle spread along the fifteen-hundred-mile border between the two countries. Tanks crawled through wretched swamplands and soldiers fired their guns from trenches in pristine sandy desert in the south. Heavy artillery fire was exchanged from mountaintops in the north. Indian and Pakistani battleships engaged in the Indian Ocean.

A few days after the president's speech, Saadia snuck away with a cousin, only a year older than herself, and walked two miles to the Mayo Hospital. They wanted to donate blood for the soldiers, but the nurse on duty told them that to do so, they had to be at least eighteen years old, which neither of the girls could claim to be. My mother pleaded with the nurse to take her blood. The truth was that blood was needed badly on the battlefield and so, eventually, the nurse gave in. Saadia watched with satisfaction as the soft plastic pouch full of her deep purple blood was carted off to another room to be spilled elsewhere on the land. Many days Saadia would stand with her college classmates along the Multan Road cradling packets of biscuits, Capstan cigarettes, candy, cake rusk, and anything else they had gathered from the neighborhood. They cried "Allahu Akbar," God is the Greatest, as they flung rations at the soldiers moving east on the road toward the border. In the evening, when Saadia would return home, exhausted, war would still hang heavy and loaded in the sky. Jet fighters would sometimes dogfight right over the open veranda of Grandfather Akhlaque's house late in the night. One evening the family saw a fiery stream in the sky left by the tail of a fighter plane that was shot down, and Saadia's younger brother darted out the door in the direction of the smoke before anyone could stop him. He returned an hour later cradling a warm shard of metal in his hands. It was a piece of the Indian jet, he said. He had salvaged this debris, and with his eyes wide open he described the heat of the battle to all family that gathered around.

A cease-fire was signed four months later in the Soviet Union, in the city of Tashkent, over the New Year in 1966. Thousands of soldiers had died on each side, but people in both countries were still gripped by the hysteria of war. They wanted to fight for many more days. So stressful was the signing of peace that the Indian prime minister, Lal Bahadur Shastri, a slight old man of sixty-two years, died of a heart attack the day after signing the document. President Ayub, on the other hand, came back to Pakistan to face a rioting public. He had made the Pakistani people so confident in the inevitability of their victory that now they blamed him for signing it away too easily and betraying their trust.

My mother continued to believe in President Ayub. Even as people protested on the streets demanding Ayub's resignation, Saadia knew he was no coward. He had fought for Pakistan as a soldier before, and he had done the right thing by quickly bringing an end to this war, she believed. A few weeks after the war ended, Saadia published her first piece of writing. Newspapers were running low on ink giving space to all the angry voices of dissent against Ayub Khan, but Saadia wrote an essay defending his decision to opt for peace. She sent it to off in a white envelope to the editor of the largest Urdu newspaper. She didn't really expect to see her words ever again, but she checked the opinion columns every day anyway. Sure enough, there it was one day, her great defense of the president in the pages of the newspaper. She read her own words carefully. They seemed so much more powerful, so true, in newsprint.

She wrote again for the paper, this time narrating an emerging legend of a major in the Pakistani army who gave his life in battle while leading a platoon charged to protect the main canal that brought water to Lahore. The war sparked a passion for writing in Saadia, and she couldn't put down her pen after that. She became the editor of *Kiran*, her college's monthly magazine, and she began dabbling in fiction and short stories for the publication. She picked up old books of poetry by the great classic Urdu and Persian poets like Iqbal and Ghalib. She joined the college debate team and wrote speeches while touring other women's colleges in the country. Three years later, at a debate, Saadia spoke one last time in defense of President Ayub. He was on his way out of power. His political opponents had at last cornered him on charges of nepotism. Ayub Khan finally resigned months before Saadia graduated from college.

Saadia's economics teacher spotted potential in my mother. As she neared the end of her bachelor's degree, Saadia's teacher told her, "You would make an excellent teacher." To teach at the college level, Saadia knew she needed at least a master's degree, and she spoke to her parents about this. With their blessings, she applied for a master's program in economics at the same college. And when the end of the master's neared, my mother spoke

Saadia graduated with a bachelor's degree in economics from Lahore College for Women in 1969.

to her parents about doing a PhD. This time there were many more questions. No woman in the family had ever gone on to receive a PhD. Was it really necessary? How long does a PhD take, anyway? Grandfather Akhlaque slowly grew more receptive to the idea, but both father and daughter knew that it was my grandmother, Sharifa, who resolutely resisted the notion. Saadia's mother was a loving and cool-tempered woman, but on this issue she said in no uncertain terms that she would not accept anything but marriage. All these big thoughts about higher education, she told Saadia, could wait. "It's your age to make your own home now," she said. My mother chose to resist with her own unflinching silence on the matter of marriage. What was in Grandmother's favor was the list of suitors, which was long.

Many days Saadia would return from college, stepping off a horse-driven *tanga* cart draped in her black *niqab*, to find a new group of women sitting in the veranda of the house visiting with my grandmother. Each time, she would pass them mumbling some polite greeting. She seldom stopped to chat and often felt the women's eyes follow her into her room. Sometimes she wouldn't even lift her veil when she stepped inside the house, even if it was only women in the room, in front of whom she had no need for it. She didn't want the women to be able to judge her attractiveness. Saadia wanted to remain unseen and unmarried. It was one such day in the fall of 1970 that Saadia walked through the gate to find two women seated on the rope bed on the veranda across from Grandmother Sharifa. My mother greeted the older woman first, who smiled gently at Saadia, and then said hello to the younger woman. As she hung up her *niqab* inside, Saadia's older cousin, who was recently married herself and was now heavily pregnant, walked in. "He has a PhD from America. He's a professor at Punjab University," she said. "He has his own car!" Saadia's final exams were coming up in October. She said she had no time to think about such things. "If you like him so much, why don't you marry him?" she shot back caustically at her pregnant cousin.

Saadia's mother was pleased after this meeting. It was a suitable match, Sharifa told her daughter in a more tender moment. The Mufti family was a lot like the Qazis, she explained. They were not so wealthy, from Lahore as far back as any one of them could remember, and they lived in a nearby working-class neighborhood. Saadia could visit all the time. My mother suspected that marriage would spell the end of her dream to be the first woman in the family to get a PhD. At the same time, this man was well educated himself, and maybe he would offer her a chance to study some more. He was seven years older than her, though, nearly thirty years old. He would probably want to start a family soon. Most of all Saadia feared that she would settle down complacently into a new and comfortable life. There was not much wrong with that life, it's just that she wanted more.

Grandmother Sharifa was insistent and my mother calculated the cost of resistance: she could confront her mother and launch a full-scale war that would divide the house into two camps. But in the end she did not go down that road. Maybe she loved her mother too much.

Or perhaps she had also learned lessons from the former president Ayub, to choose her battles carefully and retreat for a chance at peace. In the long run, things may work out for the best, she told herself. A few weeks later, she said yes without having ever seen as much as an image of her husband-to-be. The wedding date was set for later that year, on December 4, 1971.

In the midst of feverish wedding planning, Saadia's older first cousin, Yusuf, had to leave for Islamabad on a work trip. Yusuf was in his midthirties, and my mother considered him a brother. Yusuf's mother, Grandfather Akhlaque's sister, had passed away months after Saadia was born, and my grandfather and grandmother had adopted Yusuf, along with his brother and two sisters, and raised their nieces and nephews as their own. Saadia was only a year old when the adopted siblings came home. Saadia was closer to Yusuf than anyone else in the family and Yusuf spoiled her like a baby sister. He was trained as a civil engineer and traveled all over the north of the country working on irrigation projects. One specific project, he told Saadia before leaving for Islamabad, was in the ancestral village of Ayub Khan. Yusuf said that he was going to Islamabad to discuss this project with the former president, who had retired to a quiet house in the capital city after being forced out of power. He told my mother that if she could convince her parents of it, he would gladly take her along to meet Ayub. It was a radical idea to go on a road trip so close to the wedding, but Saadia wouldn't take no for an answer this time. Sure, it might have been a small battle, but she was going to win it.

My mother traveled north with Yusuf and his young wife, Tasneem, and drove several hours toward the colder climes of Islamabad. The retired president's house was tucked away in a thicket of trees, and Saadia stared out at the lush green mountains of the city as they drove up the long driveway of the house. They waited on the plush couches in the living room for a few tense and quiet moments before they heard President Ayub descending the staircase. He was dressed in a purple robe. My mother, dressed in her black *niqab*, saw him for an instant and quickly lowered her eyes, the only part of her that Ayub Khan could see. He was sniffling and coughing, clearly not in the best of health, as he sat down and spoke in an eloquent manner with Yusuf about the irrigation scheme. This was a man very different from the one Saadia had heard on the radio as a teenager. Perhaps the ruthless political ouster engineered by his opponents was still fresh in his mind. Cousin Yusuf continued with polite conversation between sips of tea, and the meeting lasted almost half an hour. My mother sobbed through nearly all of it. Toward the end of the meeting, the former president finally asked Yusuf, "Why is she crying?" My mother wept some more. "Sir, she respects you," Yusuf tried to explain. "It is akin to worship, if I might say, sir," he stuttered. The warrior president moved from his seat and came over and sat next to my mother. He gently placed his hand on her head, as a father does, and she burst out in more tears.

"My daughter, please say something," he said to my mother, lowering his voice to an encouraging whisper. At that moment Saadia could have told him, as she had told many college auditoriums full of people, that the former president had taught her the meaning of belonging to a nation. He had changed her life with one radio speech. She could have told him that she supported his decision to end the war many years ago, that selfish, opportunist politicians did a great injustice to the nation by turning against him. She might have begged him to return to the political stage and fight back, for he was the only one who could lead the nation as a civil war between the two wings was brewing. Instead, Saadia gathered every bit of courage and whimpered only, "May I please have one photograph to remember you by?" The great faded warrior nodded and instructed an aide to bring a photograph from his office. The man returned with a black-and-white photograph in his hand. In it, Field Marshal Ayub Khan wore his full military attire with all his medals neatly pinned to his chest in full glory. He smiled slightly as he looked off at the far distance as great men of history often do, as if they can so clearly see the future.

On her wedding day, Saadia woke up when it was still dark outside. Sleeping guests covered every inch of the cold floor, and she tiptoed over forms she could hardly recognize as friends and relatives. She needed to get an early start. The skies over Lahore would soon erupt into a second day of war. The groom's wedding party would arrive earlier than planned, so that all scheduled (and abridged) festivities would be completed before dark, when road travel became perilous. Saadia found her mother in the kitchen already baking fresh bread for the wedding party.

This is the signed photograph that former president Ayub Khan gave to Saadia when she visited his home in Islamabad.

Saadia sat down to help her, but Sharifa told her daughter to get herself dressed for the big day. My mother had no idea how to dress herself in her flowing purple-and-silver wedding dress and all the ornate jewelry that went along with it. Luckily, a few of her college friends arrived early in the morning and began helping her into her bridal costume. One of Yusuf's sisters did her makeup using a small mirror. They all chatted excitedly, trying to make light of the real possibility of aerial bombardment during the wedding party.

At noon, the hundred-strong Mufti party arrived at the Qazis' home. The mood was tense at first, but it soon melted into hushed but warm celebrations. Saadia sat quietly alone on a chair in her parents' bedroom waiting for the cue to make her appearance on the small stage that had been set up in the open veranda. Now that she was getting married, she would no longer wear her black *niqab*. Her husband-to-be had expressed no desire for her to cover herself up like that. Her cheeks were lightly blushed and her eyes were done elaborately with kohl, accentuating their almond shape. A purple scarf was lightly draped over her hair and a large delicate gold hoop hung from her nostril as the centerpiece for an elaborate jewelry set that decorated her forehead, neck, and wrists. She sat listening to the sounds of the Muftis and Qazis mingling and laughing outside and occasionally falling silent after the sound of a distant bombing or the roar of an aircraft.

Soon, a few of Saadia's cousins and girlfriends burst excitedly into the room. It was time to join the groom outside. As she walked out, her head bowed modestly, Saadia stole a quick glance at the groom seated on a couch. His face was concealed completely by the veil of garlanded flowers hanging off the thin metal crown that sat on his head. Saadia was seated next to him but not touching him. Soon the older women in the wedding party began to step forward to help the couple feel more intimate. An aunt picked out a yellow sweet *ludoo* from a plate and offered it to Saadia. She took a small bite, trying not to seem greedy, and she left a bit of a lipstick mark on it. The *ludoo* was then passed to the groom. The jovial aunt encouraged him to take a bite from the same spot where my mother had left her lipstick, and when he bit off a small piece, the younger girls gathered around them giggled shyly. Both bride and groom remained stiff and nervous. Next came the milk, the symbol of fertility, and the young couple split a full glass between them. In between these traditional rituals, relatives stepped forward and presented the couple with cash wedding gifts wrapped in small envelopes and wished them a safe and happy life together. The festivities soon began wearing thin as news of an imminent Indian air strike on the city swept through the party. Lunch was served hurriedly outside in tents. Akhlaque soon walked up and placed a hand on the shoulder of his new son-in-law and suggested that it was time to take Saadia to her new home.

So began the *rukhsatee*, the final ritual in which my mother's parents gave her away. The women began weeping. Saadia hugged all her relatives, who stood in line as she began the long journey out of the gate toward the car where the groom waited, holding the door open for his wife. Saadia gave her mother a long hug, her mascara, smudged by her tears, now spread all over her face like war paint. My grandmother, also weeping, would have told her daughter to wipe the tears and leave happily with her husband. He was her real family now. In her mother's embrace, my mother attempted to compose herself, but then she saw the groom's car. It was a white Volkswagen Beetle. At least, it would have been a white Volkswagen had it not been covered completely in fresh wet mud. Since the war had started the day before, white cars were no longer allowed on the streets. The military police had decided that they made for easy targets for Indian jets running sorties. The groom had been unable to arrange for a paint job at such short notice, so the only option was to cover his car, the only one in the family, entirely in sticky brown mud. Saadia froze for a second when she saw the car. It looked as if it had been dug out from a ditch. And she began weeping once again. My father helped her into the seat and crawled in and sat next to her and they drove off, newly married.

Saadia was exhausted and shut her eyes as the car began moving, but she was startled to attention when the car suddenly braked with a jerk. She recognized the road crossing. There was the unmistakable wail of an air-raid siren and horrible commotion all around. Through the window she saw military police thumping on car windows yelling at passengers to stop and jump into the trenches dug along the roadside. Indian jets were about to pound the ground with bombs at any moment. Quickly, the groom moved to open his door but then he stopped when he noticed that Saadia had not made the slightest move. She was not crying anymore. She stared down at her lap, saying nothing. He had known this woman only a few minutes, but his wife didn't need to spell it out for him: she was not crawling into any trenches in her wedding dress. So he settled back into his seat. As they waited for the startling sonic booms, which would be closely followed by the sound of jets passing overhead, it was he who broke the silence. "What happened to that ring?" he said, pointing to her left hand. He noticed that his bride wore a ring on each finger, except one index finger. Saadia straightened. Where had it gone? She remembered putting one on each finger as she was getting dressed at home. A few heartbeats passed as her husband waited for a response. Anything. "It must have fallen off somewhere," she replied in Punjabi, still looking straight down at her lap. He was surprised by how forceful Saadia's voice was. They fell silent once again. It was exhilarating, the first words they ever spoke to one another.

EIGHTEEN MONTHS EARLIER on a crisp and bright June morning in 1970, my father, Shahzad Mufti, posed for photographs at his graduation ceremony at Case Western Reserve University in Ohio. He wore a neatly trimmed chinstrap beard that went handsomely with his black graduation gown. The dark blue hood he wore indicated that his doctoral degree was from the medical school. For one photograph he posed with a close friend from Greece, with whom he had roomed for a year, and for another photo he posed with Margaret, the only black American woman in the program, with whom Shahzad had become friends early in their studies. He had graduated a few times in his life now. He got his bachelor's degree from Government College in Lahore and a master's degree from Punjab University, also in Lahore, but this celebration came with some real pomp. It was a moment of great pride for him, truly American in its grandness, and Shahzad smiled broadly for the cameras. In the photographs, it's the small details that would later stand out. Strapped high up around Shahzad's right biceps was a white armband with a black peace sign on it. Someone had handed it to Shahzad as he walked with the procession up Euclid Avenue, and he quickly wrapped it around his sleeve.

Shahzad had come to America four years earlier as a university student when campuses all over America had become hubs of antiwar political activity. The civil rights movement had also made great strides, but the fight for respect and dignity of blacks in America was not yet complete. Protests against the war in Vietnam were spreading from coast to coast, hopping from one university campus to the next. Weeks before Shahzad's graduation, forty miles down the road from Cleveland, American soldiers in the Ohio National Guard had shot and killed four college students at Kent State University as they protested the war. Like many of his classmates, Shahzad believed that the war in Indochina was unjust. He also saw glimpses of the injustices in America. Once, he and a black medical student in his class were walking across the campus late at night, returning from the library, when they were stopped by campus security. "What do you guys think you're doing here?" a couple of cops in a patrol car asked ominously. They tried to explain that they were medical students. Only after they produced their school IDs did the security officers let them off after a sharp head-to-toe inspection. Shahzad had learned not to take all this very personally. He was not white, of course, but he also knew that unlike his black friends, he was also not American.

Shahzad graduated from the medical school at Case Western Reserve University in 1970. Like much of his class, he wore a white armband with a peace sign to graduation.

My father was there because the cold war between the United States and the Soviet Union had entered a new phase. The two competing superpowers scrambled for alliances in the third world, particularly in Asia. Since India was squarely in the Soviet camp, the United States began reaching out to Pakistan in the early 1960s. Pakistan's northern border was separated from the Soviet Union by a narrow ten-mile-wide corridor, which made it all the more important from an American political-planning perspective. The two countries were getting along just fine. In 1961, President Ayub Khan had paid a visit to the United States, where he addressed a

joint session of Congress, had dinner at Mt. Vernon, and
even got a ticker-tape parade on Fifth Avenue in New York
City. Jacqueline Kennedy made a reciprocal visit to Pakistan
the following year and toured the entire country, including
the Afghan frontier town of Peshawar and Pakistan's tribal
areas. "I must say I'm profoundly impressed by the reverence
which you in Pakistan have for your art and for your culture, and for the use you make of it now," she enthused at an
outdoor dinner party in Lahore's historic walled Old City.
"My own countrymen too have a pride in their tradition,
so I think that as I stand in these gardens, which were built
long before my country was born, that's one more thing that
binds our countries together and which always will." As the
first lady departed for home, Ayub Khan presented her with
a Thoroughbred horse named Sardar (Chief), who traveled
with her to Mt. Vernon. The first lady would write in her
memoirs that the horse became her "favorite treasure."

In the flurry of civilian exchanges that followed, the government of Pakistan had advertised scholarships in 1964 for
two Pakistani students to travel to the United States for doctoral programs. Shahzad, who had only just completed his
master's degree at Punjab University, won one of those slots.
My paternal grandmother, Zubaida, burst into tears of sor-
row when her son ecstatically broke the news to her. Shahzad
was one of her twelve children, and he made sure to remind
his mother of this fact as he consoled her. But she insisted
that "each one has its own slot in the heart." Shahzad's father, Abdul Majid Mufti, had passed away very suddenly after
an accident only a few years earlier, so Shahzad understood
that leaving the nest at this time hit his mother harder than

it might have otherwise. My father received his visa and air ticket, and he was all set to fly out on September 13, 1965, when the Pakistan-India war broke out. All flights out of Pakistan were suspended and all nonessential government programs, including my father's scholarship, were indefinitely postponed. The war, my father only half joked to his mother, was the answer to her prayers. Unlike my mother, who as a young college student spent those days of the war collecting rations for soldiers, my father had spent the months of the war with his mind on the world outside Pakistan.

Shahzad landed in the United States a full year later in September 1966 with fifteen dollars in his pocket. His impressions of America when he arrived were sketchy at best. He spoke English well enough but with an accent. He had heard clips of President Kennedy's speeches on the radio and he remembered, like all Americans seemed to remember, the exact moment when he learned of the American president's death. He was shaving in the morning preparing for a class at the Punjab University when Radio Pakistan news announced that President Kennedy of America had been shot and killed. Shahzad was shocked. He did not imagine that such things could happen in America too. The government scholarship was good only for four years of study, so my father began working on his doctorate at Case Western University on a tight clock. Still, he used these years to get to know America the best way he could have hoped for: through its music.

Of the close group of friends Shahzad made at medical school, one worked part-time as an usher at Severance Hall, the home of the Cleveland Orchestra. She would invite the

My paternal grandfather, Abdul Majid Mufti, graduated with a bachelor's degree from Islamia College, Lahore, in the early 1910s. He is seated cross-legged on the floor, second from left, and the only man in the entire group wearing a bow tie.

entire gang to the discounted Thursday afternoon matinees. The orchestra performed with George Szell, one of the great American conductors of the century, and at Severance Hall Shahzad first heard the classical works of Beethoven, Mozart, and Tchaikovsky. He was often speechless after hearing a symphony for the first time, amazed perhaps that he had spent thirty years of his life without knowledge of these European treasures. He never passed up an opportunity to see a live act that passed through Cleveland: Simon and Garfunkel; the Doors; Crosby, Stills, Nash & Young. He even got the rare chance to introduce his group of friends to South Asian classical music when the Indian sitar maestro Ravi Shankar passed through town. Shahzad traveled the great country on Greyhound buses and bounced between the coasts by air, once stopping Sammy Davis Jr. at an airport for an autograph. He attended *Hair* on Broadway and a theater production about the trial of Julius and Ethel Rosenberg in San Francisco. In this new exciting country he pondered questions that he had never even thought existed, like the one on the cover of *Time* magazine a few weeks after he arrived, in big bold red letters: "Is God Dead?"

He was one of the first in his class to complete his doctoral program in 1970. It was time to go home. That white armband meant something to Shahzad but perhaps not what it meant to many others. It was the slice of America that he had lived and loved. The white armband was the America he was taking back home with him. "What's this?" asked Ron, the man who had acted as Shahzad's host-father in Ohio for four years. Ron tapped the white band dismissively with the back of his hand. Ron and his wife June had always been there for Shahzad. They were a middle-aged couple, a lawyer and a teacher, who lived in a very nice home in Shaker Heights, which Shahzad visited from time to time for meals and nice evening conversation. Ron and June said many times that they didn't like all the fighting out in Indochina, but they saw the war in Vietnam as a necessary one. "Oh, nothing," my father said as he smiled back at Ron. What was the use getting into an argument with people who had been so loving and kind to him? And this wasn't Shahzad's battle, anyway. What right did he have to talk about the direction America was taking? It was time for him to leave, and he couldn't imagine how or when he would ever be back. The furthest thing from his mind at the time was that the next decisive battle in the Cold War would be fought a decade later in his homeland.

The flight took off from New York City on the Fourth of July 1970, and there was no looking back for Shahzad. My father stepped out of the plane and onto the tarmac at Lahore and paused to take a deep breath, filling his chest with the warm, sultry air of his country for the first time in four years. One of his older brothers was waiting for him, and they laughed as they embraced. Shahzad's brother told him that he almost didn't recognize him. His hairline had receded a few inches and he looked older than when he had left. Shahzad returned to the house that his father had built two decades ago for the family, when Pakistan first became a country. Shahzad fell into his mother's lap when he saw her. She couldn't really get up when he walked in through the door. She was in her midsixties and arthritis had started to finally set in, and her knees were very weak now. She appeared much more frail than when Shahzad had last seen her.

On his first night back in Pakistan, Shahzad slept under the open sky on the roof of the house. There was no air-conditioning and it was much too hot inside. The gentle breeze helped him cool off. He had a tough time falling asleep that night. He was jet-lagged and the mosquitoes were vicious. He finally slipped into sleep, but he was woken up by the sound of the dawn call to prayer from the nearby mosque. Shahzad was no longer accustomed to the sound of the prayer call so early in the morning, and he rolled over, pulled his cotton sheet over his head, and waited for it to finish. He had never been one to pray, not so early in the morning, anyway.

Shahzad returned to the Punjab University campus. It looked just the way he had left it, spacious, bright, and lush with every shade of green. He first went looking for Dr. Muzaffar, who was his mentor during his master's degree. When Shahzad walked in, Dr. Muzaffar stood up briskly. "Doctor sahab!" he yelled out, adding an honorific to my father's newly acquired title. He walked up and hugged him. They chatted joyfully for a while and Dr. Muzaffar asked many questions about America, which Shahzad dutifully answered. Shahzad had been lecturing at the Punjab University before he left for America, and Dr. Muzaffar asked him if he would like to pick up right where he had left off and teach some courses in the fall. Shahzad was elated as he left the room. He had a job. But that wasn't all. He had also just witnessed something truly extraordinary: in all the years Shahzad had known him, Dr. Muzaffar had never before stood up to greet him. As Shahzad walked out of the office, he felt for the first time like a doctor.

In the weeks that followed, Shahzad's mother and six sisters threw themselves headfirst into the mission to find Shahzad a wife. He had failed to solidify romance in America and returned to Pakistan a single boy with a receding hairline, all of which was highly alarming to the women in the family. He was open to the idea of being set up, but he also claimed to have no opinion on any of the marriage prospects. Any woman who could impress his mother and sisters, seven women all at once, was surely good enough for him, he would say. He told his mother that he would marry the girl she chose for him. But in reality, Shahzad had lived in America for far too long and was now accustomed to blazing his own trail. Even if he did not know it at the time, this was his quest and he would find the way to my mother, albeit in a roundabout way.

It was a small matter of a brand-new white Volkswagen Beetle. During his final years in the United States, Shahzad had squirreled away enough of his university stipend to save up enough to eventually buy a car. On his layover in Frankfurt on the way back to Pakistan, he had enough to place an order for a VW Beetle, for which he paid fifteen hundred dollars in cash to the manufacturer in Germany. He had been back in Pakistan for many weeks now and still had not seen his new car. All he knew was that the vehicle was snagged in some Pakistani bureaucratic tangle. Since no one else in the family had ever owned a car, none had the slightest clue about how to negotiate an imported vehicle out of customs. Shahzad would have to figure this one out all on his own. He began navigating a dizzying labyrinth of Pakistani bureaucracy alone, day after day, made all the more maddening after four years of more straightforward dealings in America. He would collect reams of documents at one office only to deliver them to the next one across town. He signed, copied, attested to countless pieces of paper, and no matter how many thumbprints he left in little boxes at the bottom of however many pages, he felt no closer to his car.

One day the search for one elusive document led Shahzad to the Lahore city court, where his older brother Jawad worked as a judge for a small claims court. Shahzad was

sitting in his brother's damp, sweltering office amid towering stacks of files waiting for signatures, when in walked his
brother's senior colleague at the court, Akhlaque Qazi. My
father stood up out of respect for the older gentleman, and
Shahzad was introduced as the younger brother who had just
returned from the United States with his PhD. Akhlaque was
impressed by Shahzad's gentle manner and humble disposi-
tion. When he learned of Shahzad's predicament, Akhlaque
Qazi said that he had recently imported his own car through
customs and so he might be able to help.

My uncle Jawad and Akhlaque Qazi had gotten along
splendidly for many years in the middle rungs of the Pakistani judicial bureaucracy. They were both straight-edged
men of modest means, mediating meager disputes between
the not so powerful common people of the city. Both were
comfortable in their lack of any real influence. They often
discussed these court cases and politics over lunch, Jawad
with his silver tiffin carrier and Akhlaque with his *paratha*
roll fried at home by his wife. It was during one of these
ordinary lunches a few weeks after my father's appearance
at the court that Uncle Jawad Mufti suggested to Akhlaque
Qazi that the women in the two families might enjoy
meeting for evening tea someday. Jawad had earlier told
his mother that his colleague Akhlaque Qazi had a young
daughter, Saadia, who was about to graduate with a master's
degree from Lahore College. He suggested she might make
a wonderful match for Shahzad.

When the meeting took place in the fall of 1970,
Shahzad's mother saw the girl only briefly at first when she
walked into the house one afternoon covered head to toe

in a *niqab*. Grandmother Sharifa had the awkward task of explaining that their daughter had not actually yet agreed to being married, but Shahzad's mother was eyeing a few other girls in her circle, so she felt no rush either. In a later meeting, Saadia sat down without her veil with Shahzad's mother, who was greatly impressed by the girl's quiet confidence. She also felt very comfortable in the Qazis' home. "It seems to me that they are our kind of people," she told my father one day after returning from a visit. Finally, one afternoon in May, Shahzad's mother and eldest sister told my father that they were ready to formally ask for the hand of a lovely girl named Saadia in marriage for him.

The *nikah*, a modest religious ceremony, took place a few weeks later and served as Shahzad and Saadia's engagement. It was the first time my parents were in the same room, and the immediate families gathered to admire the lovely young couple. But Saadia's face was obstructed by her red *dupatta* draped over her head, and neither of my parents had the courage to turn their head to look at the other's face. The engagement ceremony was brief and concluded with the two young people still unsure of what the other looked like in the flesh. Shahzad was able to get a photograph of Saadia after the *nikah*, though, and he began carrying it in his wallet. She had a fair complexion, slender features, and large, bright, intelligent eyes. He thought she was beautiful.

That fall, he went on a work trip to the city of Peshawar and bought a few trinkets for his fiancée from the open market of the northwestern border town. He showed them to his mother in Lahore and suggested that he could deliver them to Saadia himself. It might be a good excuse to finally see

Shahzad and Saadia had their official wedding portrait done at the famous Rollo photo studio in Lahore.

his fiancée's face. His mother was not impressed. She told Shahzad that he had lived in America too long. He seemed to have forgotten how things worked. She took the gifts from him and told him to rest easy. She would personally deliver the presents to Saadia on her next visit to the Qazis' house. Shahzad realized he would just have to wait. He would not see his wife until the day of their wedding. He would speak his first words to her inside the white Volkswagen, covered entirely in mud, parked in the middle of a chaotic road crossing, as fighter jets screeched overhead. They were a young couple with big dreams, waiting to write their own tale together. But for now they waited for the war to pass.

Two

A FEW DAYS AFTER they were married, my parents moved into their own home on the campus of Punjab University. Shahzad had signed on as a superintendent in a men's dormitory and was assigned his own ground-floor faculty apartment. The first few days at home were probably not the honeymoon either of my parents had imagined. The bombs kept falling and they spent the days preparing for the nights, when the blackout would make the sounds of not so distant aerial raids seem even closer than they were. Saadia tried to get the kitchen running, but there was often no gas, which allowed her to mask a more serious problem: Saadia did not know how to cook and had not bothered to learn before the wedding. Lucky for her, Shahzad was never a picky eater and he ate all that she served, nodding forcefully, telling his newlywed wife what a truly great cook she was.

The worst of the war was still occurring in the eastern wing of Pakistan. The union of East and West Pakistan as one country was doomed from the very start. Pakistan was the only country in the world that had two equal-size wings that were not connected by land. It was as if France and Turkey were two equal halves of one country, but all of Europe sat between them as the sworn enemy of that state. It was never going to work. Historically, the lands of East Pakistan had looked east toward countries like Burma and Thailand, while West Pakistan looked west toward Iran and the Middle East. The two wings inhabited two politically divergent worlds.

Physical distance wasn't even the biggest trouble. In East Pakistan, nearly the entire population spoke the Bengali language and in West Pakistan no one spoke it. Bengali was never given the same status as Urdu, which was more widely spoken in the west. The Bengalis took a lot of pride in their language, and when Urdu was declared the national language of all of Pakistan, they were incensed by how their language was belittled and ignored by the powerful political elite in the western half. The west had always been dominant in the military, bureaucracy, business, and nearly every other sphere of political life. The east was poorer and less developed, and was often treated as a satellite state for its resources and raw industrial material. There was also a stench of racism to the whole thing: taller, fair-skinned west Pakistanis mistreating the darker-skinned, more diminutive Bengalis in the east. It was only a matter of time until they would fall out.

The real trouble between East and West Pakistan began brewing soon after military president Ayub was forced out in 1969. His departure after a decade of rigid rule left a political vacuum, which was filled by two major political parties, one in the west and one in the east. The Awami League was popular in the east among the Bengalis, and in West Pakistan the new Socialist Pakistan People's Party commanded most support. It was led by a charismatic young leader named Zulfiqar Bhutto. In the general elections of 1970, the first after Ayub's departure, the Awami League swept the polls in the eastern wing and the People's Party won the majority in the west. Since the eastern party won more votes in total, it had the legitimate right to form a ruling government, but Bhutto of the People's Party teamed up with the military elite in the west to keep the Bengalis from coming to power. The Bengalis reacted to the suppression with mass protests, which turned increasingly violent after the military sent in troops to East Pakistan to crack down on the unrest.

One night in March 1971, the Pakistani military launched Operation Searchlight. At the stroke of midnight it began a systematic massacre of Bengalis who were resisting West Pakistan's diktats, and the army committed heinous acts of brutality against thousands of its own citizens in the eastern wing. It was the beginning of the Pakistani civil war. Following Operation Searchlight, thousands of refugees from East Pakistan crossed the border into eastern India. In the Indian refugee camps, a fully armed Bengali separatist movement was born, secretly aided and trained by the Indian government. For many months in the beginning of the civil war, from the safe distance of Lahore, news of the Pakistani military battling the Bengali separatist army came to West Pakistan only through sterilized waves of state-owned radio and televised propaganda reels. In the months before their wedding, Saadia and Shahzad had separately followed the events closely, but their impressions of the brutal civil war were vague. Bhutto toured the western wing in those days, calling the East Pakistanis "sons of swine" who could "go to hell" if they wanted a separate country. His supporters cheered loudly at this divisive rhetoric, largely unaware of the massacres occurring a thousand miles away.

News reports of rape and murder in East Pakistan by the Pakistani military leaked out to the world, and nearly everyone turned out in support of the Bengalis' desire for freedom. In America, some of the biggest musical stars of the time—the Beatles, Eric Clapton, Bob Dylan—performed in the Concert for Bangladesh at Madison Square Garden in August 1971. It was a concert lineup for which Shahzad would have jumped on a Greyhound bus in a heartbeat a year earlier, but now he was in Pakistan, caught inside the war. He never even heard about the concert.

The stage was now set perfectly for India to enter the conflict on humanitarian grounds and deliver a crippling blow to its archenemy with full global support. My parents' wedding day was the official start of the war between India and Pakistan over the issue of Bengali independence. The Indian army attacked Pakistani cities like Lahore in the west, and at the same time formally joined forces with Bengali fighters and began pummeling Pakistani forces in the eastern half. Indira Gandhi, the Indian prime minister who was popularly known as the "iron lady of India," was decisively outmaneuvering her adversaries in Pakistan, militarily and diplomatically. It started to look very dire for Pakistan very quickly.

On December 15, a few days after my parents moved into their new home, they watched, on their brand-new black-and-white television set, a news report on the state-owned Pakistan Television channel that showed Bhutto speaking on the floor of the United Nations, representing West Pakistan. He was furious. Wagging his finger in the air, he lambasted the Security Council for "acquiescing to dilatory tactics" of the Indians and letting Pakistani forces weaken in the east against India. "We will fight. We will go back and fight," he yelled in his impeccable English, his voice quivering with rage as he ripped a proposed Security Council peace agreement into shreds, tossed it in the air, and stormed out of the hall followed by his entourage. It was an awesome but theatrical display of outrage. In reality, Bhutto knew West Pakistan had lost. The very next day, Pakistani forces officially surrendered to the Indians in the East Pakistani capital of Dhaka.

Saadia and Shahzad watched, horrified, as the Pakistanis surrendered. It was an outdoor ceremony. A Pakistani general was mobbed by what appeared to be hundreds of people. He undid his epaulets, removed his revolver and lanyard, and handed it over to his Indian counterpart. The two men walked over to a table and took their seats and flipped through the "Instrument of Surrender," a document drafted by the Indians in which the Pakistani military officially conceded defeat. The Pakistani general signed the document and then the Indian general examined it briefly before signing it as well. The shamed Pakistani general was led away by a mob to an Indian military jeep and was driven off to a prison camp where he would join nearly ninety-three thousand other Pakistani prisoners of war. Neither Shahzad nor Saadia said very much that evening. These were powerful and painful pictures for both of them. The entire nation would try to erase the shameful events from their collective memory, even from their history. But Pakistan had signed a written document of defeat, and when something is written down it is not so easily forgotten.

Pakistan lost half of its navy, a third of its army, and a quarter of its air force in the war of 1971. Pakistan also lost half of its population as East Pakistan broke off to form a new independent country called Bangladesh. While Bangladesh would begin the long process of healing from the deep scars the Pakistani military had left on its people, Pakistan would begin reckoning with its new reality. Pakistan was a country of nearly sixty million people, still one of the largest in the world. But now it was a single corridor of land that followed the thousand-mile length of the Indus, from its source in the Himalayas all the way south to where it drained into the deep and warm water of the Indian Ocean. Its area was more than three times the size of Great Britain. Straddling Central and South Asia, Pakistan was a new nation, perhaps even a more coherent nation than it was before. But it was a nation more uncertain of itself than ever before. And there was a lot of work to be done to fix all that had gone so wrong.

THEIR HOME SLOWLY began to take shape. It was a small two-bedroom apartment, just the perfect size, Saadia thought. The sun filtered through the large windows in the front and in the back, which looked out onto a small yard. Saadia found a spot for everything: a bed, a dressing table, kitchenware, a fridge, a television, and a tape recorder. There was an old couch from Shahzad's mother's home, and also his gramophone, along with a distilled collection of LPs, only the most precious ones for which he found space when returning from America. Shahzad often played Simon and Garfunkel songs for Saadia, as well as his favorite classical symphonies. She found them pleasing, but he soon understood that she did not like this music very much. So they settled on the old *filmi* songs from Pakistani and Indian movies that they both enjoyed and remembered from their college days in Lahore.

Their most prized possession, bar none, was my father's Volkswagen Beetle. It was a 1969 model, beige-white in color, with a strong 1.3-liter engine that bubbled encouragingly whenever Shahzad turned the ignition. A few days after they watched the surrender on television, Shahzad gave the car a good scrub in their short driveway and let it dry in the brittle winter sun. Saadia stepped out of the house to inspect it and asked my father excitedly if they could go for a drive that evening. My parents would spend many days in the Volkswagen, taking it for rides all around Lahore, the city that was home to both of them.

Lahore is situated on the eastern bank of the River Ravi, one of the five major tributaries that feed the giant Indus from the east. The river runs along the western edge of the

Saadia (left) stands with Yusuf's wife, Tasneem (right), and her children. My parents' white Volkswagen is parked behind them.

city, so over the ages Lahore has grown along the length of the river and eastward in the direction of the border with India. Lahore sits in the heart of the geographic region named the Punjab for these five rivers, a region of rich and verdant plains, similar in size to Austria. If the Punjab were an independent country, it would be listed among the dozen or so most populous nations in the world.

The Ravi's headwaters lie north of the Punjab, more than 150 miles from Lahore, high up in the Himalayas, and the river cuts rapidly through many steep mountain valleys before descending into the plains of the Punjab. By the time the Ravi passes Lahore, the first major city along this river, it has settled into an easy and lackadaisical pace. The city of Lahore, legend says, is named for Loh, the son of the Hindu deity Rama. It is believed that princes from Rajput warrior tribes established an outpost near this location on the banks of the Ravi a few centuries after the birth of Christ, almost exactly halfway between the two ancient cities of Kabul in the west and Delhi to the east.

Lahore has been an important hub of the Punjab region for nearly a thousand years. Under British colonial rule, beginning in the nineteenth century, Lahore was made the capital of the Punjab province and grew rapidly, a trend that continued when Pakistan became independent. Karachi, the port city eight hundred miles to the south, has always been Pakistan's largest city and the country's business and industrial center, as well as its original capital. Lahore is downright mellow compared to the cosmopolitan bustle of Karachi. Still, Lahore has always had an allure that few cities in South Asia can match. It is not the oldest city in the region, but it sprouts with more history—ostentatious landmarks and hidden treasures in equal parts—than any other. Every slave, saint, or savior who passed through the winding alleys of Lahore, or any traveler who rested under the bulbous canopy of a mango tree, seems to have left a keepsake in the city, as if an excuse to return.

The beating heart of Lahore is the Old City. The three square miles of the nearly thousand-year-old settlement are surrounded by a high and sturdy wall, which Emperor Akbar had built four centuries ago. All roads of Lahore lead to the walled Old City. Inside the Old City the paths begin to coil like veins. Tall and slender edifices line these labyrinthine alleys, with their oriels protruding like pot-bellies from the top floors, so close together sometimes they appear to kiss.

The walled Old City is accessible via thirteen gates whose inspired and vivid names capture the best and the worst of the character of the city and its people. The Roshni Gate, or the "Gate of Light," which leads into the great mosque, alludes to the tendency of Lahore's denizens toward romance, which can easily descend into melodrama. The Masti Gate, which translates loosely as "Drunken-Mischief Gate," is in all likelihood a corruption of "Masjidi Gate" for the mosque nearby, but you can expect such rascally wordplay from Lahoris whose unique Punjabi twang is infamous all around the land of the five rivers. The Shah Alami or "King of the World" Gate betrays Lahore's inflated and occasionally misplaced sense of self-importance. The Mori Gate, named for an unspecified bodily orifice, confirms the city's hedonistic obsessions, especially with food. He who has not seen Lahore, they insist in the Old City, was never really born.

When my parents were married in Lahore, it was a city of nearly two million people and the second-largest city in Pakistan. The campus of Punjab University, where Saadia and Shahzad lived, was on what was then the southern fringe of Lahore, eight miles away from the walls of the Old City. Punjab University was founded in 1882 under British rule. It was one of the earliest institutions of higher education in the colony and quickly gained a prestigious reputation. The original campus was on a small plot of land, less than a mile outside of the Old City, but as the city began to grow through the nineteenth century and into the twentieth century, the population of Lahore began bleeding farther out from the Old City. To accommodate the growing city and the growing institution, in the 1950s the government of Pakistan granted Punjab University a new, large plot of land far away from the walled city, and this became the New Campus.

When my parents moved to this New Campus in 1971, it was still surrounded by nothing but miles of wheat fields. Modernization of the city's road network was still catching up with the sprawl. Shahzad and Saadia would scarcely see another vehicle as they drove up the Canal Bank Road, a major north–south connector. They would most often turn left off the Canal Road in the direction of the walled city, and just before they entered its environs, they would turn into Ichhra, the working-class neighborhood where they both grew up.

Ichhra is ancient. Some archaeologists have suggested that it might be the locale where the first people settled along the River Ravi almost two thousand years ago, to form the settlement that would become the seed of modern Lahore. The Ichhra that Saadia and Shahzad grew up in in the 1940s and '50s, a few miles south of the walled city, was a diverse neighborhood where old tombs and Hindu temples and Muslim mosques dotted the crowded winding alleys. Shop fronts sold everything from bundles of cloth to hot teatime snacks. It was home to mostly low-ranking government officials, writers, teachers, and clerks. As children, both Saadia and Shahzad went to separate schools in the neighborhood, neither of which had any furniture. They both learned their alphabet and math sitting on cold straw mats, with reusable wooden tablets in their laps. They were cheaper than paper.

In Ichhra one day, Shahzad pointed to his childhood playground. He told Saadia that he learned to play cricket here with his brothers and all his friends. He impressed her by running through some bowling figures and told her about how good he still was at the game. Saadia listened carefully as my father told her this story, and she began recollecting stories from her own past. She too had memories from Ichhra from when she was a little girl: the haunted house on the corner that all kids were afraid of walking past, the film actor who lived down the alley. She also remembered going with her brothers to a cricket field and sitting at the boundary of the ground with all the other girls and some younger boys. There she would watch and admire the older boys as they played intense games. She would wait for the balls that would roll over for four runs. She remembers cheering, mindless of who was winning or losing. It was this same playground.

"I know. I remember that." She smiled. "I remember you."

When my mother was six years old, Grandfather Akhlaque was allotted a house in the government servants' quarters in the Chauburji neighborhood, a few miles north of Ichhra, closer to the walled city. Chauburji, a neighborhood exclusively for low-ranking government employees, was quieter and more residential than Ichhra. Saadia lived there until her wedding, and it was still the place where they visited

Saadia's parents every weekend. Every landmark on the way was a new story. My parents saw their shared city in this way, their collective memories, happy and painful, whizzing past in the windshield of the Volkswagen: the Canal Bank Road down which Shahzad rode to class as a student hundreds of times; Lahore College on Jail Road, where my mother would stand waiting for the horse-driven *tanga* to take her back to Chauburji; Multan Road, where Saadia threw rations at the soldiers as their armored vehicles drove to war. Bathed in their overlapping memories, my parents fell in love in the city of their birth.

One evening Shahzad told Saadia to get dressed, because they would be taking a special car ride that night. Saadia put on one of the dresses given to her as a wedding present and even some lipstick for the occasion. Shahzad wore his best pants with a collared dress shirt. They skipped the usual left turn toward Ichhra and instead drove straight north along the Canal Bank Road until they reached the major inter-section at the Mall, the glitzy thoroughfare with tall com-mercial complexes that grew westward out of the Old City and into the British colonial part of town. Shahzad took a left on the Mall and drove a mile up to Alfallah Cinema, where he parked the car in the lot. They walked up to the tiny window and Shahzad bought two tickets to the movie. It was Zeffirelli's *Romeo and Juliet*, a British production from a few years before, which had only just arrived in Paki-stani theaters. Saadia was exhilarated. She had seen only one English movie before this in her life, *Around the World in Eighty Days*, and that was almost ten years ago. Shahzad and Saadia took their seats, and once the lights were dimmed,

One of the earliest photographs Shahzad took of Saadia while they were on their honeymoon in the northern city of Abbottabad. Almost four decades later, American military forces would track down and kill Osama bin Laden in this same hill station.

they held hands, something they would have been too shy to do in public, even as a married couple. Later, after the movie and after dinner, they drove south on Canal Road back toward their home on the university campus. In the rearview mirror of their treasured white Volkswagen, they saw, shrinking and glittering, their beloved city of Lahore.

From the ashes of the war of 1971, Zulfiqar Bhutto, the founder and leader of the Pakistan People's Party, rose to become the single most influential leader in Pakistan. He was born in 1928 in Larkana, a small town on the banks of the Indus in the south, a couple hundred miles from the southern coast of the Arabian Sea. A few years after Bhutto was born, his father, a prominent landowning politician of the region, was knighted by the British colonial government. Bhutto left his home for California as a teenager and studied political science at the University of California at Berkeley, from where he graduated with a bachelor's degree in 1950. It was in California after the Second World War that Bhutto first learned about socialism and communism, and he would carry these ideals with him through to the end of his life at the gallows. After studying law at the Inns of Court in London, Bhutto returned home in 1953. His home was no longer a colony but part of a new independent country for Muslims called Pakistan. Bhutto was ready to lay claim to the vast political fortune that his powerful father had amassed for him as inheritance.

Ayub Khan came to power in a coup a few years later, and the military president quickly took note of the charming, handsome, eloquent scion of the powerful feudal family. He appointed Bhutto to a Pakistani commission to the United Nations, and from there Bhutto rose swiftly through the ranks. He became the youngest member of Ayub's cabinet as minister in charge of the country's energy policy, and he showed a keen interest in nuclear energy. Soon he was a close and trusted adviser to the president and was appointed foreign minister. It was in this position that Bhutto worked with Ayub Khan through some difficult days during the war with India in 1965.

At the end of that war, when President Ayub signed the peace accord against Bhutto's advice, the president and his young adviser had a public row. Bhutto believed Pakistan could have extracted more from the war by delaying peace.

A few months after the accord, Bhutto abruptly quit the government and created his own political party, the Pakistan People's Party, and vowed to take down the regime of President Ayub for his egregious "crime" of signing a peace treaty with the Indians prematurely. As would become a repeated pattern in Pakistani politics, the apprentice turned against his mentor.

Bhutto became Ayub's loudest critic and led the street movement that took Ayub Khan out of power in 1969. Bhutto's slogans of "power to the people" and "bread, cloth, and shelter" for everyone proved to be groundbreaking. Millions of factory workers, laborers, and famers flocked around Bhutto as he rolled up his sleeves and delivered his populist message in the language of the street. As he traveled from village to village under a grueling sun along the length of the Indus River, he became the first political leader since the founders who had true national political appeal across ethnic and linguistic groups, at least within West Pakistan.

After the war of 1971 and the breakaway of the eastern wing, the military chief who was left in charge of the country appointed Bhutto interim president of the newly dismembered Pakistan. Bhutto was charged with the colossal task of bringing his country back on track. He had his hands full. As one of his first tasks, he signed a peace accord with Indian Prime Minister Indira Gandhi in the summer of 1972. The two countries agreed to respect the Line of Control that divided Kashmir, caught between India and Pakistan, as a de facto border. More important from a political point of view, Bhutto won an agreement to repatriate the nearly one hundred thousand Pakistani prisoners of war who were, a year after Pakistan's surrender, still languishing in prison camps in Bangladesh.

Bhutto's peace with India was perceived differently from the peace signed by Ayub Khan. In 1965 Pakistanis believed that their country had made territorial gains that were worth fighting for. This time, six years later, Pakistan had decisively lost half the country. So Bhutto returned to Pakistan to throngs of admiring supporters. People admired Bhutto for whatever little he was able to scrounge for the country in the negotiations. A few months after the signing the peace accord, Bhutto gathered the smartest scientists and engineers in the country in a secret meeting and told them that he had learned about India's plans for building a nuclear bomb. He asked the Pakistani scientists how much money they would need to build a bomb of their own, and then he green-lit the project.

More than any bomb or a peace treaty, the country was in dire need of a new constitution. Now that the country was half of what it used to be on the map, it needed a new written document to guide its path. This, more than anything else, would prove to be Bhutto's toughest assignment. To write a new constitution he needed all of Pakistan to come together and agree on a way forward. This was one thing he could not get done by the sheer force of his tremendous diplomatic skill or his endless political cunning, will, or charm. Pakistan was only twenty-four years old, and it had already seen two constitutions come and go. The first one, from 1956, took nine years after independence to complete and lasted only a few years, ending when Ayub Khan overthrew the

Saadia's brother, my uncle Afaq (second from right), poses outside the Chauburji home in 1974 with a friend (far right) who had returned to Lahore the day before, after years as a prisoner in Indian prison camps.

government in a military coup. Then Ayub Khan drove through his own new constitutional order that lasted only as long as he was in power, just over a decade. Now Bhutto had a chance at a third one.

The blueprint for both previous Pakistani constitutions was a document called the "Objectives Resolution." It was a list of nine points that Pakistan's earliest leaders and the country's first "constituents assembly" had submitted two years after independence, in 1949, as a guide for any future constitution-making endeavor. When Pakistan first came on the map in 1947, it was the world's fifth-largest country by population and the largest Muslim country. The Objectives Resolution had declared that any constitution must ensure that the government would be "chosen representatives of the people" and would function on "principles of democracy, freedom, equality, tolerance, and social justice" as they were "enunciated by Islam." The state would ensure that "Muslims shall be enabled to order their lives in the individual and collective spheres in accordance with the teachings and requirements of Islam," but minorities could "freely profess and practice their religions." The constitution must also "guarantee fundamental rights" like "equality of status, . . . social, economic, and political justice, and freedom of thought, expression." Finally, the objectives demanded the need for the "independence of the judiciary."

The document was endorsed by nearly all leaders of the freedom and independence movements, but even back then, a few people in the assembly criticized it for being too Islamic and unduly influenced by ulema, or religious clerics. Pakistan should be a purely secular state, they argued, where Islam had no real role in law and political society. But this was a view very much in the minority. The leader of the constituent assembly, a well-known Oxford-educated lawyer by the name of Liaquat Ali Khan, who was Pakistan's first prime minister, said that his hope was that the resolution would set the stage for a country that "may prove to be a laboratory for the purpose of demonstrating to the world that Islam is not only a progressive force in the world, but it also provides remedies for many of the ills from which humanity has been suffering." Pakistan, in other words, was the world's first experimental laboratory in Islam and democracy.

In 1970, if Bhutto represented a more secular strand of politics in Pakistan, the religious strand was probably most explicitly expressed by the Jamaat-e-Islami, or the Congregation of Islam Party. The Jamaat, as it was called, was founded a few years before Pakistan's independence, in 1941, in Lahore. Its founding leader was a religious-minded journalist and activist from the Punjab named Abul Ala Maududi. He was one of the most prominent intellectuals in the world at that time writing about modern national politics and Islam. He assembled a group of like-minded people in Lahore at a time when the British were beginning to withdraw from their colonies in Asia. His aim was to create a political front that could successfully represent political Islam in South Asia after colonialism ended.

Initially the Jamaat did not support the demand for the creation of a separate country for Muslims, because many of its members did not view the European conception of a modern nation-state as compatible with the political goals of Islam. But when Pakistan was finally a reality in 1947, Maududi and his party lobbied aggressively for a strong emphasis on Islam in Pakistan's law and constitution. From the very beginning, the Jamaat was an assembly of mainly middle-class and educated but religious folk. The Jamaat's middlebrow intellectual vision for an Islamic society didn't resonate very much in a poor and agricultural economy, and it never really had the numbers or financial resources to compete against wealthier and more populist political fronts like Bhutto's. As decades passed, politics in Pakistan became increasingly the domain of the wealthy and land-owning elites. But what the Jamaat lacked in real electoral

prospects it made up for with its impassioned and energetic following—street muscle.

The Jamaat was not the only group claiming to represent
Islamic thinking. There were several other religious groups
led by more traditional religious clerics and even men in
Bhutto's own close circle of advisers who had their own vision for an Islamic democracy. In reality, when it came to
Islam, it was always only a question of degree. Any player
on the national political stage with a hope of success or
any leader with dreams of transformative change needed to
include Islam in his political agenda. This was the founding vision of the country and the legacy of the Objectives
Resolution. This is what Bhutto had to work with.

The breakaway of Bangladesh came as a real blow to the
national idea of Pakistan. The state had been created at the
end of colonial rule on the claim that Muslims needed a
separate state in South Asia. But now that half the Muslims
of Pakistan had broken off because of their linguistic and
ethnic differences, what would hold the rest of the nation
together? The question hung over the constitutional project
like a gloomy cloud. But Islam was not the only, or even the
biggest, challenge. Bhutto needed the men and the women,
the Socialists and the nationalists, the farmers and the industrialists to come together to agree on one single document.
He needed the people of Pakistan, who spoke more than a
dozen different and mutually unintelligible languages, and
were of many different ethnicities and cultures, to define the
rules for their shared state. They needed to define how the
thread of Islam tied together the Muslim-majority country
and how the religion must define political life. But even the

most basic questions needed answers: How many provinces would there be in the new Pakistan? Would it be a parliamentary system or a presidential system? How would power be distributed throughout the federation? In some ways, Pakistan needed to be rebuilt from the ground up.

Shahzad began teaching an undergraduate course in developmental biology and another one in ecology in the winter of 1972. In the cold, hard schools of Ichhra he had learned to be deathly afraid of his teachers. They would lash out without warning and smack students unexpectedly with heavy wooden sticks. But in America, Shahzad became enamored with his professors' teaching styles and he brought them home to his classes at Punjab University. He was a hit with his own students. Soon he was also able to obtain a few grants to set up his own research laboratory. He hired several students as assistants, and in one corner of the lab he carved out his own office and installed an air conditioner for the grueling summers.

The professorship started off excellently, but the work of a superintendent of a student dormitory, looking after the daily needs and problems of the hundreds of students living in the building, was a little more complicated. Punjab University had become extremely political after the civil war of 1971. As different political groups organized on the national stage to influence the future course of the country, the campus of the largest university in Pakistan became the grounds for an epic turf battle between student groups loyal to different competing political parties. Two student groups in particular were turning the campus, quite literally, into a battleground: the student wing aligned with the Jamaat, known as the Islami Jamiat Taleba or the "Islamic Students Congregation," and the People's Students' Federation, which operated under the umbrella of Bhutto's People's Party.

Shahzad, freshly returned from a euphoric antiwar left in America, took a great liking to the ideology, energy, and charisma of Zulfiqar Bhutto. In his Socialist and populist ideology, Shahzad saw a man he could relate to, but this wasn't an opinion he could express freely on campus. He did not want to get caught in the middle of the heated student politics. The Jamaat's student wing was a powerful force that did not shy away from violence. And on a bad day, Bhutto's students could be every bit as ruthless. So Shahzad learned to keep his political opinions to himself. Luckily for my father, the zoology department, like most departments of the natural sciences, was less politicized than others. These were research hubs, known more for producing eccentric scientists than calculating or charming student political leaders. As a result, the scientists often found themselves stuck between disputing parties, neutral arbitrators of hot political exchanges on campus. Shahzad found out quickly, though, that this didn't necessarily guarantee safety.

A few months after he began teaching, Shahzad was appointed one of a dozen election commissioners for the student union elections at the university. It was a prohibitively hot September day when Shahzad and his colleagues gathered in the Senate Hall across from the Law School to begin counting the ballots for the president of the student union. By eleven at night, there was an imposing throng of Jamaat's student activists gathered outside the building, chanting slogans in anticipation of their candidate's victory.

Then, just before midnight, the raucous slogans suddenly turned into panicky commotion. There was yelling and then the unmistakable sound of gunshots. Shahzad and his colleagues in the Senate Hall froze. Before anyone even had a chance to react, one of the windows in the hall shattered and crashed; a spout of blood splattered across the white wall. Shahzad looked a few seats over at Dr. Omar, a chemistry professor, as he dropped to the floor, bleeding from a head wound. The bullet had grazed his skull and it was only a superficial wound, but he still needed help. An ambulance arrived a few minutes later, and the professor was loaded up and taken away. The firing resumed. The chief election officer told the faculty to suspend the vote count, as he began making phone calls from a sheltered corner of the room. My father and his colleagues scrambled under the long conference table and sat huddled there for hours to avoid any more stray bullets. Soon, the police began firing tear gas at the crowds. In the early hours of the morning, when the crowds finally dispersed, my father and a few colleagues crawled out from under the table and snuck out through the back door.

By the fall of 1972, it was clear that the new Pakistani constitution would be unlike anything else in the world. Bhutto, finally confident that he had hammered out a blueprint for a constitution that would please everyone, presented the draft to the members of the national assembly, who had been elected in the fateful election a few years earlier that had led to the civil war in the first place. A passage based on the points of the Objectives Resolution served as the preamble to the new constitution. Article 1 declared that the country would be named the Islamic Republic of Pakistan, as it did in the first constitution of 1956. But unlike any previous constitution, anywhere in the world, this one stated in the very next article that "Islam shall be the state religion of Pakistan." The document, written in English, outlined a parliamentary system of government with a prime minister at its helm, and it guaranteed the necessary "fundamental rights" to all citizens regardless of race or religion. In its essence this was not very different from any constitution for any parliamentary democracy anywhere else in the world, except for the very major difference that the laws and principles of Islam would guide this parliamentary constitutional democracy.

In its original constitution of 1956, Pakistan had become the first independent Muslim democratic republic. Now with this new constitution, Pakistan became the first democratic country in the world to declare Islam as the state's religion. At a time of crisis after the 1971 civil war, when the nation had questioned the very idea of being built in the name of Islam, the leaders of Pakistan decided to double down, becoming even more emphatic about the experiment in Islamic democracy. On October 17, 1972, Zulfiqar Bhutto invited the leaders of all political parties, Islamic, non-Islamic, secular, regional, left, right, conservative, and liberal, to come together and meet in Islamabad, the capital. After a full day of final negotiations, with some brusque walkouts and some cliff-hanging drama, all political leaders signed the "Constitutional Accord." Pakistan finally had an agreement on a new constitution that would guide the country's path into the future.

Later that same night, Saadia was rushed to the delivery room at Lady Willingdon Hospital in Lahore. Thirty-six hours later she gave birth to my sister. They brought her home ten days later, and Shahzad spent the entire first night at home awake, staring at his daughter in awe. She was asleep through most of it, and he fanned her obsessively to keep the mosquitoes away. A year after they were married, Saadia and Shahzad were now parents. They had brought life into this world and they were elated, but also overwhelmed. They knew that they would now spend every minute of every day for many years to come protecting this life until it could protect itself. The real work lay in the days, years, and decades ahead when great sacrifices and a good amount of luck would be required to succeed and survive the harsh realities of an unpredictable world. My parents decided to name my sister Afia. It is an Arabic word taken from the Quran, and it means "tranquil."

LESS THAN FIVE YEARS later, on the morning of July 5, 1977, Saadia woke up to news that would change her life, and that of her family, forever. Zulfiqar Bhutto, who had been prime minister of Pakistan ever since the constitution passed, had been arrested by the military late in the night.

The elected government had been toppled. On television, a man wearing thick-rimmed glasses was reading coldly from a prepared script in nasally Urdu. He was a military general by the name of Zia-ul-Haq. Saadia had never seen him or heard him speak before.

General Zia explained that the infighting between political parties had forced the military to step into the political arena once again, in the interest of national stability. He said that he had ordered the arrest of all major political leaders including Prime Minister Bhutto. "I have accepted this challenge only as a soldier of Islam," Zia said. "My one and only goal is free and fair elections." He promised that elections would be held within ninety days. This strange general with a long pencil-thin mustache and one lazy eye concluded his address on this note: "in the recent upheaval the spirit of Islam that has come forward is commendable. This is proof that Pakistan, which was founded in the name of Islam, will remain standing in the name of Islam. For this to be an Islamic system is extremely important." It was the second time the military had taken over in the country's thirty-year history.

Saadia went through the motions of the morning, numbed by the sudden political upheaval. My parents now lived in a much larger house on the university campus, one that Shahzad had been allotted recently after several years of work. Saadia prepared eggs and *paratha* bread in the spacious kitchen for the large cast of characters that now occupied her home. Afia was almost five years old, and my older brother Shehryar had been born the year before. My paternal grandmother Zubaida had become very ill lately, and she was also living with my parents. Saadia broke the news to her bedridden mother-in-law as she laid breakfast out for her by her bed. "They've unleashed the apocalypse on us," Saadia said.

Saadia's thoughts dwelled on her husband. Shahzad was on a work trip many hundred miles away, but my mother was sure he would be watching the news too. She knew that his blood would be boiling. The past few months had been very tense at home, and one of the main reasons for this was Shahzad's mounting frustration in dealing with the Jamaat's influence on the Punjab University campus. Saadia was not coping well either. She had started to feel very depressed and was getting through her days only with the aid of several sedatives. She knew that this news would make things worse.

In the five years since working out the constitutional deal and becoming prime minister, Bhutto had forcefully implemented a unique social, political, and economic plan. True to his Socialist leanings, he nationalized all industry. True to his aspirations to make Pakistan a global power, he triggered a nuclear program, handing its reins to a young, ambitious, and industrious European-trained scientist by the name of Abdul Qadeer Khan. He attempted to make the military generals subordinate to his political office, but then had to rely on those same generals to quell another separatist movement in the southern province of Balochistan. He carried out massive land reforms that targeted large feudal landowners, not very different from ones in his own family. He also passed a series of laws empowering factory workers and unions. Bhutto's cocktail of policies was largely a disaster. Although his land reforms pleased a lot of small farmers, they upset the economic interests of the influential feudal landowning class. His nationalization project crippled a great number of very powerful business owners too. And as unemployment rates shot up, he lost his core support from the working class.

In his foreign policy, Bhutto naturally gravitated toward the Communist bloc and also oriented Pakistan more toward its western Muslim neighbors, like Iran, Turkey, and the Arab Middle Eastern countries. He began speaking of "Islamic socialism" and made diplomatic moves to position Pakistan as a leader among Muslims countries. In 1974, he hosted the second gathering of the newly formed Organization of Islamic Cooperation in Lahore. It was a maneuver to get closer to Pakistan's Arab and Muslim neighbors by bringing in a star-studded cast of Middle Eastern political heavyweights. Colonel Muammar Gaddafi of Libya addressed a packed house at Lahore's cricket stadium and called Pakistan a "citadel of Islam." He told the thousands gathered that "our resources are your resources," referring to his country's newly discovered and vast oil reserves. The Pakistanis named the cricket stadium after him. On the sidelines of the conference, Anwar Sadat, the president of Egypt, helped broker peace between Pakistan and Bangladesh, and Pakistan finally recognized its former other half as an independent country. King Fahd of Saudi Arabia was there and so was Yasser Arafat of Palestine.

Short of friends at home, Bhutto had also tried to buy favor with domestic Islamic political groups by pandering to the very parochial concerns of a few religious political

Zulfiqar Bhutto (in the middle of the front row, wearing a Jinnah cap) gathered the most prominent Muslim leaders from around the world for a conference in Lahore in 1974. Here he is praying at the Badshahi Mosque in the Old City with Colonel Muammar Gaddafi and King Faisal of Saudi Arabia to his left and Yasser Arafat, who sits in sunglasses, to his far right. (Source: AP)

leaders. He helped pass a law that declared a small minority religious group, the Ahmediyya, non-Muslim and heretical. He ordered the closure of all bars and nightclubs and restricted the sale and drinking of alcohol. Parties like the Jamaat accepted these favors but knew they were token gestures. They remained deeply suspicious of Bhutto, who became increasingly notorious for his personal habits, which were anything but strictly Islamic. Over his years in power, Bhutto had cultivated a notorious reputation for womanizing, drinking, and living a plush life while preaching austerity.

On the campus of Punjab University, the Jamaat's student group started ruling student politics with impunity. As Bhutto's hold on power started to weaken, the Jamaat's students became increasingly brazen and menacing. Shahzad saw tenured professors addressing activists from the student group as "sir," and it made his stomach churn. They were amateurish thugs when Shahzad had first started work, but now they were cold-blooded murderers. A few months before Bhutto was arrested by the military, a student at a medical college in Lahore was shot dead in his dormitory one day. He was a prominent worker for Bhutto's student wing, and everyone knew that it was the students from the Jamaat's group who had killed him. When Shahzad bumped into one of the Jamaat's student leaders on campus one day, he could not stop himself from confronting him: "Why did you do it? Why didn't you just beat him up, shake him up a little instead? Why did you have to kill him?" Shahzad asked him, trying to keep his cool. The student didn't lose his cool either. He didn't have to. "We found a girl in there with him, doctor *sahab.*" He added the honorific at the end sarcastically. "You see, he had turned away from Islam. And the punishment for an apostate is death." The Jamaat's student activists were convinced that in this turf battle they had God on their side.

My father was bubbling with horror and anxiety as he navigated the campus grounds every day. He wanted to speak out, like he had seen people do in America in the '60s, but he had two little children now. He couldn't even express himself freely to any of his friends, because he feared that if the word got around, the Jamaat's students would not waste time making an example out of him as an outspoken professor recently returned from America. Some days he would come home trembling with anger, and it worried Saadia. She had no desire to get involved in politics anymore, especially not when it pitted one countryman against another. "Leave it," she would plead with my father, trying to play down the political troubles. "We have our children now. Who cares for all that happens in the world outside?" But as Shahzad was becoming more distant and angry, she was becoming more depressed.

Meanwhile, as more people abandoned Bhutto's camp, he started to become paranoid. And this revealed a not-so-subtle authoritarian streak. In some ways he became even more heavy-handed than President Ayub, the military ruler he replaced. By the time the next scheduled elections of 1977 rolled around, nearly all political parties in the country had banded together in opposition, forming a single front that took to the streets and attracted huge crowds of disgruntled people.

Bhutto finally brought about his own demise in the March elections. When the People's Party won in a massive landslide, it was clear to everyone that Bhutto's government had rigged the elections. The united opposition took to the streets again and demanded that Bhutto step down immediately. They called strikes that paralyzed the major cities. In Lahore, Bhutto ordered the police and military to fire on protesters. Seven years after the civil war, Pakistanis were again being killed by their own military. By April, some cities were starting to look like war zones.

In Bhutto's mind this was all a plan hatched in Western capitals aimed at removing him from power. The street agitation was not indigenous, but a "huge colossal conspiracy against the Islamic state of Pakistan," he said in a speech at the parliament in April. It could be that these were just paranoid ramblings of a man on his way down, but he did have reasons to be suspicious. The United States had made very clear on many occasions that they did not like or trust this Pakistani leader with Communist leanings and nuclear ambitions. Only months before, during a visit to Islamabad, American Secretary of State Henry Kissinger had engaged in a heated exchange with Bhutto while discussing the country's nuclear program. Kissinger had reportedly threatened Bhutto: "We will make a horrible example of you."

When Bhutto was finally arrested that night in July by the military, and the mustachioed general spoke on the TV screen, and my mother had told her mother-in-law that "an apocalypse" was upon them, she was speaking very personally. Zubaida understood this too. General Zia-ul-Haq's speech on television, in which he spoke as "a soldier of Islam," might spell disaster at Punjab University. Saadia feared that all this would finally push Shahzad over the edge.

For a few weeks everyone kept hope alive. The general had promised elections within ninety days, and perhaps sanity would prevail. But that wasn't how things turned out at all. The situation spoiled quickly, losing all recognizable form. Bhutto was released on bail, rearrested, and released again. The elections kept getting postponed month after month. In September 1977, Bhutto was finally arrested

one last time, this time on the very serious charges of murder of a political opponent. It was a grim turn of events.
The penalty for murder was death. Bhutto was thrown into
a prison cell, and he now dedicated all his resources to his
legal defense.

With Bhutto out of the way, General Zia's path to power
was cleared. He settled into his role as supreme ruler and
began unrolling his own program for the country. As many
would have guessed after the general's first televised speech,
the Jamaat-e-Islami became Zia's favored political party in
the early days. He began cultivating the Jamaat's support and
consulting closely with its leaders. The Jamaat had never enjoyed any electoral success, nor did it expect any to come its
way soon, but the sudden attention from a military dictator
catapulted the party onto political center stage.

The Jamaat presented the general with a laundry list
of transformations they wanted to see. And as Bhutto had
done earlier, Zia picked the most simpleminded and myopic
changes and moved forward with them to win the Jamaat's
favor. After declaring himself president of the country a little more than a year after the coup, one of Zia's first reforms
was the introduction of the Hudood Ordinance in February
1979. The order added a series of new statutes to the Pakistani penal code, specifically punishments for extramarital
sex, theft, and alcohol consumption, which were considered
crimes beyond the realm of humans and thus "crimes against
God." The punishment for these crimes had been described
in the Quran: whiplashes for drinking alcohol, stoning to
death for adultery, and cutting off the hands for theft. These
were the only punishments for any crimes described in the

Quran, and General Zia decided to include these laws verbatim in Pakistan's penal code. Even though the laws remained largely unenforced at the time, they signaled Zia's intent to use punitive Islamic laws to fortify his rule.

It was in these days that my parents first began talking about leaving the country. With another military ruler in charge, Shahzad became more pessimistic than ever about Pakistan progressing through the next decade. He started mailing out applications for jobs he saw in his academic zoology and anatomy journals. He heard back first from Kenyatta University in Nairobi in the spring of 1979. They offered him decent pay and a senior rank. At first, Saadia was not impressed by the thought of living in Kenya. She knew nothing about Africa, but her sense was that it was difficult living, and the children would be exposed to many new tropical diseases. At the same time, she knew that the most important thing for the health of the family was to leave Pakistan. After some thought, she told Shahzad that she was ready and happy to move to Kenya.

They were still mulling options when one day Shahzad received a letter at his office from the University of Michigan. Shahzad had applied there for a postdoctoral research position, and when he saw the envelope his heart began racing. It was a thin letter and he could not bring himself to open it alone, so clutching the letter tightly, he made the short drive home. He barged through the door and showed the letter to Saadia. She tried to calm him as he tore open the envelope and extracted the piece of paper. Shahzad began reading from it: "'Dear Dr. Mufti, We are delighted to inform you . . .'"

So my parents began preparing to leave the city they loved in the country that was their home. It was their country that was pushing them out, Saadia and Shahzad concluded after many hours of conversation. Michigan was an opportunity to start fresh. It was best for the children too, they agreed. And so they began packing up. Zulfiqar Bhutto was hanged on April 9, 1979 after being convicted of murder. Days later, Shahzad, Saadia, and their son and daughter boarded a Pan-Am plane at Lahore airport bound for Detroit. This time, in his mind, Shahzad was leaving Pakistan permanently. He would not return, he promised himself, not unless the country changed. Now thirty, Saadia too was excited to be leaving. She was looking forward to America, the country she had seen in movies and on television. More than anything, she hoped this move would bring her family some much-needed comfort.

They settled into their seats on the airplane. Afia and Shehryar sat between them. The plane roared as it sped down the runway. As the wheels slowly peeled off the ground, Saadia peered out the window and watched the treetops and homes of Lahore shrink beneath her. The coiling vein-like streets disappeared, and the outlines of the city's many neighborhoods began coming into view—Ichhra, Chauburji, the Old City. Then, suddenly, Saadia was overcome by the strangest sensation. It was unlike anything she had ever felt before. Her heart began sinking, as if it were being pulled by some invisible string back down toward the ground. She felt a lump in her throat. She was making this move for her family, her own flesh and blood. She had not even fully left yet, and the land was already pulling her back in.

Three

I WAS BORN on the morning of January 22, 1981, just
before dawn, in the small town of Athens located along the
southeastern edge of Ohio. It was one of the coldest days
of the year. The ground was freshly blanketed with several inches of snow from the night before when my father
rushed my mother to the hospital. It wasn't a long drive.
The hospital was on the grounds of Ohio University, where
my father had months earlier taken a job as a professor at
the medical school. My father paced in the waiting room
and soon after sunrise, a nurse walked in and smiled as
she told him that he had a new baby boy. He followed her
into the nursery ward, and from across the glass pane saw
two newborn babies lying in cots. He recognized me in an
instant: I was the one with a full head of black hair. A little
later, he picked me up and carried me back into my mother's arms, and my two older siblings were waiting there to
see me for the very first time.

The previous spring, as Shahzad neared the end of his postdoctoral research in Ann Arbor, he and Saadia decided that they wanted to stay in the United States. From this long distance, Pakistan still looked like the same place they had fled, and neither felt ready to return. Shahzad began interviewing for teaching jobs, and he received offers from the medical schools at the University of Chicago and Ohio University. Saadia and Shahzad flew out to both cities to explore. In the end they settled on Ohio because it was offering a higher rank and Saadia felt more comfortable sending the children to school in a small town rather than on the south side of Chicago. That spring, as my mother's pregnancy progressed, she planned the move while my father rushed to finish his lab work in Michigan. Saadia was still in the first trimester of her pregnancy when my parents finally drove their belongings down to Ohio and moved into their new home.

Athens was a much smaller college town than Ann Arbor, with fewer than twenty thousand people. It was a town of mostly white people compared to the slightly more cosmopolitan Ann Arbor. On the map, they had moved a few miles closer to Lahore, but they now felt much farther away from Pakistan. Saadia's nausea got worse and she began to subsist on a diet of 7UP and almonds, the only two things she found in combination that would not make her sick. The real problem, of course, was that this was her first time bearing a child alone, far away from her mother.

The day after I was born, the *Athens Messenger* carried a small announcement at the top of page seven under "Hospital Notes": "Saadia and Shahzad Mufti, Athens, a son."

Shahzad teaching a class at Ohio University.

My parents had already decided on my name and my father had spelled it out for the attendant filling out the hospital records: "Shahan Mufti." My given name is a Persian word, and it suggests royalty, "like a shah." The word "shah" is derived from the ancient and much more complex word "*khshayathiya*." The word was used as a royal title by ancient Persian kings who ruled Central Asia hundreds of years before the birth of Christ. The derived title "shah" was adopted not only by later kings of Persia but also by sovereign monarchs of the many empires in South and Central Asia. The great kings of the Afghan kingdom called themselves "shah," and the title "shahanshah," or "king of kings," was used by emperors who ruled the lands of South Asia too. Why I received this uncommon, rather ostentatious, Persian name in a small university town in Ohio, I am unsure. My father's name, Shahzad, comes from the same root, but his name means "son of shah." Maybe my parents wished for some continuity. Or perhaps it was the fact that at the time of my birth, the lands of Persia ruled over the thoughts of all those who lived in America.

Saadia and Shahzad were still in Pakistan in January 1979, closely following the drama around Zulfiqar Bhutto's murder trial, when in Iran, Pakistan's neighbor to the west, the last Persian shah, Mohammed Reza Pahlavi, was facing a popular revolt. The shah had ruled Iran with an iron fist ever since the British and American spy agencies had helped him topple an elected government decades earlier. But recently, Iranians had started fighting back against the shah's repressive regime. Beginning in 1978, millions of Iranians started to spill out onto the streets to demand that the king step down from power. At first the shah responded to the dissent by letting loose the draconian secret police on the protesters and organizers, but the Iranians did not back down. Finally, when the powerful military stopped accepting the king's orders, and the young conscripts refused to shoot at other Iranians, the shah was outflanked and rendered toothless. On January 16, 1979, military officials in Iran announced that the shah had flown to Egypt for vacation and medical treatment, but Iranians knew he would never return. He left on an Evergreen Airlines aircraft, a company that had long been a CIA front.

With the shah gone, an Iranian Muslim cleric by the name of Ruhollah Khomeini made plans to return to Iran after many years of exile. Khomeini, whose first name means "spirit of God," had been fueling the revolt against the shah with his moving sermons, which were secretly distributed throughout the country on cassette tapes. He flew to Iran from Paris a few days after the shah had escaped and was greeted by millions of adoring Iranians on the ground. They had suffered badly under the shah's rule, and Khomeini offered hope for change. Weeks after he landed, the people decided in a popular vote to abolish the monarchy and replace it with an Islamic government. Before the end of the year, Iran had passed an Islamic constitution. And so Iran became the second country, after its neighbor Pakistan, to become an Islamic republic. Unlike Pakistan, which was a country of mostly Sunni Muslims, Iran declared Shia Islam as its state religion. Khomeini was declared a lifetime supreme leader of Iran.

America, which had strongly backed the shah for decades, was stunned by the swiftness of the Iranian revolution. In Iran, the course of the revolution was turning decidedly anti-American. When the shah arrived in America nine months after he left Iran, Khomeini demanded that the former king be returned to face trial, but the American government ignored and resisted these demands. Then, on November 4, 1979, weeks after Saadia and Shahzad had landed in the United States with their two children, a group of Iranian students stormed the American embassy in the Iranian capital, Tehran. They captured the sixty-six Americans inside. Three of them were CIA agents, and the rest were regular embassy employees. But now they were all hostages of the Iranian regime. The very next day, for the first time, Khomeini publicly used the phrase "the Great Satan" to describe America. Riding the popular anti-American sentiments that had been building over decades, Khomeini decided to channel his country's despair and turn it into anger at one meddling foreign power.

The trouble in Iran was only one of the many crises gripping the region. Days after the mobs of students had taken American hostages in Tehran, the Kaaba, Islam's holiest site, which is in Mecca, Saudi Arabia, was taken over by armed militants from a messianic Islamic cult. They announced the arrival of a new prophet of the end days and declared jihad against the Saudi monarchy, another close ally of the United States. The group, which included members of Saudi Arabia's own military, chose the center stage of Islam's most sacred site at a special time—the annual hajj, when millions of Muslims from all over the world gather there. It was also the new year of the fifteenth century of the Islamic calendar. The militants took hundreds of hostages inside the holy site and laid out demands for the establishment of a true Islamic government in Saudi Arabia to replace the corrupt monarchy. A tense standoff lasted several days, and the Saudi government eventually had to invite foreign troops to clear out the Islamic holy compound.

In Iran, Khomeini wasted no time using this episode to turn the shock of Muslims all over the world into anger against America. "It is not beyond guessing that this is the work of criminal American imperialism and international Zionism," he said on Tehran radio on November 21, 1979. The next day, Pakistan's own radio stations began quoting Khomeini in reports suggesting that the United States and Israel were in fact behind the attacks on Islam's holy mosque. That day, hundreds of students, many of them workers of the Jamaat-e-Islami and other political parties, began gathering outside the American embassy in Islamabad yelling, "Death to America." Thousands kept arriving as the day went on, unloading in waves off buses. They finally stormed the compound. They smashed windows and toppled cars and poured gasoline and set fire to everything, razing the embassy building. Other mobs launched attacks on a few American-owned locations in Islamabad, including the American School and the American Information Center. Some of the young men attacking the embassy carried rifles and small pistols. A bullet pierced the chest of one of the six U.S. Marines who were standing guard on the rooftop, killing him instantly. Panic spread inside, and more than a hundred embassy officials locked themselves in a secure vault, waiting for help.

Pakistan's military president Zia would have been torn about how to react to an angry mob burning down the American embassy in his capital. A few months earlier, the United States had cut off all economic aid to Pakistan, to punish the country for its nuclear program. American plans to attack Pakistani nuclear facilities had also been leaked in the press only days before, and Zia read all this as signs of intimidation. On the other hand, from the dictator's point of view, it was not wise to let unsupervised mobs rampage through Pakistani cities like they had in Iran. Who knew where all this could lead? Conveniently, Zia didn't have to make any tough decisions right away. He'd taken that day off, enjoying a daylong bicycle ride through the city of Rawalpindi to raise public awareness about the healthy mode of transport. A good part of the military brass was there with him for his protection, and so no one was around to answer the frantic calls from the U.S. embassy throughout the afternoon. Pakistani troops finally arrived four hours later. By that time, the protesters had left, after gutting the entire compound, leaving only a heap of ash and debris. The embassy officials hiding in the vault were recovered safely, but four embassy workers, including two Americans, were killed that day. It was the worst attack on any U.S. embassy ever.

My parents had barely touched the ground in their new home in America when they were bombarded with pictures of these events out of Iran, Saudi Arabia, and Pakistan. On their first color TV set, they watched ABC's *World News Tonight*, showing footage of blindfolded American hostages in handcuffs in Tehran. Young Pakistani men were shown ransacking the American embassy in their country's capital, Islamabad. They saw Iranian students in Tehran carrying out garbage in American flags. Chilling images of the stern-looking Ayatollah Khomeini, dressed in a loose dark-colored robe, were a regular fixture on the evening news. His stern hawklike features, which grew around his piercing eyes brimmed by thick bushy eyebrows, became the very face of evil in America. His jet-black turban was instantly recognized as trouble. In Washington, protesters would gather outside the White House, holding signs like DEPORT ALL IRANIANS: GET THE HELL OUT OF MY COUNTRY. Middle Eastern–looking men were beaten in the streets of America.

"America Held Hostage" became a nightly segment on ABC News over the next year. CBS's Walter Cronkite, American television's most trusted man, added to his famous sign-off—"and that's the way it is"—a count of the days that the American hostages had endured captivity. The count ticked over: ten, twenty, fifty, one hundred, three hundred days. *Time* magazine declared the ayatollah its man of the year in January 1980. He was "The Mystic Who Lit the Fires of Hatred," and his revolution had jolted America out of its self-doubting "Vietnam syndrome." The article stated that "worries about America's ability to influence events abroad are giving way to anger about impotence."

It was not a good time to be Muslim in America. But with my birth, there was finally some good news to cheer about. My parents brought me home three days after I was born, and that evening my father sat down with a bowl of popcorn to watch the Super Bowl—football was the only American sport he found interesting. The entrance to the Louisiana Superdome was decorated with a large yellow bow, eighty feet tall and thirty feet wide. The spectators in the stands all wore smaller yellow bows too, turning the entire stadium a bright hue of yellow. It was a day of great celebration all across America. That morning, fifty hostages from Tehran had arrived back home in America. After 444 days, the hostage crisis was finally over. "The Star-Spangled Banner" would have sounded extra special that evening. But the damage was done. The seeds of fear and hatred of Islam and Muslims had been sown in America in the extraordinary year before my birth. In time these seeds would grow tall and big, casting a dark shadow over my family's life in the country.

WHEN I WAS less than two years old, my family traveled to Pakistan, my first visit there. They had settled decently in Ohio. Soon after my birth, Shahzad had bought a house on a tree-lined cul-de-sac a few miles from Ohio University. It was much larger than anything my parents had ever lived in, with a sprawling front yard and a backyard that opened into a thicket of trees along a small stream. It had four spacious and sunny bedrooms on two floors. Parked in the driveway was a brand-new beige Datsun. The house was in a good school district too. But all the creature comforts didn't lessen the strong pull of home. The weekly exchange of letters, and occasional audiotapes and Polaroid photographs, between Lahore and Ohio eventually wore thin. So when my mother's youngest brother decided to get married, my parents saw a good excuse to make the journey back home for a visit.

We landed at Lahore airport in October 1982. A group of a dozen or so relatives were waiting on the tarmac as we descended the gangway. My parents had not seen their families in nearly three years. They had experienced leaving home, but this was the first time they experienced homecoming together. They embraced their loved ones and shed some tears. My parents would see little of their three children from this moment onward during their stay. Afia disappeared with a bevy of cousins her age and my brother busied himself with the younger boys. I too was whisked away by aunts and uncles, cousins, cousins of cousins, all kinds of Mufti and Qazi relatives. Naturally, I remember nothing from this trip. I was too young. And I could not have comprehended how defining this trip would be for the future course of my life.

I spoke not a word of Urdu, but I did speak English with a strong American accent, and this, I am told, provided hours of entertainment to my extended family who were unfamiliar with this way of speaking. There is a stack of photographs from this trip, which my mother has kept safe in an album, that offer clues to my life during these weeks in Pakistan. Apparently, I ate a lot. In one photo I am discovering the pleasures of the *ganderi*, a cube of raw sugarcane, and in another I am enjoying a mango, the sweetest of the sweet fruits of Lahore. There is a photo from our visit to the zoo, where I hold an ice cream cone in my hand standing in front of a zebra enclosure, and there's another of me playing my first game of cricket with my brother and cousins. In another photograph, from the roof of the house in Chauburji, I look on as my mother's youngest brother, my uncle Asdaq, launches a paper kite into the sky with a swift upward motion of his straightened arm.

While I strayed off, wide-eyed, plunging myself into the tastes, sounds, and sights of this new and strange place, my parents would have returned to view their old home with a more tentative eye. Zia-ul-Haq, the general with the lazy

Grandfather Akhlaque brought home two goats for a ceremonial sacrifice when I entered his Chauburji home for the first time. Here, he holds me in his arms, standing in the same courtyard where my parents were married.

eye, was still the military ruler in charge. There was a time, a couple of years earlier, after the attack on the American embassy in Islamabad, when things would have felt very uncertain for the general. It would have seemed that Pakistan, like Iran, was ready to embark on a path of hatred and bitterness toward the United States and face international isolation. Zia-ul-Haq must have felt wobbly in his seat. But then only weeks after the embassy attack, an extraordinary development completely changed the course of Pakistan's history and made General Zia more powerful than ever before.

Over the New Year weekend of 1980, the Soviet army invaded Afghanistan, Pakistan's other neighbor along its western border. The Soviets helped topple a newly elected Afghan government and replaced it with a Communist regime. Panic ensued in Washington. The Soviets had been expanding their influence in Central Asia for decades, and Afghanistan, which bordered several Soviet states, had been in the crosshairs of the Soviet empire for many years. Some American military analysts speculated that the Soviets were expanding southward in order to eventually reach the warm waters of the Indian Ocean. But Afghanistan had no coast. So, the thinking went, the invasion was actually only a layover to get through to the real prize: the southern coast of Pakistan near the Persian Gulf, the world's outlet for petroleum. American planners would have looked over the map of Asia that year and wondered how it all went so wrong. They had no ally left in the region. Most of Indochina had been lost; China was already Communist; the Indians were close allies of the Soviets; the shah of Iran had fallen among chants of "Death to America"; and the Soviets had now taken over Afghanistan too. The domino theory suggested that all of Asia would soon fall to communism, unless it could be stopped in its tracks.

Desperate for help, America reached out to the only country it could hope to befriend: Pakistan. It wasn't an easy task. America had shunned Pakistan for attempting to build the bomb, and President Zia's personal leaning toward Islamic rule would have frightened some Americans after watching the scenes in Iran. But neither the bomb nor Islam necessarily meant anti-Americanism at that time. President Jimmy Carter kicked off negotiations in 1980 by offering a four-hundred-million-dollar aid package for two years, but General Zia rebuffed the offer, calling it "peanuts." It was a slight against the American president, who was a peanut farmer in his early days, but it also indicated that if the price were right, Zia might be willing to come on board. Zia's negotiations paid off. Two years later, in the year I was born, President Ronald Reagan offered Pakistan an aid package of more than three billion dollars, eight times the size of Carter's offer. This time Zia signed on the dotted line. When we flew to Pakistan in 1982, Pakistan had become an important ally of America, second only to Israel in the amount of American taxpayer money it received as aid. Pakistan was now America's front-line ally in the Cold War.

America's deal was simple: half of the American aid was meant to boost Pakistan's economy and the other half was to beef up the military arsenal. In return, Pakistan agreed to train and arm thousands of fighters for a guerrilla army and send them across the border into Afghanistan to battle and expel Soviet troops. The United States was able to lure the oil-rich rulers of Saudi Arabia into the deal as well, and they contributed millions of their petrodollars to the project. Thousands of young, often unemployed, Muslim men from Arab, African, and Central Asian countries began descending on Pakistan in the early eighties. Many of them ended up in northwest frontier towns near the Afghan border where, with American and Saudi money, the Pakistani intelligence agencies and military had set up training camps for them.

Here the men and boys were trained in the use of automatic weapons and military equipment and the best strategy to conduct guerrilla warfare in the rugged and mountainous Afghan terrain. They were also indoctrinated with Islamic religious fervor to motivate them to fight fearlessly. Special textbooks for these holy soldiers were printed in Urdu by the University of Nebraska, to teach these warriors about the importance of jihad, the Islamic ideal of struggle, and hatred for the "godless" Soviets. Battling the Soviets, they were told, would win these fighters a place in heaven.

This guerrilla army became known as the mujahideen, or "wagers of jihad." They crossed over into Afghanistan by the tens of thousands. Convinced that they were on a holy mission and trained by a top-notch Pakistani military, the mujahideen proved to be a fearsome fighting force. They began giving the Red Army hell in Afghanistan, and the American government loved it. When a few important mujahideen commanders visited Ronald Reagan, the president brought them out onto the White House lawn to introduce them to the U.S. news media. "These gentlemen," Reagan said, "are the moral equivalents of America's founding fathers."

In 1982, Pakistan and America's covert war against the Soviets in Afghanistan was in its third year. My parents would have seen the very real impact of the war in Afghanistan on Pakistan. To begin, there were great demographic changes. The war had forced millions of ordinary Afghans out of their homes and they began spilling across the borders into neighboring countries. Many of them went into

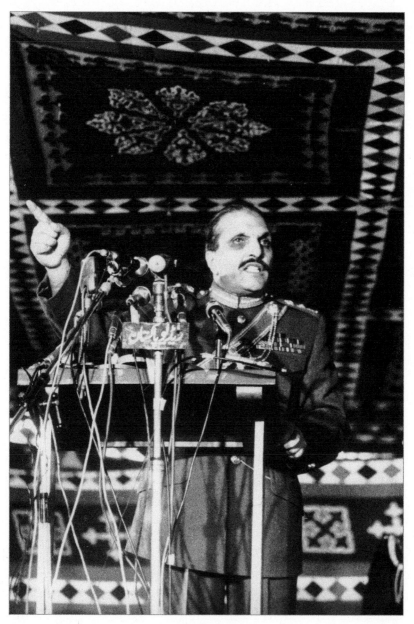

General Zia-ul-Haq speaks at a conference in Peshawar for Islamic foreign ministers on January 1, 1980. (Source: Central Press/Getty Images)

Iran, but a majority arrived in Pakistan. With nearly three million Afghans on its soil, Pakistan ended up hosting the largest population of refugees anywhere in the world at that time. Some of the young Afghan men in these refugee camps were recruited for the mujahideen army, some families moved to various Pakistani cities to begin rebuilding their lives from scratch, but most of the refugees simply languished in refugee camps.

Opening the borders to refugees from a country that was not only flush with weapons due to a violent guerrilla war but also the source of a vast majority of the world's heroin supply took a special toll on Pakistan. For the first time during this visit, Shahzad and Saadia heard stories of young men in extended circles of relatives and former students falling prey to heroin addiction. Friends were using the term "Kalashnikov culture" to describe a new wave of violence, driven by automatic weapons, that was sweeping through the cities. These weapons, supplied by America, were meant for killing Soviet troops in Afghanistan, but instead, thanks to the thriving black market for weapons run by corrupt Pakistani middlemen, many guns found their way into the hands of criminal gangs, who turned them on rival groups and on innocents.

Pakistan also became the battleground for a protracted regional power struggle. The Saudi-backed militias being trained for the anti-Soviet war brought with them a puritanical vision of Sunni Islam, which was extremely hostile to Muslims from the Shia sect, a minority in Pakistan. When the Saudi-backed militias began targeting Shias in Pakistan, Iran began forming its own Shia militias in Pakistan to battle the Sunnis. As a result, urban gang wars for control of turf between Sunni and Shia militias, backed by Saudi Arabia and Iran, respectively, erupted in all major cities, including Lahore. In the background, billions of dollars' worth of heroin was being grown in Afghanistan, bankrolling the Afghan war against the Soviets, and much of it was also being funneled to the rest of the world through Pakistani ports after going through the hands of local drug dealers. This meant that the cash incentives were high on all sides, and the mafia wars between Shia and Sunni inside Pakistan were claiming hundreds of lives every year.

As the transnational web of violence continued to spiral, Zia became increasingly comfortable in his position as military ruler with full American support. He was also moving forward swiftly with his "Islamization" campaign. He announced a definitive-sounding plan for introducing a *Nizam-e-Mustafa*, or the "Order of the Prophet," as the new Islamic vision for Pakistan. On paper, it appeared as a series of sweeping reforms. The punishments for extramarital sex, theft, and alcohol consumption introduced by Zia in 1979 through the Hudood Ordinance were already in the books. Zia made a few additions to the penal code, which became known commonly as the blasphemy laws. These prescribed punishments such as life imprisonment for defiling the Quran and the death penalty for anyone who "defiles the sacred name of the Holy Prophet Muhammad." The laws were mostly abused to target religious minorities. In 1981, the government added a new apex court called the Federal Shariat Court, which operated parallel to the regular Supreme Court and was tasked with adjudicating this new religious class of crimes. The Respect of Ramzan Ordinance made it illegal to eat or drink anything in public during the fasting period during the month of Ramzan. The government also created a new tier of law enforcement, a moral police, which was charged with helping to strengthen people's "moral values" by staging public interventions and encouraging people to pray and women to cover up "properly." There were minor changes as well. Female newsreaders on TV now covered their heads with a scarf. The *azaan*, or call to prayer, was aired on radio and television five times a day.

Besides some of the obvious violations of constitutionally guaranteed freedoms, the laws sometimes wandered into the absurd. The daily news was now also telecast in Arabic each day, for example, but almost no one spoke Arabic in Pakistan. So what was the point? Other laws only confirmed what Shahzad had suspected earlier, when Zia had first come to power: that the military general was interested in Islam only as a tool to cement his political power. Zia was all too happy to introduce moral police to check on people's eating and drinking habits and clothing, and he was quick to prescribe harsh punishments for violating narrowly defined behavioral codes, like public lashings for drunkenness. His laws targeted the more vulnerable members of society, like women, the poor, and religious minorities. But there was little, if any, focus on the promises of an Islam-inspired democracy, the social and economic justice, the freedom of expression, and the judicial independence that were outlined in the Islamic constitution. Corruption remained rampant and even worsened in some places. Many of the old opportunistic and corrupt politicians, secular and Islamic, surrounded Zia; despite vast amounts of American aid, social safety nets were in deplorable shape. Hospitals remained understaffed and people continued to die of easily curable diseases and malnutrition as Zia's cronies lined their pockets with dollars.

When it came to real change on larger social, political, and economic issues, Zia had little to offer. He was far more careful than his predecessor, Bhutto, and stayed out of the way of the powerful landed elite and wealthy industrialists and business owners. This meant that even the more fundamental political and legal reforms were designed to not rock the boat too much. The rulings of the Federal Shariat Court, for example, were often overturned by the common law Supreme Court for being unconstitutional. As a result, there were frequent judicial tussles between the two courts. It was the same with his economic policy. In accordance with the letter of the Islamic law, Zia ordered the abolition of monetary interest from Pakistan's domestic banks, but this went unimplemented, leading to more confusion as two parallel financial systems emerged, one with interest and one without. In education, Zia gave madrassas autonomy to teach their own independent curricula, which widened the gap between regular primary and secondary education and madrassas.

For all the apparent changes as part of the Islamization campaign, Shahzad was struck by how little things had changed where it mattered the most for him. When he visited his old friends at Punjab University, they told him that the Jamaat's student group still had an iron grip on affairs of the university, just as they did before Zia came to power. Islamic government or not, the group was still running the affairs of the university as always. There was some news, his friends told him: President Zia had inaugurated another major university in Islamabad, called the International Islamic University. It was built on the campus of the new Faisal Mosque that was constructed using millions of dollars in investment, and was named after King Faisal al-Saud of Saudi Arabia.

For most of the trip, Saadia and Shahzad busied themselves visiting family all over the Punjab. They also saw old friends from Ichhra and Chauburji, classmates from Lahore College and Punjab University, some of whom they had not seen in more than a decade. They were home again. Saadia went shopping in Anarkali bazaar near the walled Old City and then at the newer shops in Liberty Market. Shahzad watched a cricket match, and it had been so long he barely recognized anyone on the team anymore. Yet he savored every moment of the daylong game. The radio still had many of the same songs playing that Shahzad and Saadia remembered listening to on Shahzad's gramophone when they got married a decade ago. They watched as their children took to life in Lahore with natural ease and mixed with generations of family.

We spent our last evening in Pakistan with my paternal grandmother. My grandmother's arthritis had become much worse over the years and she was now in a wheelchair. It was the starkest reminder of her general failing health. She was happy to hear about my father's success in Ohio, but that night she broke down into tears as I sat in her lap.

Shahzad found time for a cricket game with friends during the trip to Pakistan in 1982. Here he's throwing the ball at a batsman. The graffiti on the wall in the background reads: "Long Live Ayatollah Khomeini" and "We Are with Khomeini," in support of the Islamic revolution in neighboring Iran.

"Shahzad, what do you have there that you can't have here?"
My father knew nothing he said would persuade her, so he
stayed silent.

It was time to go back to America. The next morning, a
small group of relatives traveled to the airport once again to
see us off. It was a miserable occasion. No one knew when
we would be together again. My grandmother Zubaida held
me in her arms and cried, even though she had met me
only eight weeks ago. Not fully aware of why everyone was
crying, I too began to sniffle as my father snapped a photograph of me in my mother's lap, while she mustered a smile
for the camera. The last photograph was taken outside a
railway station on the way to the airport, and it appears
absurdly morbid. We all stand in line wrapped in shawls,
my parents, us siblings, my aunt and uncle and my paternal
and maternal grandmothers and Grandfather Akhlaque
Qazi. Not one of us could manage a smile in the dark, dull
morning haze of the cold winter.

Saadia and Shahzad checked in the half dozen suit-
cases at the airport and worked their way through customs
and passport control and into the departure lounge. They
were exhausted before the thirty-six hour journey had even
begun. We had a bite to eat as we waited. Finally we boarded
the plane quietly, amid hundreds of other people leaving
or returning in various stages of disconnect and disrepair.
Saadia's eyes were red and swollen from saying goodbye
again, and my sister still quietly wept with her head in my
mother's lap. No one had said a word in quite a while when
finally Shahzad turned to Saadia and broke the silence.
"Saadia, we should return home." Saadia knew what he

meant. Home was Lahore, not the house on the cul-de-sac in Athens. Saadia said she agreed completely. She gave him a tired smile and fell asleep instantly. This time, she didn't even feel the plane taking off.

WITH ONE EYE on the past and one on the future, Saadia and Shahzad wrestled with the idea that my father presented on the plane. *Home.* It was a decision that could change everything once again. They had now lived in America for five years. The children were completely at home in Ohio and easily slipped back into their life in Athens. But it was more difficult for the two of them. Shahzad, a zoologist by training, thought about this during the long hours at his lab. Some animals have a strong migratory instinct that lures them periodically across oceans and continents to find home and build a nest. It could be the smell of the soil, or perhaps some memory encoded in their DNA that guides these journeys. Maybe it is the same function that allows newborn animals to recognize their kin before their eyes are fully open or their senses are sharpened. It feels like an invisible force that acts on the pit of the stomach, deep inside the gut, and pulls people toward the one spot on the planet that is the nucleus of their life. It is the place where memories and history and blood have coagulated into a tight mass, so dense that it seems to exert its own gravitational pull. *Home.* Or maybe it's not biological at all. Perhaps it is simply faith. A faith that one path leads to a

better outcome or faith in a mission that justifies uprooting and moving from one place to another.

But it wasn't all pull. There were also forces pushing
Saadia and Shahzad away from the small college town where
they had bought a house and tried to make a home. America was still hostage to the memory of the Iranian crisis, still
haunted by what had occurred at the embassies in Tehran
and Islamabad a few years earlier. Those attacks were just the
beginning of a stream of shocking assaults against the United
States in many other Muslim countries. The American embassy in Tripoli fell to rioters next, and then the bombing
of the U.S. embassy in Beirut killed more than sixty people.
In Beirut a newly formed organization named Islamic Jihad
targeted an American military barracks in the middle of the
country's civil war and killed 220 American Marines. With
every passing month, Americans learned of new reasons to
be suspicious and afraid of Islam and Muslims. This fear was
recent. Shahzad had not felt this during his time in America
in the sixties. He had fit in with such ease then, but now he
found it impossible to construct a social life with colleagues.
He had been very close to his friends at his medical school,
and at Ann Arbor he regularly visited his professors' homes.
My mother made friends with many of the women she met
too. But in Athens, Saadia and Shahzad felt isolated, even
more so after the trip to Pakistan. They rarely invited anyone
over and rarely got invited out. Was it Saadia and Shahzad
who were being cold? Or was the air of hostility they felt
real? Perhaps it was a bit of both.

Many years before I would receive that phone call as
a college student in Vermont, my father fielded a phone

During the short trip to Pakistan in 1982, I am sitting on my uncle's motorbike in the courtyard where my parents were married. A couple of charpoys are laid out behind me.

call that similarly made him wonder about his place in the world. Late one Sunday night, the phone rang and my father crawled out of bed to the living room. Perhaps it was a call from Pakistan, he thought. The man at the other end of the line was obviously drunk and there was loud music playing in the background. "Is this Shazz?" said the man. "Who is this?" my father asked. There were only three bars in town and he was probably calling from one of them. "Well, guess what? I'm with the Ku Klux Klan," he slurred. "I'm sending one of my guys over to get some money from you . . ." My father hung up the phone. It immediately rang again. "Get the fuck out of my country you fucking Iranian," the man bellowed this time.

My father hung up once again and now he left the phone off the hook. He sat down on the couch in the dark and wondered why the man had called this number. Did he find it in a phone book? Maybe in search of "Muhammad" the man had come across "Mufti." Or maybe in search of "Shah" he had spotted "Shahzad." As he thought about how his name appeared in the phone book, Shahzad suddenly realized something more important: the phone book also listed the home address. He scurried back to the bedroom and woke up Saadia to tell her about the phone calls. The bars in town would close in about an hour. Was there a chance this man might come to the house? The children were asleep in the two rooms whose windows faced the street. They thought about waking the children and moving them all into their own room, but that might needlessly scare them. They tried to dismiss the idea that the drunken man would actually show up at the door, but what if they

The entire family in front of the house on the cul-de-sac in Ohio. I am in Saadia's arms looking to the left.

were wrong? They sat next to one another on the couch in the living room staring at the front door until the sun rose. Then they stood up and began packing lunches for the kids before the school bus arrived.

Sometimes they wondered about what the children were facing in school. My sister was late to come home one day from a playdate at a friend's house, so my mother called to ask if she was still there. The friend's mother picked up the phone and Saadia asked if she could speak to Afia. The woman put Saadia on hold and then she heard the woman saying to someone, "Tell that brown bitch it's her mother calling." Saadia felt a tingle through the length of her spine. She knew that she was meant to hear those words. When my sister came back home, my mother told her that she would never be allowed to visit this friend's house again. Afia cried for hours, confused.

There were real reasons to stay put. My father was up for tenure review soon. While I was the only one in the family born in America and an American citizen, the rest had been green card holders for almost four years now. In another year they might all become citizens. And then there was the house. They had bought it only a few years earlier, right before the housing market in America took a nosedive. They could lose tens of thousands of dollars if they tried to sell it now. Saadia and Shahzad discussed all this and kept talking in circles. Eventually, they stopped pressing each other for a specific date. Soon the memories from the trip to Pakistan began to fade a little, and so did the impassioned urgency with which Shahzad and Saadia had first spoken about their plans to return to Pakistan.

Then one day, the memories came flooding back to sweep us all away. It was a few days before my third birthday. Athens was blanketed in fresh powdery snow. The schools were shut for a snow day and everyone was home that morning. At around eight o'clock the phone rang in the living room. Saadia answered it.

"Are you Saadia Mufti?" the woman on the line asked.

"Yes I am."

"I have a telegraphic message for you that I'll read out: 'Yusuf has died STOP We are all going to the village STOP Akhlaque.'"

Celebrating my mother's thirty-fourth birthday at our home in Athens, Ohio, in 1983.

Saadia heard the message clearly, but her mind did not register it immediately. Yusuf, my mother's adopted brother, whom she had seen less than a year ago in Pakistan, happy and healthy, was dead. Saadia walked into the bedroom and told Shahzad the news with an expression so blank that it scared him. As she said the words out loud, Saadia fainted and collapsed to the floor. She came back around but Shahzad gave her a sleeping pill, so she slept for the next several hours. When she woke up, it was dark outside. She called for my father from the bed and asked him whether what she remembered had actually happened.

He sat by her side and told her that it was true and then he showed her the telegram that had arrived. Saadia read the letters on the page and began weeping uncontrollably, just the way she had when Yusuf had taken her to President Ayub's house. My father told her that Yusuf had died suddenly of a heart attack. He was only forty-nine years old. He was gone and Saadia never had a chance to say goodbye.

For days afterward, Saadia walked around the house not saying much. She was devastated, and she had actual difficulty stringing together sentences. Eventually, she went mute, turning deeper into her shell. Shahzad struggled to understand what was happening to his wife, but he did know that this was all much bigger than the grief over Yusuf's death. What would happen when the next person passed away in Lahore? Would they be caught on the wrong side of the globe once again? They realized in those days of mourning Yusuf that it was not for the sake of the young that they needed to return to Pakistan. The children could be brought up anywhere. The truth was that they needed to be there to bury their old into the earth. There was no choice. They needed to be home.

With an eye on two generations, my parents finally made the decision: they would return to the country along the Indus. They would live in the city of Lahore on the Ravi. Shahzad told his department chair in Ohio the following month that he would not be looking for a renewal of his contract at his tenure review. He had a work opportunity in Pakistan, he explained. His chair said that he understood. My parents put the house up for sale and took the first decent offer they got even though they did lose thousands of dollars. They had a big garage sale and sold off nearly everything, the beds and crib, the couches, pots and pans, and even the toys that were too large to pack and carry. My father handed over the keys to the beige Datsun to a friend. Days before the flight, as Shahzad emptied out his drawers, he sifted through the many plastic cards he had collected in America: his faculty ID from Ohio University, his MasterCard, and the four green cards for the four Pakistani members of the family. He had no use for these anymore, but he packed all these things safely in a plastic bag anyway and tucked them in with his clothes in the suitcase. They were good memories.

Shahzad and Saadia were changing the course of the family's history. The Pakistan they were returning to would not be like the old Pakistan. They were giving up one life and embarking on a completely new one. Shahzad had faith that this was the best thing to do. The children and the generations after him would thank him for this decision, he told himself. But this was only what he wanted to believe at that time. Deep inside, he knew as well that no one really knows what the future brings. How would he look back at this moment and retell the story to himself? And how would his children remember this moment? He did not know; the future hadn't happened yet. And at the end of it all, it is what happens in the future that molds the story of what passed.

Four

MY EARLIEST MEMORY is from Pakistan. It was the winter
of 1985. I was four years old. I stood at the front gate of
my home in Lahore, peering out through the tilted blue
slats at the neighborhood children playing cricket on the
street. The ball would get hit with a sweet *thok* with the flat
paddle bat and sail over the lush treetops. The boys would
chase after it, kicking up tufts of dust and shouting out at
each other in a language I did not understand. Then one
boy, noticing me spying from behind the gate, called at me
to join the game in inviting tones of friendship. I did not
speak his language, I did not know the rules of the game
yet, and I did not have the courage to go outside and learn,
so I turned around and darted back indoors as quickly as
my legs could carry me, panting, frightened.

This is what I believe to be my first memory, anyway.
I do have a handful of older memories from my life in
America, but they are dubious. All people are capable of

conflating the real with the imaginary at all stages of their lives, and I am unsure whether those old memories are real or simply figments of my imagination, or perhaps figments from someone else's life that I heard and sewed like patch-work into my own story. They are faded, like old Polaroids, so it's hard to tell. In any case, I've discarded them, and the blue gate is where my real memory begins. That is what I decided a long time ago.

When I landed in Pakistan in 1984, I spoke not a word of Urdu or Punjabi, my family's languages and the major languages spoken in Lahore. It wasn't just the rules of cricket that I was unsure of; everything else in my environment was equally new and strange. I did not belong to this place, not yet. My father returned to a job at Punjab University, this time as a full professor in the department of zoology. My mother was offered a job teaching English at a nearby high school. She never did get that PhD she wanted, but she was finally a teacher like she had always wanted to be. She was ecstatic. We moved into an independent single-story house on the university campus. It had three bedrooms and, lucky for me, a large front yard, where I went to work refining my cricket skills. When we did leave the university campus, it was in our family car, a green Datsun not unlike the car my father had left behind in Ohio. We most often went to visit grandparents or one of my dozen-odd aunts and uncles in the city, where I would spend the days playing with cousins.

In those early days in Pakistan, my grandfather Akhlaque Qazi, who appeared like a big mound of a man to me, be-came my first best friend. I believe this was because he was the only one in my extended family who was fluent in

English and enjoyed expressing himself in the language. It wasn't the English I was used to hearing. It was heavily accented on the *d*'s and the *t*'s. His intonation was British, which was unfamiliar but pleasant to my ears. He joked with me in English and made me feel part of the group of his half dozen grandchildren when we gathered at his home in Chauburji. He said I was his "Yankee" in the family, and this made me feel special.

Weeks after my family landed in Pakistan, I began elementary school. My siblings began taking the school bus with my mother, but for the longest time my father insisted on dropping me off and picking me up from school himself in his new Datsun. Week after week he found me waiting for him, sitting quietly alone after school in the corner of the schoolyard. He worried about the language barrier between me and the other children. Then one morning when my father dropped me off, a taller boy walked up to us and took my hand and led me to a group of children gathered around the monkey bars. The boy became my new best friend at school, much closer to my age than my grandfather. After that, I started taking the bus to school.

Elementary school was where I began learning the rules of life in Pakistan. My school was privately owned, one of the largest nongovernmental schools in the city, and mainly drew children from the large working and middle class in Lahore. The wealthy studied at the American School or other international private schools, but my friends' parents were teachers, doctors, engineers, artists, and small-business owners. In retrospect, the varied economic classes represented among my friends made for interesting schoolyard dynamics, but at that time we were all tied together by our collective fear of the unpredictable tempers of our teachers and our love of cricket.

I slowly learned to love the sport. Within a few years I had the many and complex rules of the game all sorted out in my head. I could now see the sprawling beauty of the game, which is invisible to outsiders. I could field at deep backward square leg position if required, and I could bowl a googlie. As a batsman I hit the ball through the cover region of the field with fine balance. I also developed a taste for the corn on the cob with sharp spices and lemon that all the other children ate after school. I learned a lot of Urdu and began peppering my English with the new language, mimicking the hybrid language my friends and teachers spoke so naturally.

President Zia was still in power. Early during his rule he had started to encourage the privatization of education. Some of these privately owned schools like mine used English as the primary medium of instruction. Yet regardless of whether a school was public or private, or whether the language of instruction was English or Urdu, the state closely regulated the curriculum, especially the subject of Islam, which was required through high school. A few years after coming into power, Zia had introduced a new National Education Policy, which gave "the highest priority" to the "revision of the curricula with a view to reorganizing the entire content around Islamic thought." This would give "education an ideological orientation so that Islamic ideology permeates the thinking of the younger generation and helps them with the necessary conviction and ability to refashion society according to Islamic tenets." Pakistan had always been an Islamic state. It had an Islamic constitution, and almost 99 percent of the population was Muslim. But Zia felt that the national ideology was not Islamic enough. The youngest Pakistanis were naturally the most important targets for a new, more Islamic, national narrative.

I was constantly playing catch-up. I had not grown up with the same innate sensibilities about nation and religion and society that the other children in my class seemed to possess, and my thoughts were convoluted. I had trouble separating even the very basic concepts to which I was introduced. There was a man named Muhammad Ali Jinnah, for example, the founder of the nation who we learned had "made Pakistan." We were shown a portrait of him in class. He had a bony face and he stared back with the gentlest of smiles. The trademark Central Asian "Jinnah-style" wool cap he wore on his head was exactly like the one my grandfather wore. (The reverence we were expected to show to Jinnah in school was not unlike what my parents required of me for Grandfather at home, and I briefly but seriously considered whether the two might be related.)

One day, when I was asked in class to identify the person in the painting, I replied, "Muhammad." It was technically the correct answer—Jinnah's first name was Muhammad, and I could have narrowly escaped trouble if I had just stopped there. But I didn't. I followed the name with a prayer, "May blessings and peace of Allah be upon him and all of his family." This was a prayer said exclusively and only after uttering the name of another Muhammad, the

My brother and I played cricket for hours on end in the front yard of our house on the campus of the Punjab University. I am at the far end waiting to hit the ball.

Prophet of Islam. In saying the prayer I had revealed a dangerous confusion resting in a dark corner of my mind: I did not know that Pakistan's founder and the Prophet of Islam were two different people. It was an honest mistake to confuse the two men who loomed so large in our national school curriculum and I, all of six years of age, had no malicious intent at all. But I remember the stunned silence in the classroom that followed my answer. Some of the kids gasped and others covered their wide-open mouths with their palms. The teacher was so shocked she went mute for a few moments and then went on with the lesson as though she had never heard my answer. I said nothing for the rest of the class until I was called to the principal's office.

Muhammad Ali Jinnah and Muhammad the Prophet are two very separate people, the principal explained to me. She was very calm but serious, and my teacher sat next to me looking on gravely. No one knows what the Prophet Muhammad looks like, I was told, and so there are no images of him. It is very, very important, my teacher told me, that we never try to draw a picture of the Prophet in art class, nor should we ever confuse anyone else's portrait for his. I promised that I understood and that I would always remember all of this. In truth, I did not completely understand; it would take some time and much effort to sort all these new ideas into their respective places. Pakistan was Islamic, and somehow so was I. Muhammad was the Prophet of Islam and Muhammad Ali Jinnah was the founder of the Islamic country. And Jinnah wore a cap like my grandfather's. The line between Islam, Pakistan, and my family was not clear to me at all in those early days. Little did I know that over the years, as I learned more and more about Islam, Pakistan, and my family, these lines would only get more ambiguous.

Each of the family names I inherited from my parents, "Mufti" from my father and "Qazi" from my mother, appear in the *Oxford Dictionary of Islam* in distinct entries. The dictionary defines "mufti" as "a jurist capable of giving, upon request, an authoritative although nonbinding opinion (fatwa) on a point of Islamic law." Mufti is an important position in Islamic judicial bureaucracy, the entry explains, and "in some contexts, muftis are appointed by the state and serve on advisory councils." The word "*qada*" is defined as a "court judgment," which is "issued by a *qadi* (judge) in response to a specific case and circumstances." A "qadi," or "qazi," the entry goes on, "may request a fatwa to help determine the legal outcome of a specific case but is not bound to follow it." A separate entry for "Islamic law" explains that in the courts in the Islamic legal tradition, "a mufti's rulings could be given to individuals, qadis, and/or agents of government, and could either legitimize policies or restrict their practical effect." Simply put, a mufti is a jurist, trained in the formal legal tradition of Islam, whose job it is to interpret the true will of Allah, which is the singular true God in Islam. Qazis, on the other hand, are fair-minded judges, responsible for passing down judgment and enforcing Allah's will on the people in the court of law.

But what exactly is Allah's will? To answer this question, I will use a word you have heard before. You might understand "sharia" as a set of laws, perhaps like commandments, collected and written somewhere and easily available upon request. You might even imagine it as a laundry list of vicious and barbaric acts like the cutting off of hands and feet, or beheadings, the taxing of religious minorities, or the stoning of defenseless women until their skulls crack open and their brains ooze out. But this is not sharia; these are just some awfully old laws. Sharia is much more enigmatic than all this. Literally, the Arabic word "*sharia*" means a road or pathway. The *Oxford Dictionary of Islam* describes it as

My grandfather Abdul Majid Mufti (second from left) with a few work colleagues. While they all wear suits, three of them also don hats that would have made them identifiably Muslim under British colonial rule.

"God's eternal and immutable will for humanity, as expressed in the Quran and Muhammad's example (Sunnah), considered binding for all believers." It is probably best to imagine sharia as a combination of those two ideas: a road or path, which is God's, and, if followed, leads to a utopian social order, which the one singular God willed for its earthly creation.

Do beheaded torsos, brains oozing from cracked skulls, the covering of women's hair, or minority taxation lead to a utopian social order? Some muftis and qazis have said that they do. But others disagree. They might say that mandatory charity for the less fortunate, protecting religious minorities, equal rights for women, helping a poor and suffering animal, giving water to a thirsty traveler, an independent judiciary, or socioeconomic justice and even capitalism are the real paths of sharia. At different moments in Islamic history, different points of view of sharia have been dominant in different places.

So where does the path of sharia begin? What contours does it trace? And what do you do when you encounter a fork in the road? There are no easy answers to these questions. The reality is that outside of a handful of specific examples, Allah's will is never clearly spelled out as laws in the Quran. Muslim jurists believe that God has woven his will into the text of the holy book and into the actions of the Prophet Muhammad, whose tradition has been recorded by many historians. So understanding the path of sharia requires understanding the layers of the writing that describe God and the character of his Prophet. And this is where muftis, qazis, and other scholars of Islam come in. By plunging themselves in sacred text and written history, the muftis and qazis emerge with answers to the questions of the faithful. They navigate mundane and sometimes unearthly territory in search of the path that leads humanity to the perfectly harmonious society as imagined by Allah.

Like any developed body of law, sharia is expansive, cosmic, and endless. Like all societies, Islamic civilizations treated their jurists and lawmakers with respect and some deference. But of course the muftis and qazis of Islam are only human. Each mufti may interpret the path of sharia differently; each qazi may implement it differently. Over a thousand years, they have worked in Islamic societies in places as far away as Córdoba and Calcutta, where they have been pillars of Islamic legal bureaucracies and of lawful societies. In each place they have helped shape particular and unique societies, all Islamic. They have often disagreed with their contemporaries and with their predecessors, but then that is the nature of sharia. For all its apparent holiness, it is a most human of projects.

How did my parents end up with these Islamic titular names? They descended from people who held these posts at some time in history. Muslims first arrived along the Indus River in 711 CE, eight decades after the Islamic Prophet died. An army, under the leadership of a young military general named Muhammad bin Qasim, was dispatched by a Muslim governor of an early Arab Islamic empire after the Muslims had conquered the lands of Persia, which lay east of the Euphrates. A tale of the conquest of this region, which the Arabs knew as Sind, written in Arabic and found centuries after the invasion and translated into the Persian language, tells of the Muslim army assaulting the coastal city of Debal near the spot where the Indus drains into the ocean. The city was ruled by a local Hindu emperor, but the southern river valley was diverse in religious belief. Buddhists inhabited much of the region, while some others followed the ancient prophet Zarathustra (Zoroaster). Over a few years, the Arab conquerors continued claiming towns farther north up the Indus well into the Punjab region. They left behind small autonomous kingdoms led by Muslim princes flourishing all along the southern course of the river. These kingdoms survived several decades. Some muftis and qazis may have remained in Muslim trading colonies, but the Islamic legal system or bureaucracy did not really take root.

Muslim armies would begin to come again to the Indus, this time to stay, beginning in 1000 CE. These Muslims were mostly Persian speaking and arrived from the north, rumbling in on horseback from the obscure mountain highlands beyond the Oxus River in Central Asia. The first Muslim ruler to capture Lahore, a man named Mahmud, hailed from the Central Asian region known as Ghazna and is remembered in Pakistan as Mahmud Ghazni. Lahore was the first major city east of the Indus to be captured by any Central Asian Muslim ruler and it became so important to Mahmud Ghazni's empire that he moved the capital from Ghazna to Lahore. When Mahmud's rule ended, waves of other Muslim conquerors came over the northwestern mountains and ventured farther east deep into the lands of present-day India. Within a few generations, Lahore and the larger city a few hundred miles to the east, Delhi, had become bustling cosmopolitan medieval cities of Muslim empires.

In sub-Himalayan cities like these, curious travelers and adventurous young men—Central Asians from the north, Persians from the west, Hindus from the east—arrived to find work. Many of them were recruited for the vast militaries, and these military camps became melting pots for people from all across Asia. Over time, the military camps developed a unique vernacular—a mixture of Turkic, Indio-Aryan, and Arabic languages—and this slowly became the popular street language in many major cities east of the Indus. It was called the *Zaban-e-Urdu,* or the "Language of the Camp." The Urdu that I learned in Lahore when I first moved there as a boy is derived from this same language that developed at the turn of the millennium.

It was around this same time that the first professional class of mufti and qazi would have settled in the Punjab and in Lahore. The office of the qazi, in particular, became an important one. It was not simply a judicial office; the qazis became bureaucratic point men for an emperor and his trusted regional governors. The qazis were responsible for laying out local city bureaucracies from top to bottom. The muftis, meanwhile, were always on hand to advise the qazis on what Allah's will might be in the face of any given legal or bureaucratic question.

Emperor Timur, remembered by some as Timur the Lame or Tamerlane (he had one lame leg), a surly Turkic general, invaded the lands of the Indus in the late fourteenth century from his home across the Oxus in Central Asia in present-day Uzbekistan. Timur claimed descent from the fearsome Mongol Genghis Khan, and his armies conquered all the lands between the Euphrates and the Indus rivers. On his way to capture Delhi, which had become the most important city east of the Indus, Timur dispatched a unit to Lahore. "The princes and nobles whom I had sent to Lahore returned from that place, bringing with them much wealth and property," it is written in a first-person Persian-language biography of Timur written in 1425. "I received them with due honor, and the plunder which they had brought from Lahore, in money, goods, and horses, they presented to me, and I divided it among the nobles in attendance at my court."

While Timur's men had robbed Lahore of its wealth, his descendant Babur brought glory to the city of a kind never seen before. Babur's empire in South Asia would go on to become one of the largest, most powerful empires in the world at the time. Babur's descendants, who called themselves the Mughals, would rule much of the lands of South Asia, including all of present-day Pakistan, India, Bangladesh, and beyond, for four hundred years. It was a spectacular empire at the cutting edge of developing arts and sciences. Babur's grandson, Akbar, for example, established several specialized *Unani* medical hospitals in Delhi and its environs; a laboratory in Lahore became one of the world's best for astrological instruments; Shah Jehan, Akbar's grandson, ordered the construction of the Taj Mahal in Agra; and Shah Jehan's son, in turn, built the Badshahi Mosque in Lahore, one of the largest mosques in the world. Lahore became one of the Mughal Empire's most refined cities and even its capital for some time.

As I read this history in my school textbooks, about Qasim, Timur, Mahmud Ghazni, and the Mughals in the modern city of Lahore, I also imagined the muftis and qazis of the past sitting at the side of the great emperors, helping lay out efficient bureaucracies and courts, writing down the law of the land with their quills on lengthy scrolls. There were no people in my Mufti or Qazi families who actually did the work of muftis or qazis anymore. There were hardly any muftis or qazis in the country anymore. These professions had been stripped of any importance a long time ago, replaced by modern constitutional lawyers and judges in the state of Pakistan. I had chemists and doctors and soldiers and hydrologists and psychiatrists and zoologists in the family, but none who actually worked as qazis or muftis. These were simply surnames now, vestiges of a long lost past but one that was not quite forgotten. Still, I could not help but feel pleasure in reading about it all in school. More than anything, it made me feel grounded.

THE ERA ENDED in the blink of an eye, when General Zia-ul-Haq died suddenly and violently one hot afternoon in August 1988. For ten years, the dictator had carefully charted his course to power, one strategic step at a time, situating himself as one of the most important leaders on the global stage. The Soviet invasion of Afghanistan had been a godsend for the military ruler—without it he might not have lasted more than a few years in power. By the late eighties the Soviets were beginning to withdraw from Afghanistan, accepting defeat at the hands of the mujahideen. During the eighties in Pakistan, Zia had become increasingly unpopular. With the mission in Afghanistan now accomplished, the Americans did not have much use for the Pakistani dictator either. When he departs, people would say bitterly, not many will miss him. But Zia did not die alone. He perished among dozens of others, including an American ambassador and also my cousin Zahid.

Zahid was married to Erum, the daughter of Yusuf, my mother's adopted brother. Erum was one of Saadia's favorite nieces. She was born in 1968, a few years before my parents were married. I remember Erum from when I first arrived in Pakistan. She seemed to me like Tinker Bell out of a Pakistani fairy tale. Her eyes were sparkling gems, she spoke in chirps, and she was beautiful. I remember the older boys whispering about her all the time and accusing each other of being in love with her. But everyone knew that Erum loved only Zahid. She was just fifteen years old when she met the twenty-year-old army cadet who was training in the Pakistani military academy. Zahid was also very good-looking. He had rosy cheeks and hazel eyes and a sharp jawline, the clichéd clean-cut young military officer. They made a beautiful couple, like in the movies, people in the family would say.

It all passed quickly, as if it really was a movie. By the time they married in 1986, Zahid had steadily risen through the ranks of the Pakistani military and had become an aidé-de-camp to General Mohamed Afzaal, a high-ranking military officer and General Zia-ul-Haq's right-hand man in the army. On the morning of August 17, 1988, Zahid accompanied General Afzaal to Bahawalpur, a small town in the south of the Punjab, where they joined General Zia to witness a demonstration of an M1 Abrams tank that the United States had recently supplied to the Pakistani army as part of the broader military pact between the countries. It was probably the last place any of them wanted to be that day, watching a single tank firing at distant targets in the sweltering heat.

President Zia, in particular, was reeling from many crises at home. A huge arms depot of mujahideen weapons had blown up in the suburbs of Islamabad a few months earlier, killing at least ninety-three people. The rubber-stamped government, which Zia had brought in to power in a recent election, accused Zia of a cover-up after the catastrophe, and Zia had responded by dismissing the entire government in one fell swoop. Zia was also getting paranoid about his control over the military in the closing days of the Afghan war, and there were persistent whispers of dissent in the lower ranks. The Americans were getting weary of Zia's continuation of the Pakistani nuclear program. With the Soviets out of the region, the Americans had started asking all kinds of bold questions. Where was he routing American weapons? How closely was he keeping track of where all the aid goes?

Zia would have had a nagging feeling that the Americans had found someone else to support in Pakistan. Benazir Bhutto, Zulfiqar Bhutto's eldest child, had been in exile for years after Zia had hanged her father on murder charges, but she had recently landed back in Pakistan, and a million people had come out on the streets of Lahore to welcome her. They shouted slogans not only in her support and in the memory of her father but also against General Zia, her father's killer. "How many Bhuttos will you murder? Every home will spring a new Bhutto!" they chanted on the streets. Benazir had started saying that "democracy is the best revenge" for her father's "judicial murder," and these words must have chilled Zia.

Still, Zia had no real choice when it came to attending the tank exhibition that day. The American ambassador had already been invited, and another American official, in charge of military aid to Pakistan, would be present. Zia's closest military advisers had warned him that the ranks within the military were getting shaky and his absence from

President Ronald Reagan, Muhammad Zja-ul-Haq, Nancy Reagan, and Mrs. Zja in the White House's Cross Hall posing for photos during Zja's state visit on August 12, 1982. (Source: Reagan Archives at the University of Texas)

a ceremony where the entire military brass had gathered would send the wrong message at a precarious time. So Zia had arrived against his best judgment. It seemed fitting that the tank demonstration was a disaster: all ten shots from the cannon missed the target.

Soon after the demonstration, my cousin Zahid would have waited outside Pak-One, a C-130 Hercules military cargo plane. As military protocol dictates, General Afzaal and President Zia would have boarded first and strapped themselves into their seats in the air-conditioned cabin, along with their two American guests and other notables. Another eight generals would have filled the benches in the VIP area behind them. Zahid, a young captain, would have sat in the back without any air-conditioning with a dozen or so junior military officers. The C-130 took off from the airstrip before four o'clock in the afternoon. A few minutes later, local villagers near the town saw the president's giant airship do loops in the sky like a roller coaster and dive nearly vertically, nose first, toward the ground. Seconds later Pak-One crashed into a deserted field and exploded in a huge ball of fire, killing everyone on board.

I drove with my family to Zahid's funeral in the city of Sargodha, a few hours north of Lahore. The house was darkened and I remember walking into a room filled with women dressed in white. They were all wailing and screeching. The loudest screams were those of my young cousin Erum. It was the most chilling sound I had ever heard in my short life. In her womb, my twenty-year-old cousin was carrying a baby. Zahid and Erum had found out about the child only weeks before his death. Then, six months after the funeral, Erum gave birth to a healthy baby boy. She gave him the name that Zahid had picked out: Changez (Genghis), after the Mongol warrior and ancestor of Timur, who had ruled northern Punjab along the Indus a thousand years ago.

It was a long season of death in my family. My grandmother Zubaida, who spent the last several months of her life on a rope bed in the room next to my bedroom, had died months before the crash. My grandmother Sharifa followed soon after the crash. Watching her granddaughter through an adopted son experience such tragedy had weakened Grandmother Sharifa's spirits and she never really recovered. She fell very ill and died less than a year later of kidney failure. Just as they had planned, my parents were there in Lahore for these deaths, to lower their mothers' bodies into the ground.

In the weeks after his wife's death, Grandfather Akhlaque started to wilt too. He lay in bed for weeks and stopped eating and refused to go to work, insisting that his legs could carry him no longer. Then one day his friends and colleagues from the newspaper office came to his bedroom, looked at him sternly, and told him that he was needed to get the next morning's newspaper out. Somehow they managed to get him on his feet. It must have taken every ounce of my grandfather's strength to do that. It must be difficult when you know you're the last of your generation standing.

Months before the election of 1988, my mother hung up a charcoal portrait of Benazir Bhutto in the entranceway to our home. Shahzad and Saadia had rarely ever seen eye to eye on political issues. When they first got married, my father admired Zulfiqar Bhutto and my mother greatly resented him for his dirty political campaign to oust President Ayub in the sixties. Neither of them was especially happy with the dictatorship of General Zia, but my father had an especially hard time during his rule. When Benazir returned to Pakistan in 1986, though, my parents agreed that this was a leader who offered hope for the political future of their country. She was eloquent, extremely sharp, intelligent, beautiful, and charming. She spoke of freedom and peace after many years of oppression and violence and war, and millions of Pakistanis loved her for it.

In the election, held a few weeks after Zia's death and a few weeks before the tumbling of the Berlin Wall, Benazir's People's Party faced off against the Islamic Democratic Alliance, a group of parties with Islamic leanings. That party was led by a man named Nawaz Sharif, the scion of a prominent Punjabi business family, which had turned to national politics when its ventures in the steel industry were crippled by Zulfiqar Bhutto's nationalization scheme of the 1970s. Sharif's animosity toward the Bhutto family and his personal religious leanings endeared him to General Zia, and under his wing Sharif became the chief minister of the Punjab province in 1985. For this election, Sharif formed his own party and partnered with the Jamaat-e-Islami and a few others to offer a commanding alternative to Benazir. It was a close contest, but in the end the People's Party came away with more votes. Benazir was the new prime minister of Pakistan. She was the first woman elected to lead a Muslim country, and that too in the world's oldest Islamic republic.

I remember my parents being very happy with the election results. We all watched Benazir being sworn in on our TV at home. She looked striking in her costume—matched to the colors of the Pakistani flag—a regal emerald green flowing *shalwar kameez* dress and wispy white scarf over her head in traditional fashion. She was a youthful thirty-five years old, and she winked at someone in the crowd—her husband, perhaps—as she approached the stage to take her oath. A few months later, President George H. W. Bush, newly elected president of the United States, invited Benazir Bhutto to Washington as the first state guest of his presidency. It was a proud time for many in Pakistan. In that year, between my cousin Zahid's death on Zia's airplane and the election of Benazir Bhutto, I remember developing, for the first time, a sense of how close our ordinary peripheral lives could come to those who rule us. I began to understand the importance of that thing called "politics" that played out in the newspapers and that grown-ups used to stay up late talking about.

Benazir was less religiously inclined in her politics than Zia, and many expected her to roll back some of the changes in Pakistan's penal code, especially the ones that targeted women. But the conditions never seemed right to tackle a sensitive issue like religious law. Benazir had been in office only a few weeks when thousands of people marched to the United States Information Center in Islamabad to protest *The Satanic Verses*, the novel by Salman Rushdie that had been published a few months earlier. Muslims all over the world were already organizing to have the book banned, because

Benazir Bhutto casts her vote in the first general elections after the death of General Zia, on November 16, 1988. (Source: Zahid Hussein/AP)

they believed it denigrated the Prophet Muhammad and maligned the religion of Islam. The protests in Islamabad turned violent. The crowd attacked the American building and broke windows and set fire to vehicles. The police fired tear gas and live ammunition to disperse the crowd, killing six people. Though no one inside the American complex was hurt, it was the worst anti-American violence in Pakistan since the attack on the embassy in 1979. The religious political parties of Pakistan had used the international literary controversy to make an important point at home: Zia might be gone, but they were still around.

When Ayotallah Khomeini of Iran heard about the violence in Islamabad, he decided to issue a fatwa on Valentine's

Day, 1989: in his opinion it was incumbent on Muslims to murder Salman Rushdie. The whole affair involving the Muslim author was transformed into an international diplomatic crisis. Benazir, meanwhile, lasted in office barely twenty months before President Gulam Ishaq Khan dismissed her government after her political opponents and the military conspired against it. Her party and family's own corruption made it easier for her opponents to get rid of her. Over the next decade, Benazir and Nawaz Sharif, who represented a more religiously conservative and business-friendly political alternative, took turns getting elected, getting ousted, and then engineering the other's demise.

My father decided to install a satellite TV antenna on the roof of our house. The new democratic governments that followed Zia approved of this technology and it meant that, for the first time, we finally had something to watch on television other than state-sponsored programs. There were a few Indian satellite channels that had started broadcasting around that time and there were also American channels like HBO, MTV, and CNN. In the summer of 1990, I was one of the millions of people around the world who watched Bernard Shaw's live broadcast on CNN from Baghdad as America's first war in Iraq began. "The skies over Baghdad have been illuminated . . . This is thunder, this is lightning, this is death—this is hell." It was the first time I witnessed war in my life, and it was riveting and alarming from such a short distance.

But all this domestic and international geopolitical turmoil was, at best, background noise to me at the time. For a young teenager like me, the nineties were a blast. I was inspired by the new wave of rock-and-roll bands that started popping up in Pakistani cities and decided to learn the guitar. I started a band with my brother and two best friends from school. We were the first rock band in our school, and after we explained this unusual concept to our principal, she agreed to gather the entire school in the library for twenty minutes for a mandatory concert. We played popular American rock songs that we had heard on MTV, as everyone sat listening quietly, cross-legged on the library floor. It was a great show. Even though I went to an all-boys' school, our principal allowed the girls from the nearby girls' school to attend. And we played our hearts out for them. It was true rock-and-roll.

When the cricket World Cup of 1992 was played in Australia, life came to a standstill. The Pakistani side was going into the tournament as underdogs, but when they managed to scrape through the early rounds and made it to the semifinals, we all allowed ourselves to dream. I remember little else from those few months other than playing cricket, talking about cricket during lunch, and passing notes about it during class. Pakistan met England in the final, and the Pakistani team captain, a national sports hero by the name of Imran Khan, said in an interview before the game in Melbourne, "We really have been through the fire, it looked like we'd been knocked out and suddenly to come back, it has given me the greatest pleasure and satisfaction." That's how a lot of people in Pakistan felt in those days. Pakistan went on to win the final and Imran Khan and his team brought back the World Cup.

In the tenth grade, I finally made it onto my school's cricket team. I was a batsman, and since I had a solid defensive style, I opened my team's innings to lead through the initial period when the ball could swing unpredictably in the air. Toward the end of the year, I even got a chance to captain my side for a few games. I didn't pile up a great winning record as captain, but it was still an important moment for me when the coach first called me into a meeting to ask me if I wanted to lead the side. I had arrived in Pakistan more than a decade earlier, and I remembered watching the boys outside my gate playing cricket. I had run away from the game then, scared of being discovered as an outsider. Now I was fluent in Urdu and Punjabi, just like a native speaker, and I had read the great writers of Urdu literature in school, and I knew all the taboos and sensitivities of Pakistani society like second nature. But more than anything, it was this old British colonial sport of cricket that was my measure for how truly Pakistani I had become.

And like clockwork, just as I became captain of my school side, I also began thinking about going back to America. MTV and HBO did their part, but it was more than that. I was, after all, American. I was the only person in my family who was born there, and I had the blue passport to prove it. Yet I was also the only one in the family who had no real memory of America. Years after we had moved to Pakistan, my brother and sister and my parents still recalled life in Ohio. They told the most mundane stories: the time at the restaurant when the ketchup bottle fell and smashed on the floor; the time when the snake showed up in the backyard in Athens. But I shared none of these memories. Now that I was fully and confidently Pakistani, I realized that, more than anything, I wanted to be back in America, to collect my own stories for myself.

I applied to a boarding school, one with many international students, in the mountains of northern New Mexico and was offered a scholarship. My parents had been supportive when I applied, but now that it was a real option, they both got cold feet. My father had left it all behind in America and returned to Pakistan because he found he could not leave his past behind. And now, a little more than a decade later, I was ready to leave Pakistan for the same reason. Grandfather Akhlaque, my oldest best friend, came to my rescue as he always did. He spoke to my parents encouragingly and told them that it would be the best experience for me. He had lived in the United States in the 1960s for one year on a government exchange program, and he spoke fondly of his time there. "America will teach you many lessons," he told me before I left, "but no matter what, you can never forget Pakistan."

I landed at Albuquerque International Airport in the fall of 1997. A few months later I heard that Pakistan had conducted nuclear weapons tests. It was prompted by India, which had tested its own nuclear weapons the day before Pakistan did. The two neighboring countries became the sixth and seventh in the world with nuclear weapons. I watched the news in the TV room at my school. The reports showed raw footage of the nuclear tests in the mountains in the south of Pakistan, and I was struck by how it looked so much like the arid landscape of northern New Mexico that wrapped itself around my school campus, nestled in the southern Rocky Mountains. There was a thunderous tremor when the nuclear device went off, and the mountains on the TV screen started to glow like a giant pyramid lit up by a million fluorescent lights from the inside. As Zulfiqar Bhutto had envisioned decades earlier, Pakistan became the first Muslim country to become a nuclear power. I could hear the chatter in Urdu around the camera that recorded the scenes. "*Allahu Akbar*," Allah is the Greatest, the men cried.

IT WASN'T UNTIL AFTER the attacks of September 11, 2001, that I too would think about returning to Pakistan. When I graduated college with the class of 2003, many of my friends took jobs at banks and law firms in New York City, Boston, and Washington. I might have tried for the same, but the war had changed me. The phone call from the federal agent the day after the attacks, the talk of a clash of civilizations in the classroom, a focus on Islamic society and law—it was all too personal for me to tune out. Sitting far away in Vermont, I was being pulled back closer to the foundations of Pakistan's national story. I wanted to explore it up close.

The mastermind behind the attacks on America, it emerged, was a man named Osama bin Laden. It was a name few in the world were familiar with. Bin Laden was part of the mujahideen army who had been trained in guerrilla training camps in Pakistan under the rule of General Zia. He had fought with thousands of others in the battle against the Soviet Union in Afghanistan. He was a special figure in the war. He was not only a fighter on the front lines inside Afghanistan but also one of the wealthy Saudi donors who provided hundreds of millions of dollars to the American and Pakistani project to deliver a decisive blow to the Red Army.

Once the Soviets had been defeated in 1989, everyone lost interest in Afghanistan. Just like the United States turned its back on the war-ravaged country after using it for a decade, Osama bin Laden left Afghanistan too. He wandered the globe in search of a new enterprise. Pakistan naturally had no choice but to remain tied to Afghanistan in geography. In Afghanistan, a full-fledged civil war erupted after the Soviets left, as competing subgroups of the mujahideen fought each other for supremacy. Pakistan had important stakes in Afghanistan's future. Not only did Pakistan host millions of Afghan refugees who were waiting to return, Pakistan also shared Afghanistan's longest international border and had a sizable local Pashtun population, who had deep bonds of kinship with the Pashtuns who lived in Afghanistan as a majority ethnic group.

Through the early nineties, while Pakistanis were experimenting with electoral politics, electing a female head of state like Benazir Bhutto, churning out rock-and-roll anthems, and winning a cricket World Cup, Pakistani military and intelligence were busy pulling strings in Afghanistan, attempting to end a bloody civil war in that country. There were more than enough arms to go around in Afghanistan, and a handful of warlords were destroying whatever was left of the country after a decade of war. For a few years, Pakistani governments tried to broker a peace between the warring factions. Prime Minister Nawaz Sharif took all the Afghan warlords to Mecca in 1992 and had them perform the holy pilgrimage together, and it actually looked promising for a few days. But then every time there was any chance of peace, the Afghan leaders would begin fighting again.

Eventually, the Pakistani military took a different tack. If reconciliation wouldn't work, it was simpler to back one group to the hilt and help it eradicate all other opposition in the Afghan civil war. The Pakistani military and intelligence agencies chose a Pashtun group from Kandahar, in the south of Afghanistan, which called itself "Taliban," or "The Students." It operated under the leadership of a man named Mullah Omar. With the backing of the Pakistani military, the Taliban marched victorious into Kabul in 1996 and the Afghan civil war finally ended, six years after it started.

The Taliban declared Afghanistan an "Islamic emirate" and set up a bizarrely brutal regime. The regime had no Islamic scholars of reknown and the lawmakers introduced astonishingly violent punishment for the smallest crimes. Women were the prime targets of this new regime: they were not allowed to leave home, go to school, be seen in public, or even visit doctors. The Pakistanis officially recognized the Taliban government and turned a blind eye to its brutality. The rest of the world simply ignored it altogether, and this allowed the Taliban to rule as they pleased. The Taliban did little postwar reconstruction and millions of Afghan refugees stayed in Pakistan. But from a Pakistani perspective, at least the nearly two decades of war on its border had finally ended.

Osama bin Laden had lost a fortune after the Soviet-Afghan war traveling around the world as a freelance militant adventurer, and he returned to Afghanistan in 1996. He was still not a widely recognized figure internationally, and the Taliban allowed him to stay in the country as a guest. During his itinerant years, bin Laden decided to turn his attention to the United States, his former partner in crime. He concluded that with the Soviet Union gone, it was America that now presented the biggest threat to Muslims like himself. From his base in Afghanistan, bin Laden helped plan, fund, and coordinate the attacks on America in 2001. Once the dust from the crumbled towers settled, all eyes in Washington turned back to that long-forgotten country neighboring Pakistan: Afghanistan.

By the time of the attacks, a new military general, Pervez Musharraf, was ruling Pakistan. He had launched a military coup, the third in Pakistan's history, against the elected government of Nawaz Sharif a year after the nuclear tests in 1998. He was generally admired in the West as a "modern" and "secular" man and known for his verbose and lofty proclamations, but now none of that mattered. After September 11, it was time for action. Pakistan was in a familiar place: at the front lines of an American war inside Afghanistan. Even the cast of characters was loosely the same this time: the American military and intelligence, the Pakistani military and intelligence, and Afghan warlords and loosely coordinated Islamic guerrilla fighters. The big difference was that the good guys during the last American war, the mujahideen, were now the bad guys.

America presented its demands to Musharraf: Pakistan must withdraw its support from the Taliban government in Afghanistan immediately. The Americans told Musharraf that they were sending ground troops to invade Afghanistan and they needed Pakistan to cooperate fully in this military mission. The Americans needed to use Pakistani seaports and the country's network of highways to supply food and ammunition to the thousands of American forces landing in landlocked Afghanistan. In return, America promised, like before, to pay Pakistan billions of dollars in aid each year.

A little more than a week after the attacks, George W. Bush announced the beginning of a War on Terror at a joint session of Congress to thunderous applause. It was not just a war in Afghanistan, he said. This war would "not end until every terrorist group of global reach has been found, stopped, and defeated," Bush said. The rules were simple in this war: "Either you are with us or you are with the terrorists." A few hours later, General Musharraf sat in front of a camera at the studios of Pakistan Television to address his own nation. He spoke in Urdu, describing how the fates of Pakistan and America had become entangled once again. He explained that the Americans wanted intelligence, airspace, and logistical support from Pakistan. "I ask you to trust me," he said in a pleading tone that was unlike him. "We in Pakistan are facing a very critical situation, perhaps as critical as the events in 1971," he said, referencing the earlier civil war that had dismembered Pakistan.

Musharraf ended his address with a cryptic Islamic tale. It was the story of a treaty that the Prophet Muhammad

signed with Jewish tribes for strategic advantage against a
common enemy in another nearby city. When the treaty
expired, Musharraf explained, Muhammad was able to lead
an army against the same Jews and defeat them badly in
battle. "Therefore, on this occasion, a strategic decision is
to be taken. It is not a question of lack of strength. I have
fought two battles. My whole life is dedicated to Islam, and
I have never shown any cowardice," he said. It was like a lesson in a classroom that only the Pakistani kids understood.
Most of them reluctantly went along.

Months after the attacks, I saw in a college circular that
the American Fulbright program was introducing a new
Islamic Civilization Initiative. All the talk of a clash of
civilizations had spurred a sudden interest in an Islamic
civilization in America. The institute was inviting applications to travel and study in countries with large Muslim
populations. So I decided to apply. At that time there was
no opportunity to go to Pakistan—it was deemed too "dangerous" by the U.S. State Department. It was strange, because for me it was just home. But I had to think of other
places I might go. I thought back to my social studies textbooks from school in Lahore. I thought about the Indus,
and of Muhammad Ali Jinnah, and of the great Mughals.
I thought of my grandfather Qazi and of the muftis and
about cricket. I thought about my parents and about their
wedding in 1971 and I thought about war. And I looked
at a map and saw the mammoth country of India all along
Pakistan's eastern border. It was so opaque to me that it
might as well have been a blank space on the map. I knew
that in that country of a billion people there were nearly

as many Muslims as there were in Pakistan. So I sent in my application listing Delhi, the city three hundred miles east of Lahore, as my preferred location.

A few months later I told Grandfather Akhlaque over the phone that I had received the award. He was very intrigued by the journey I was getting ready to begin. He was the only person I knew who had lived through the colonial times when India and Pakistan were all one colony under British rule. He sounded excited about my plans and told me that he had lived briefly as a child in a small town that was now on the Indian side of the border, not far from Lahore. "I wish I could tell you what it was like," he said in English, "but after all these years, I'm afraid I have little memory of it."

Five

GRANDFATHER AKHLAQUE QAZI DIED on March 15, 2005. He passed away lying in bed in the home that he had built with all his life savings on a small plot of land close to the campus of Punjab University. Gathered around his deathbed were his two sons with their wives, several grand-children, and a few lifelong friends. His legs went limp shortly after midnight, and as he took his last breath he clasped my mother's hand tightly, staring right into her eyes with a loving gaze. I wasn't there. I learned of his death the next morning, as I sat hunched over on a chair in my small studio apartment in New Delhi. The warm early morning sun was trickling through the panes of the singular window as I listened to the sound of my mother grieving over the phone line.

Alzheimer's had started to set in months ago. I was still in America when my parents first told me in grave tones that Grandfather was retaining very little new information.

It started off mildly. He would forget where he had left his wallet or, when he was at the office, he would forget where he had left a particular folder. His reactions to these episodes were unusual. He was always composed and extra meticulous, but he began to snap and grumble. Everyone in the family and at work noticed these changes. Then he began repeating his thoughts. "Have you checked the door?" he would ask several times before turning in for the night. When I spoke to him on the phone, at times he would be sharp and expressive, but then at other times there was a mysterious blankness to his voice. He almost sounded ashamed, like he had been caught unawares. The muteness in his expression would leave me flattened and sad. But right at the end, in the moments before he died on the bed, as he gripped my mother's hand tightly, she sensed recognition. "He remembered," Saadia sobbed into the phone.

My father finally took the phone from her. "Son," he said, "your mother can't really talk right now," and then, as a matter of fact, he added, "This is just the order of the world." A generation faded, in its order, and the next one emerged to take its place at the helm of time. My parents' generation was a special one. This generation, born after the horrors of the Second World War, was the first to be born in, to grow up in, to give birth in, to leave and then return to a country called Pakistan. And as the torch was passed between generations of my family, I was on the wrong side of the border, in India. If there was one country anywhere in the world that was the exact opposite of Pakistan, this was it. The phone line cut off and my grief quickly turned into frustration. I was only a few hundred miles away from Lahore, but I knew I would not make it there for the funeral. I was walking on crutches with a crushed leg and was in no condition to fly. I could barely venture a few blocks from my run-down four-story apartment building in the south side of New Delhi.

How did I land myself in such a miserable suspended state? I had arrived in India three months earlier at a time when relations between the two South Asian nuclear powers had never been warmer. Pakistan and India had fought four wars, one in nearly every decade since the two countries became independent in 1947, but in the months before my arrival, Pakistan and India inaugurated a bus and a train line connecting Lahore and Delhi. Islamabad and Delhi opened up a nuclear hotline, to expedite the exchange of quick and frank information in case of any misunderstanding regarding the countries' nuclear weapons. Most important, the two countries had started playing cricket against each other for the first time since the tit-for-tat nuclear weapons tests of 1998. Still, it was virtually unheard of for a Pakistani civilian to be living in India, or vice versa. A tiny fraction of people from either country would ever get a visa to travel across the border, and even those who did could stay for only a few days at a time. For both Pakistanis and Indians, the neighbor was always like an itch in a phantom limb that could never be scratched. The technicality of my being an American enabled me to spend a full year in India. Here was an opportunity like none other, and I could not wait to plunge right into it. In retrospect, it was that attitude that probably got me in trouble in the first place.

It took me only three days to find an apartment. It was a small studio in a leafy neighborhood near a block of foreign embassies, and I signed a lease on the spot. My landlord was a towering but jovial Punjabi Sikh man with gray eyes who wore a magnificent blue turban. He didn't budge much on the price, but he insisted that he had given me a good deal because his grandfather, like mine, was from Lahore. Early the next morning, I left my apartment to meet a group of local outdoor adventurers for a rock-climbing trip. I had picked up rock climbing years ago, exploring the wilderness of the American Southwest. If cricket was my Pakistani badge, this thrilling and deeply personal adventure sport was my American one. I thought I was going out for the day and so I packed a banana and a water bottle. Little did I know that morning that I would not return to my apartment for almost two weeks.

It was just before noon when I fell off a tall rock face and came crashing to the ground. *Caa-rrrack.* It sounded like a thick branch snapping off a tree. At first, it didn't seem like a noise that could have possibly come from a human body. It did not hurt either. But as soon as I tried to stand up, my left leg gave way, and I collapsed to the ground. That's when I saw that my leg was dangling at a right angle halfway up the shin. Then I saw the rhythmic spurts of blood sprouting through my track pants. The bone had torn right through the skin. I felt a numbing current run up my body and I began to scream, very loudly. My memories from the next several hours register only in flashes. The horrified faces of the people I had met only hours before crowded into my vision as I lay on my back. I panicked when I realized that I had not learned the name of a single person yet. Someone wrapped my leg in a dirty insulation pad and I was hauled to and laid out in the backseat of a van. The smell of sweaty climbing shoes stuffed my nostrils and mixed with the metallic taste in my mouth. A woman wearing a parka peered over my face and apologized for the traffic we were apparently stuck in. It was the beginning of Divali, the most important annual Hindu religious holiday, she explained. Delhi was experiencing some of its worst traffic jams of the year.

An hour or more later, my lower half now soaked in blood, I was wheeled into the emergency room of a barren-looking hospital. A broadly built young doctor with closely buzzed hair and a thick mustache appeared at the foot of my gurney. He didn't even look at my face, just lifted the bloodstained sheet over my leg. His face got all screwed up when he saw the wound. I chuckled. It wasn't funny in the slightest to see my doctor cringe, but by this time someone had already injected some very potent drugs into my system. Someone told me to count to ten, and I don't recall if I even started.

When I came to, it was very dark and quiet. My mouth felt like it was lined with thick paper and I had barely enough strength to open my eyes. I saw my left leg suspended in the air, wrapped up in white bandages, lifted off the bed by a wire. "*Paani*," I called out for water, using the word common to Urdu and Hindi. A woman briskly approached my bedside in the dark and poured water into my mouth with a pipette. "Is it over?" I asked in Urdu. "You need to rest, go back to sleep," the young female voice instructed me in strongly Indian-accented English.

The same doctor who had operated on me walked in the next morning and introduced himself pleasantly as Dr. Dey. I fired all the questions I had been pondering in the hours I had lain there awake and alone. "Will I walk again? Will I walk with a limp? How long will I have to stay in bed?" He told me that I was bedridden for at least eight weeks. It was a long surgery, six hours in total. I had lost many ounces of blood in the hour I was stuck in traffic. I had lost a small piece of my tibia and now had a pound of metal rods and screws inside my leg holding it together. I would have to stay in the hospital for about ten days. He didn't answer my other questions. "You're very weak right now and you need time to recover," he said in English. Then scanning the empty room he asked, "Don't you have anyone coming for you?"

I grew weaker with every passing day. I had noticed that the doctors had started to whisper outside the door to my private room. On day five, Dr. Dey burst in, dressed in a white coat, studying a clipboard of notes, and without missing a beat declared, "We need to get blood in you." He explained that my hemoglobin had dipped below the point where my system could lift it up again on its own. I had hit a slippery slope.

"I don't need it, Dr. Dey," I lied. "I feel better today."

He repeated himself, this time looking straight at me. Within minutes, a tall rickety rack was carted over by my bedside and a needle was inserted into my forearm. I traced with my flailing eyeball the stream of ruby-colored blood up to a plump plastic pouch. It sat there, resolutely dripping, one drop at a time, and I felt a chill crawl over me. It was the first time someone else's blood had run through my body. I began to shiver and a nurse walked over and placed a blanket over my chest. It was normal to feel cold, she whispered. I didn't respond. My heart did not even have the energy to race, and I closed my eyes. I began imagining, like a movie, a story my mother had told me about her life as a young teenager. It was the war of 1965. The fighting on the border was intense. Hundreds were being killed every day, and Saadia had snuck into the Mayo Hospital in Lahore and pleaded with the nurse on duty to let her donate her blood. I pictured my mother's forearm being drained of its blood by a needle. I pictured it filling a transparent pouch until it was taut full. I imagined it being carted away. Now I opened my eyes again to see myself in India receiving the blood of an Indian.

I must be honest with you. For a brief second, this thought did cross my mind: Is this the blood of a Hindu? Or is this a Muslim's blood? I know, I know, you must find this thought repulsive. You must believe me when I say that I do too. I know it does not matter whose blood got injected into my body. I should have felt nothing but deep gratitude to the human who had donated blood for me. But you must also understand that this wasn't a rational thought triggered by concerns of bloodlines or race or religion. No, this was rooted in something completely separate, something much more powerful and primordial than any of that. This was a matter of nation.

The partition of Britain's South Asian colony, which created the independent nation-states of Pakistan and India, was one of the most violent episodes recorded in history. After the end of the Second World War, more than thirteen million people in the British colony were torn from their homes and moved to some other place on the land, over a period of mere months. Some of the homeless refugees traveled hundreds of miles by horse cart or train, others traveled thousands of miles across the sea in ships, and some simply walked a few miles to cross an imaginary line in the sand. Some were driven away because their neighbors were out for their blood, but others moved of their own free will. These people would have believed that their home had somehow slipped away from them. They probably felt a tug deep inside their gut, an invisible force that pulled them across desert, rivers, and mountains. Some might have acted on a blind faith that the direction they moved in was the right direction, toward a people who were more familiar.

The partition, as it is remembered, occurred on the geographical landmass commonly known as the Asian subcontinent, because it is a continent but not quite. Geographers tell us that over the course of many millions of years, the roughly diamond-shaped Indian tectonic plate drifted due north and finally, some fifty million years ago, began colliding with the Eurasian Plate, or the rest of Asia. Over the next several million years, the two landmasses crashed into one another in slow motion—they still are to this day— and the Indian Plate became part of Asia. The collision thrust some of the youngest and highest mountains on the planet up toward the sky. The Himalayas rose in the north where the Indian Plate collided into what is today Tibet,

Muslim refugees cram into coaches and the roof of a train bound for Pakistan from an area of New Delhi, India, on September 26, 1947. (Source: AP)

the Hindu Kush and Karakoram ranges shot up in the west along what is today Pakistan's Afghan border, and highlands also formed in the east near present-day Burma. The Himalayas became covered in ice and snow, and two great rivers began flowing from here. The Ganges river system branched out into the eastern lowlands. And along the western edge of the subcontinent, the Indus River carved a southbound path toward the ocean.

The Indus River became the great western frontier of the subcontinent. Archaeologists have found physical evidence of the human species living on the subcontinent for tens of thousands of years, and they believe that it was along the Indus that the first organized human societies on the subcontinent first formed. The thousands of ancient artifacts collected at the site of Mehrgarh, west of the Indus in present-day Pakistan, are thought to be approximately seven thousand years old and belong to one of the earliest agricultural communities in all of Asia. A few thousand years later, one of the world's great early human civilizations began settling along the Indus. The people of this Indus Valley Civilization began developing orderly cities, art, and written code nearly three thousand years before the Christian era, at around the same time as the Egyptian civilization was thriving on the banks of the Nile, and the Mesopotamians flourished between the Tigris and Euphrates. From the ruins of the Indus Valley Civilization, now strewn along the path of the Indus, we know that it was remarkably modern. It had walled homes, communal baths, granaries, and in some places even what archaeologists believe to be citywide drainage systems.

Over a few thousand years, the subcontinent, half the size of Europe, became one of the most densely populated places on the planet. The people living there developed in diverse ways. They began speaking many different languages. Their blood mixed with the various people who came from across the highlands to the north, east, and west or from across the seas in the south. Countless different empires, kingdoms, and principalities fought over and shared the space for thousands of years. In this long history, there are only a handful of instances when the subcontinent was united under one rule. Emperor Ashoka, a Buddhist king, was the first to extend his kingdom from the mountains in the east to the mountains in the west and all the way down to the Indian Ocean, a few centuries before the birth of Christ. Ashoka's kingdom disintegrated after his death, and for another two thousand years not a single ruler would conquer the entire subcontinent. It was near the end of the seventeenth century that the last of the great Mughal emperors, a haughty Muslim king by the name of Aurangzeb, succeeded in extending his dense web of bureaucracy to cover the whole of the subcontinent from north to south, and east to west.

The third and last time that the subcontinent came under one rule was during colonial times. It took the British many decades to take over the entire land. The British East India Company, a corporation established in the early 1600s, won a charter to trade there in 1617 from the reigning Mughal emperor. It set up a trading post in the eastern region of Bengal, and from there, the British engaged in heated battle, economic and military, with the other European powers that had set up trading posts—the French, the Portuguese, the Dutch—for domination of the region. By the middle of the eighteenth century, the British trading company had beaten out and outmaneuvered everyone else to become the most powerful European presence on the subcontinent.

Mughal rule was weakening by this time. The many local rulers once again began ruling autonomously of the central power in Delhi. The Marathas, led by a Hindu prince in the south, carved out their own independent kingdom. The British East India Company had amassed a sizable private security force of its own, made up of British mercenaries and local recruits, and it joined in the land grab of Mughal territory. Moving westward from its trading post, the company's army began conquering all the lands along the Ganges River and south of it. In the 1840s, they arrived at the final western frontier of the subcontinent: the Indus. Over the following decade, the Punjab and surrounding areas also fell to the British company after fierce fighting. And so, the British finally controlled all the lands down to the Indian Ocean. A brief war between the company and the local rebels ensued after that. The war is remembered as the First War of Independence by many South Asian historians, but the British simply termed it a mutiny. In any case, the British Crown decided to take over the ownership of the subcontinent from the East India Company in 1857 and made it part of the mighty British Empire. The British named their newest colony India, after the Indus River. It was their "jewel in the crown."

During the centuries that the British occupied the subcontinent, a revolutionary and wondrous idea was sweeping Europe. It was called nationalism, and it was changing the very map of that continent. Nations, Europeans were proclaiming, were large groups of people who were tied together by innate, almost instinctive, primordial bonds of kinship. A nation could be recognized by common ethnic origin revealed by the shapes of people's faces or the color of their skin, or a nation might recognize its own by the sounds the people make with their mouths, speaking similar languages. It did not have to be something so obvious. Sometimes, a nation was formed on nothing more than a shared belief in a fantastical story, about God or man or earth.

And what was the purpose of finding and identifying and recognizing these nations? In it was the real prize: land. In Europe, each nation was entitled to its own piece of land, a place called state. Without nation, there was no state, and without state, nations argued, there was simply no way to express nationalism. So an essential factor in creating any nation was to identify the piece of land that belonged to it and that it belonged to. It also became as important for nations to identify the "other" who did not belong to the land or the nation. That other not only reinforced what made a nation special and different, it also allowed the nation to draw an invisible line called a national border where the claim to the land ended. Through the eighteenth, nineteenth, and twentieth centuries, the political leaders of Europe negotiated, often in very violent ways, these invisible lines that separated one nation from another, which created the modern political map. As kings and monarchs bowed to the new leaders of nations, the nation-state became the new primary unit of measuring space on the planet.

The people on the subcontinent were introduced to this idea of nation in the nineteenth century by their first physical, emotional, and intellectual contact with the British colonists. Soon, they began asking the same questions that Europeans had been asking the century before: What are the nations living on the subcontinent? The varied people had thousands of years of history living on the giant landmass. They spoke dozens of different languages; there were dozens of distinct ethnicities and races. There were several religions: Hinduism, with its epic sagas laid into the entire geography of the subcontinent; Buddhists, who followed the teachings of Gautama Buddha; people who followed Islamic religion; and Sikhs, Zoroastrians, and many others. In many ways, the subcontinent was even more diverse than Europe, and it could claim to have many more distinct nations. But making a case for a nation is no easy task. It is a project for acquisition of land and resources and space, and no one gives up any of that without a fight. So in the end, nations belong only to those few who can muster the most compelling story and then tell it tenaciously.

The Indian National Congress was the first organized nationalist movement on the subcontinent, started by a group of British and native men and women in 1885. It captured the imagination of many people with a nonintuitive nationalist story. The subcontinent, the congress said, was the common home of a people with myriad languages, ethnicities, races, and religions. All three hundred million of them were a singular nation tied together by their shared geography. This idea of a single nation dominated the political conversation across the British colony for a few decades in the late nineteenth century, but it was far from the only national idea competing for people's hearts and minds. Along the eastern edge, near the territory of modern-day Mayanmar, this feeling of one Indian nation never took root. In the southern tip, the Tamil people, ethnically distinct from the northerners, became concerned about the language they spoke, and they found a special bond with others who spoke it, recognizing in it a separate nation.

But the only real challenge to the congress's idea of one nation came from a cadre of Muslim intellectuals who founded a political party called the Muslim League in 1906. The league's leaders argued that the subcontinent was actually more of a continent than a state. They claimed that the Muslims, a third of the population of the British colony, were in fact a separate nation from the rest. The Muslims were concentrated along the western Indus River, along the north rim, and all the way to the far eastern wing. To the league, the idea of one single subcontinental nation bound by its natural geographical boundaries was a Hindu religious conception, derived from the empire of Bharat that was described in ancient Hindu mythology. The Muslims were as diverse in language, ethnicity, and culture as the population of the subcontinent taken as a whole, but the league's leaders argued that what tied the Muslims together in its farthest past was the tradition of the Prophet

Muhammad, who had walked the earth fourteen hundred years earlier. All Muslims, regardless of their race or language, looked west to their common roots, to the highlands of West Asia and beyond to the birthplace of Islam.

In the face of the congress's one composite subcontinental nation, the league's ideas became popular as the "two-nation theory." They were two conflicting conceptions of the subcontinent: the congress's idea implied one single state; the league's vision necessitated more than one. In the end the two-nation theory presented by the leaders of the Muslim League won out. Pakistan appeared on the map in 1947 as the separate state for a separate nation of Muslims. The rest of the subcontinent retained the name the British had given to their colony: India. Pakistan was a product of the earliest expression of nationalism based on a shared relationship with the tradition of Islam. To this day, it remains the only nation of its kind.

MONTHS AFTER GRANDFATHER AKHLAQUE was buried in March 2005, I traveled from Delhi to Lahore. My accident had badly derailed my research plan, and Grandfather Akhlaque's death had made me even more distracted. I felt stuck in India. I had come to this country along Pakistan's eastern border to research the history of one of the earliest experiments in political Islam. But over the first few months in India, with the accident and my grandfather's death, this history of the land and its people had all started

*Grandfather Akhlaque's father, my great grandfather, Qazi
Mushtaq Hosain.*

to feel a little too personal for me. I decided that a few days
back at my parents' home in Pakistan would do me good
and clear my head. I could spend some time with family,
finally process my grandfather's passing, and then I would
resume my research and travel in India.

My mother's youngest brother, along with his wife and
daughter, now lived in my grandfather's house where he
died. When I visited the house a few days after arriving, I
found Grandfather's bed still in the same place in his bedroom, covered with the same plush blanket that I last saw

him use. But he was gone, along with all the other traces of his life. In a large storage room upstairs, I found Grandfather's belongings piled up. I opened a large steel trunk that sat along a wall and it creaked open to reveal stacks of photographs, reams of loose papers, and thick files and binders full of documents. They were covered with careful notes in my grandfather's neat blocky handwriting. Grandfather Akhlaque was not always very good when it came to sharing intimate stories of his life experiences. On the other hand, he was an extraordinary record keeper. As I sifted through the contents of the trunk, I recognized that I had found a meticulous record of his life. Over the next several days, I carefully investigated what was left of him. It was my chance to get to know my grandfather better than I had ever known him in his life.

My grandfather's official government employee record, preserved in a brown file stained and crumbling at the edges and barely held together by a string tie, listed his name in neat English cursive as Qazi Akhlaque Hosain Faruqi. His "date of birth by Christian era as nearly as can be ascertained" was 19 November 1922. This was strange because we had always celebrated Grandfather Akhlaque's birthday on November 21. Similarly, I had always thought that he was born in Lahore, but the place of his birth was listed as Sodhra.

I had to look up Sodhra on a map. It was a small town seventy-five miles northeast of Lahore, on the bank of the Chenab, another eastern tributary of the Indus River. Sodhra was a rural town when my grandfather was born; a census from forty years before his birth put the population at only four thousand people. My grandfather was the fourth child born to his parents. My great-grandfather's name was listed in the papers as Qazi Mushtaq Hosain. I know very little about him. I found a photograph of him taken in 1940, years before his death. He wore a *pagree*, a tall and ostentatious typically Muslim headdress, and a worn tweed jacket. He had piercing eyes and a bushy beard and mustache. My grandfather had described him as a man of meager means, working in the lowest rungs of the British colonial bureaucracy as a revenue collection officer in the Punjab.

The Punjab, in which my grandfather grew up in the 1920s, was a hotbed of political activity. When my grandfather was born in 1922, the allied powers had already won the Great War in Europe, but the British were still tied up in a protracted postwar conflict in the Middle East and other lands of the former Ottoman Empire. It was more than the fate of the Islamic holy lands that was at stake over there. The Ottoman Empire had also been the seat of the Islamic Caliphate, the supreme political office that had passed from one ruler to the next since the death of the Prophet Muhammad. Over the centuries, although the caliphate had lost its political power, it remained a potent symbol for many Muslims all over the world, especially when Europeans had already colonized many of them. After the Great War, the Muslims of the subcontinent launched an international campaign to protect the caliphate, but the new secular Turkish republic finally abolished the institution in 1924.

Grandfather Akhlaque's was the first generation of Muslims to grow up without a caliph in the world. Since

My grandfather, seated for a portrait with two of his nieces in the mid-1930s. He is wearing jodhpurs, which became trendy among British gentry in the early twentieth century. He is also proudly displaying his oxford shoes of the kind that he continued to wear until the end of his life.

Muslims were a major part of the British Indian army at the time, the loss of the caliphate after the First World War was felt uniquely by them on the subcontinent. But as a result of the political wrestling around the caliphate issue in the colony, the Muslims learned that they could rally around something new and much more powerful: nation. As this consciousness of nation began to grow, so did the recognition of the "other." The foreign British colonial power was an obvious other, but the Muslims also began to see the Hindus, who were a vast majority, as the other. Hindus and Muslims had lived side by side for centuries as subjects of different empires, but now there was great potential for violence, as there is with all national movements. This violence first began to become apparent in the Punjab in the summer of 1924 with the murder of one man. It was all triggered by a piece of writing.

A few months after the caliphate was abolished, the owner of a small bookstore in Lahore's Old City, a Hindu man by the name of Rajpal, published and began selling a book with the titillating title *Rangila Rasool* (The Colorful Prophet). The book was an unabashed assault on Muhammad, the Prophet of Islam. It was written, ironically, as an admiring ode to Muhammad, but the story focused on the Prophet's sexual relations with his many wives and described Muhammad as a depraved sexual deviant. The first thousand copies flew off the bookshelves; Rajpal published a second edition and then many more. Soon it was being read in translation across the entire subcontinent. It was truly a literary phenomenon.

Muslims were incensed. They saw it as a deliberate instigation and began protesting in the streets. Even Mohandas Gandhi, a Hindu and at the time political leader of the Indian National Congress, was bewildered. "I have asked myself what the motive possibly could be in writing or publishing such a book except to inflame passions," he wrote in a magazine article that year. A case was lodged against Rajpal in the colonial court of Lahore. In July 1924, street fights broke out between Hindus and Muslims in the Punjab over the book. The violence soon spread to the northwest of the

Indus then to all other parts of the subcontinent. Muslim and Hindu gangs began looting each other's homes and businesses, and hundreds of people were killed on both sides, thousands injured.

In May 1927, the Lahore high court exonerated Rajpal of any crime. He was a free man, but many Muslims weren't convinced that justice had been done. Some attempted to take Rajpal's life and the publisher had to take on round-the-clock police protection. Then two years later, in the spring of 1929, a young Muslim man named Ilam Din, the poor son of a local carpenter, set out for the bazaar and purchased a dagger for one rupee and arrived at Rajpal's printing shop. Ilam Din found the publisher sitting outside and lunged at him, sinking the dagger into his heart. Rajpal died instantly. It became the stuff of international news: "100 Hurt in Lahore Riot," read a headline in the *New York Times*. "Feeling has been whipped to white heat here by the murder yesterday of Mahasha Rajpal," the story said, adding that "his assailant, a Moslem named Ilam Din, was captured." British "troops and armored cars were immediately drafted into Lahore." Ilam Din was arrested by the police and swiftly sentenced to death.

Ilam Din suddenly became a symbol for a much larger cause: Muslim nationalism. A prominent Muslim lawyer from the southwestern city of Bombay decided to appeal Ilam Din's death sentence. Muhammad Ali Jinnah was a fifty-three year old, sharply dressed, slender man. He was the most important Muslim nationalist leader in the entire subcontinent. Jinnah grew up in a wealthy Muslim family which, like my father's family, claimed to be descendants of the old Rajput warrior tribe. He had studied law at the Inns of Court in London, and after practicing as a barrister for a few years, Jinnah returned to the subcontinent at the turn of the twentieth century. He was quickly drawn into the nationalist political activity and joined the Indian National Congress. Alongside Mohandas Gandhi, another former lawyer, Jinnah rose as a forceful advocate for the colony's struggle for independence from British rule.

A few years later, Jinnah joined the Muslim League and became its president in 1913. At first, he was an ambassador for Muslim-Hindu unity. He brought the two nationalist movements together to work closely during the First World War, helping them present a united front against the British colonists. But the mood changed decisively after the fall of the caliphate in the 1920s. Jinnah began talking of Muslims as a separate nation who required separate electorates and guaranteed representation in the local bodies. He had support from the Muslims scattered all around the many provinces. Many of them began referring to Jinnah as *Quaid-e-Azam*, or "The Greatest Leader."

Jinnah, the central spokesman for Muslim nationalism, was not a very traditional Muslim man. He was an Anglophile in many of his manners. He was more comfortable making speeches in the Queen's English than in any of the native languages of his family and tribe. He had a taste for finely tailored suits, was known to enjoy his drink, and was a chain-smoker of 555 brand cigarettes. In one of his most memorable photographs, Jinnah leans over a billiards table, cuing up a ball for a strike, with a freshly lit

Jinnah and Gandhi, two leading figures in the movement for independence from the British, did not get along very well. In this 1939 photograph, Jinnah, the representative of Muslims, smoking a cigarette and dressed in a white three-piece suit, argues with a more piously dressed Gandhi. (Source: Kulwant Roy/Getty Images)

cigar clenched between his teeth. In all likelihood, Jinnah himself probably did not share any of Ilam Din's religious convictions, nor did he sympathize with Ilam Din's violent acts. But in taking up Ilam Din's appeal, Jinnah, the most passionate advocate of Muslim nationalism, was making a powerful political statement: Muslims stuck together. Muslims were different; Muslims were a nation; the Muslims' interest must be protected.

In his appeal, Jinnah attacked the testimony and evidence submitted against Ilam Din as unreliable. He then argued that since his client was "only nineteen or twenty years of age," and had committed the act to protect his religious prophet's honor, he should be spared the death penalty. It was not surprising that Jinnah lost the appeal. Ilam Din was hanged in the fall of 1929. News reports from the time describe his funeral as the largest procession seen in Lahore in memory. The entire cadre of Muslim political leadership attended. Jinnah stayed away. He had done his job. He was a man of politics and did not have much taste for religious ceremony.

Less than one year after Ilam Din's funeral, in December 1930, Jinnah invited a man named Muhammad Iqbal to deliver an important keynote address at the annual meeting of the Muslim League. Iqbal was a poet and philosopher who is today considered by many as one of the founding fathers of modern political Islam. He was a pivotal leader of the Muslim League and inspired an entire generation of Muslim politicians, including Jinnah, to embrace Muslim nationalism. If Jinnah was the political muscle behind the Muslim nationalist movement, Iqbal was its mind and heart.

Iqbal was born and raised in the Punjab and, like Jinnah, he earned a law degree in London. But his mind dwelled on the larger philosophical and historical questions, so he moved to Germany to study philosophy, where he read the works of modern European philosophers and earned a doctorate. Through it all his true passion was always poetry. Before Iqbal left for Europe he was already an accomplished poet. He showed a fine lyrical mastery in his early age at *mushairas*, competitive public poetry recitals that were a cultural institution in the north that combined the spectacle of sport, politics, and art, all into one. But when he returned from Europe, Iqbal was no longer writing about lighthearted matters. He was spouting incredibly moving poetry in Persian and Urdu, which grappled with the ideas of self, nation, and statehood, and how all this might fit into an Islamic construct. "With an impatient eye and a hopeful heart," Iqbal wrote in 1923, "I seek the end of that which is endless."

Iqbal took the stage at the annual Muslim League conference in front of a packed house of scholars, politicians, and activists. He chose to speak in English. He thanked the league for inviting him to preside over the meeting at "one of the most critical moments in the history of Muslim political thought and activity in India." He opened with a brief dissection of the political and philosophical history of Europe and Christendom. He dwelled specifically on the works of Luther, Rousseau, and Renan. The Islamic experience with nation and religion, he went on to say, would differ from Europe's. Muslim society, "with its remarkable homogeneity and inner unity, has grown to be what it is, under the pressure of the laws and institutions associated with the culture of Islam." The only logical extension, in Iqbal's mind, was a separate land where Muslims could experiment with their particular tradition, as a nation. "I would like to see the Punjab, North-West Frontier Province, Sind, and Baluchistan amalgamated into a single state," he said. It was uttered as a poet's dream at that moment, and perhaps even Iqbal did not suspect that ten years later a country with roughly the same contours would appear on the map with the name "Pakistan."

My grandfather Akhlaque Qazi photographed as a teenager.

Despite his call, Iqbal was ambivalent about what this experiment might yield. "I do not know what will be the final fate of the national idea in the world of Islam," he said. "Whether Islam will assimilate and transform it, as it has before assimilated and transformed many ideas expressive of a different spirit, or allow a radical transformation of its own structure by the force of this idea, is hard to predict." But he ended with this lesson he had learned from his historical and philosophical exploration: "At critical moments in their history it is Islam that has saved Muslims and not vice versa." Muslims, in other words, needed a separate space for themselves on this earth not to preserve Islam, but rather to escape the failures of the rest of the world and be saved by Islam. It was, in a strange way, an optimistic message of hope. My grandfather would have been an eight-year-old boy at the time, constructing his first memories, when in the bustling teahouses of Lahore, the older men reading newspaper reports, quoting Iqbal, would have started using the words "Islam," "nation," and "state" in the same breath.

By the time Britain declared war on Germany in 1939, my grandfather had moved into a small apartment in Lahore, the city where he would spend the rest of his life. Lahore was the right place to be for a young and ambitious Muslim boy with few resources to start a career. The movement for a Muslim state that Iqbal had suggested was now a full-blown political reality, and the Punjab looked like it might become a center of just such a state. Reading through a faded thick file folder, which Grandfather Akhlaque had labeled CAREER

DEVELOPMENT (MAY BE DESTROYED AFTER MY DEATH), I learned that in 1940, Akhlaque took a test for the "recruitment of junior clerks in the Punjab Civil Service." He was eighteen years old. He placed fourth on the exam and began work as a clerk at a university later that year. Two years later, he married my grandmother Sharifa, a highly educated woman with a degree in Persian literature, in a solemn ceremony.

Through the course of the Second World War, the Muslim League stepped up the campaign for a separate and independent state. Iqbal died in 1938, and now Jinnah, surrounded by a cadre of Muslim intellectuals and powerful landowners, spearheaded the demand for Pakistan. By the time the war ended in 1945, and as the British prepared to leave the subcontinent, it seemed inevitable that a separate state for the Muslims would be created. What exactly this new state would look like on a map, and how independent it would be, no one knew for certain. Over the next few years, the leaders of the congress, the league, and the British government shuttled among London, Delhi, Lahore, Calcutta, and other cities, trying to hammer out an agreement. But a final deal on land and power division remained elusive.

As the British began to withdraw, millions of people were left guessing and anxious about their fates and the fates of their nations. Partition hung like a sword, especially over the Punjab, one state that was demographically very evenly split among Hindus and Muslims and Sikhs. Lahore, Punjab's largest city, where Akhlaque and Sharifa lived, was at the center of a gathering storm. As the clock ticked, and the leaders failed to push through a decision about who would own the city, nerves became frayed. People

My mother's mother, Grandmother Sharifa, photo-
graphed on the day after her wedding in 1942.

began making decisions for themselves. Mass killings, the
most brutal of the whole partition, began in Lahore in
the spring of 1947. Street gangs of Muslims, Hindus, and
Sikhs turned on each other, burning down businesses and
houses, dragging bodies into the streets and leaving the
corpses for everyone to see. Each group was viciously trying to drive the others out of the city. Two miles north of
where my grandparents lived, the neighborhood of Shah
Alami inside the walled city of Lahore, had become a center of Hindu resistance. One night in the summer of 1947,

Muslims attacked it with Molotov cocktails and burned the entire neighborhood, killing hundreds. Nothing was left. For many Hindus, this was the realization that Muslims had finally won the city of Lahore. They began migrating eastward in droves. At the same time, in the city of Amritsar, a few dozen miles to the east of Lahore, hundreds of Muslims were being slaughtered every day and thousands began moving west toward the Indus. Trainloads of dead bodies, hacked into pieces, would arrive daily at each city's train station, dripping blood on the tracks.

A new map of the subcontinent was finally unveiled in June 1947. A separate state for the Muslims was carved out of the northwest corridor of the colony along the length of the Indus. An eastern wing of Pakistan was created in the Bengal province, a thousand miles away on the other side of the subcontinent. The Punjab had been sliced right down the middle, with a border running between Amritsar and Lahore. It was the "moth-eaten" map Jinnah had feared and had fought for many years to avoid. But the old lawyer knew that the situation on the ground was spiraling out of control. He also knew that his health was failing. Both the Indian National Congress and the Muslim League hurriedly accepted the partition plan. That summer, millions began moving across the invisible line to join their new nations. All in all, it is estimated that nearly two million people were killed during the partition.

My grandfather was fortunate to have been on the right side of the border. The partition turned out to be a real boon for his professional career. In an appointment letter dated August 1, 1947, two weeks before the partition,

My grandfather Akhlaque Qazi photographed as a
young professional.

my grandfather was suddenly transferred within the Punjab
government to replace one L. Sita Ram, a Hindu man, as a
cashier in a local government office. It was an unscheduled
transfer, and I can only guess that L. Sita Ram had escaped
Lahore in the dark of night like many hundreds of thousands
of Hindus. That, at least, is the best I can imagine of his fate.

On August 14, 1947, the new state of Pakistan appeared
on the world map and its green-and-white crescent flag
was raised. It was the world's largest Muslim country and
it promised to become a liberal democracy. The other
country formed retained the colonial name India, even if
the river for which it was named was now nearly all inside
Pakistan. The day after independence, Akhlaque Qazi was
promoted to the position of "senior clerk." At the end of

the year, Akhlaque's supervisor wrote this about my grandfather in an annual review: "This assistant has, I confess surprised me beyond all measure. I had the feeling that he would take years to equal his predecessor as cashier, but I found, a fortnight after partition, that I really had a better cashier than L. Sita Ram." Through all the gloom, murder, and misery of partition, the independence of Pakistan let Grandfather Akhlaque shine and rise through the lower ranks of Punjabi bureaucracy.

The birth of Pakistan had an almost magical effect on my grandparents. After seven years of marriage, they had almost given up on having a child, but within a year of independence, my grandmother became pregnant. My mother was born on November 5, 1949, the first person in the family to be born a Pakistani. Then one year later, my grandmother had become pregnant again. She recorded this peculiar episode in her personal diary:

> I dreamed that I was sitting in the lap of "The Great Leader," like some young child would. I woke up suddenly. I was embarrassed and in a sweat. Now, I could not even tell anyone about this dream. So I waited a few days and then finally told my husband about it, in hushed tones and in a manner most secretive. He put me at ease. He said this is nothing to be worried or embarrassed about. He interpreted the dream to me: "by the will of Allah, he will grant us such a son who will be in the truest sense a lover of the nation of Pakistan."

IN 2005, people in Washington and in capitals around the world began to mutter that Pakistan was turning into a "failed state." No one completely understood what that phrase meant—they still don't—but the implication was certainly ominous. Using data from 2005, *Foreign Policy* magazine, a publication based in Washington, D.C., decided to rank the most failed states on earth. The "Failed State Index" crunched heavy numbers by placing numeric values on issues like "demographic pressures," "refugees," "group grievance," "poverty," "public services," and "security apparatus." It all had a vague air of science to it. When the numbers were added up, Pakistan turned out to be the ninth most "failed" state in the world, after a handful of sub-Saharan African states and Haiti. It ranked just a notch *below* Afghanistan.

It was remarkable that Pakistan landed on this unfortunate list, considering a few realities: Pakistan's population was more than twice that of any other country near the top of the list. Its national wealth, which ranked as the twenty-eighth largest in the world that year, was 50 percent more than all the wealth of all the other nine "failed states" combined. Pakistan was one of seven countries in the world with nuclear weapons. It was one of the oldest constitutional democracies in Asia. It had one of the world's six largest standing armies and one of the most technologically advanced military forces.

That same year, Pakistan's economy grew at a rate of 8.4 percent, second only to China among the world's large economies. A World Bank report on the business outlook in Asia called Pakistan "the top reformer in the region."

That same year, Pakistan was the second-largest producer of milk in the world; it harvested the fifth-largest crop of onions and eighth-largest crop of wheat. It produced more cotton yarn than any other country, along with being one of the world's fastest-growing cellular phone markets. Such doom and gloom about Pakistan was not new. In January 1948, only a few months after Pakistan's independence, *Life* magazine ran a photograph of Jinnah, who was in advanced stages of tuberculosis, on its cover. He was the "sick old ruler of a young but equally sick country." Pakistan, the article read, "might lose its battle for survival." In six short decades, Pakistan had come a long way since my grandfather began working in the central government office as a clerk and had to use a cardboard box as a desk because the state had no money for furniture yet.

Of course, there were many reasons to worry. Pakistan had always battled extreme poverty and malnutrition. It had struggled with poor infrastructure, and almost every Pakistani government had left in some form of political crisis. But Pakistan looked nothing like the Sudan, Ivory Coast, Iraq, Somalia, or Haiti in 2005. For all its many weaknesses and volatility, the Pakistani state was capable of pulling off wonders. It had built some of the world's largest dams on the Indus. It designed and built a nuclear program from scratch, consistently managed one of the largest agricultural outputs in the world, and was in the business of manufacturing its own fighter jets. Pakistan's malaise was unique. It wasn't the state that appeared to be the problem; it seemed that the problem was with the nation, the imagined community of Muslims.

Here was a nation of nearly two hundred million people who lived along the path of the Indus River. The Punjabis and Kashmiris lived in the northeast, and the Pashtuns in the northwest. The Baluchis sat in the southwest, and the Sindhis lived in the south alongside millions of Mohajirs, who had immigrated during the partition from what is today northern India. They all looked different, spoke dozens of mutually unintelligible languages, and had their own long-standing cultural traditions. Their narrowly defined political interests often conflicted and they quarreled over the smallest procedures, often paralyzing governments. Yet their national story said that they belonged together be-cause they were all Muslim. This imagined community of Muslims was failing to gel and work efficiently. So many people in Pakistan began to wonder too: Is there a problem with the very *idea* of Pakistan?

I returned to India that summer to investigate how this idea of a Muslim nation began in the first place. Was a na-tion of Muslims even a viable idea? India was a good place to explore this question for a few reasons. First, while a separate state for Muslims was created in Pakistan, India still had nearly as many, if not more, Muslims living in it in 2005. Also, the seeds of Muslim nationalism were sowed centuries earlier in a handful of religious educational in-stitutions, and nearly all of them remained on the Indian side of the border after partition. Over the next several months, I traveled through half of India's two dozen states, over thousands of miles, meeting dozens of Muslims at these institutions, read through countless archives—all in the hope of finding answers to Pakistan's present.

When the British formally took over the subcontinent
as a colony in 1857, the entire empire had been touched by
the dense web of bureaucracy woven by the Muslim ruler of
the Mughal Empire, which had lasted for several centuries.
To call it an Islamic system wouldn't be completely accurate. In some ways, the bureaucracy looked much like early
modern Chinese bureaucracy, but it was still a bureaucracy
built by a Muslim empire, and it carried symbols that drew
a connection to an Islamic past and a system that was often
unmistakably part of a larger Islamic civilization. So when
the British began to replace this bureaucracy, the changes
stung the Muslim subjects of the empire most deeply.

In 1860, the British Parliament passed a new penal
code for British India. In 1861, the High Courts Act was
passed, which promised "Justice, Equity, and Good Con-
science," and that same year the Indian Police Act created
a new police force in the subcontinent. There were new
laws for land acquisition and new standards of evidence.
In 1864, the British Parliament passed Act XI for its Indian colony, in which it finally declared it "unnecessary"
for Muslim law officers to serve in the bureaucracy. For
the first time in perhaps a thousand years, the muftis and
qazis lost their influence. Muslims in India suddenly went
from being part of the ruling elite in a Muslim empire to a
struggling minority in "British India." Illiterate in the new
official languages used by the British, unqualified to par-
ticipate in the highest levels of bureaucracy, the Muslims
began to withdraw from political society.

Educational institutions were a natural place for the
Muslims to retreat to. Madrassas were old and tested civil

institutions that had existed in all Islamic empires from Spain to Baghdad, and they were the only recognizably Muslim institutions that had survived the British takeover. Madrassas had long been incubators of religious philosophy, but now they also became hubs of political activism. In the later half of the nineteenth century, madrassas began mushrooming all over the subcontinent. Here, Muslims took stock of their new political reality as colonial subjects and started to think of responses to their sudden and crippling encounter with Western civilization. Here, the very early seeds of Pakistan were sown.

Two institutions in particular, both founded in the nineteenth century, had long-lasting influence. The madrassa in the city of Aligarh, in the northern Uttar Pradesh province of present-day India, was my first stop. I traveled six hours by train, east from Delhi to Aligarh. The university, today known as Aligarh Muslim University, was established as a madrassa in 1876, one year before the poet Iqbal was born. The redbrick buildings of the university strike a perfect balance between traditional Mughal Islamic architecture and the Victorian Gothic towers of Cambridge University. This architecture, more than anything else, conveys the essence of the institution. It was founded with the idea of bridging the great chasm that had opened between the British rulers and their Muslim subjects.

Syed Ahmad Khan, the founder of the madrassa, hailed from an influential Muslim family in Delhi. His father had been employed in the Mughal court system and Khan himself was educated in Muslim seminaries. After the British takeover, he formed a very pragmatic approach with the view of making the best of the colonial presence. With the madrassa at Aligarh, he wanted to create students who were Muslim "gentlemen," educated equally in Islamic religious philosophy and the modern sciences developed in the West. An "Aligh" would be equally comfortable debating the finer points of theology with Islamic scholars and talking politics with the British gentry. "Philosophy will be in our right hand and natural science in our left," the snow-white-bearded Syed Ahmad Khan said to his students, "and the crown of 'there is no God but Allah' will adorn our head." He was interested in Islam as a cultural identity as much as a religious code of life.

Another important madrassa, Darul Uloom, or "Abode of Knowledge" was in the city of Deoband, a little more than a hundred miles up the road from Aligarh. It was established a few years before Aligarh and had a different view on how to negotiate Muslims' new political and social reality in the nineteenth century. A student of Deoband told me that their institution began when a single pupil and a single teacher, both named Mehmood, began the study of the Quran under the shade of a pomegranate tree that still stands today in the spectacular white marble campus. The architecture is a stark contrast to Aligarh. While Aligarh meticulously fused Victorian and Mughal architecture, the Deoband campus is designed unmistakably as an Islamic mosque, with striking and beautiful domes and archways.

Muhammad Qasim Nanotvi, the founder of Deoband, was not as welcoming of British influence. The Deobandis saw the colonists as usurpers of the subcontinents' resources, and they viewed the new colonial institutions that replaced the Mughal system as instruments to disrupt the indigenous Muslim culture that had developed over centuries. Deoband focused on training scholars in scriptural Islam. They trained muftis and qazis and other religious experts. Since there were no state structures to use them, Deoband tried to absorb them into its own bureaucracy. As other madrassas inspired by Deoband popped up, the graduates of Deoband became prayer leaders, preachers, and teachers all across the subcontinent. They were tasked with disseminating their learning and preserving an Islamic way of life, which, from Deoband's point of view, was under assault from Western Christian and secular thought.

In the dusty library of Nadwatul Ulama in the city of Lucknow, another nineteenth-century madrassa, which was formed to bridge the Islamic thought of Aligarh and Deoband, I found a flimsy bound volume from 1890 that contained an exchange of letters between Nanotvi and Syed Ahmad Khan, the founder of the Aligarh school. The book was in archaic Urdu, which both institutions propagated as the new language of Muslims in the subcontinent after the British abolished Persian as the official language, which was the Mughal court language. The letters did not discuss Muslim nationalism or any political matters explicitly; it was too early for that conversation. Instead, the two scholars debated the comparative values of Quranic scripture and prophetic tradition; the different theoretical levels of knowledge from the divine to the human; the limits of *ijtihad*, the process of logical reasoning using religious scripture. They contemplated the limits of human agency, and even explored the fundamental differences between good and evil. Like all philosophical conversations, there were no concrete conclusions. These debates only left more questions.

Such conversations about religion and man and society pushed Muslims of the subcontinent into modernity. Deoband insisted that Islamic scripture was essentially the key to spiritual advancement and self-betterment, while Aligarh argued for applying Islamic principles to broader cultural practice. Aligarh absorbed some Western influence and Deoband stood to preserve Islamic institutions from decay. And there were dozens of other institutions that contributed their own bit to the conversation. Regardless of their stance on Islam and modernity, these institutions were the seeds of modern Muslim identity in South Asia. The Muslim nationalist movement blossomed by borrowing from all this in the generation that followed. The conversations created a Muslim intelligentsia in the subcontinent that was diverse and confident. How else would Muhammad Iqbal, the father of modern political Islam, and Muhammad Ali Jinnah, the billiard-playing Anglophile lawyer, become the twin founding fathers of the Muslim nation?

The institutions at Aligarh and Deoband formed in the aftermath of the colonial encounter became the double helix of Pakistan's DNA. The modern state inherited all these debates and theoretical conversations, but it did not inherit any concrete answers. Pakistan, after all, was the experiment. The country itself was destined to become the practical test of grand hypotheses, a laboratory for ideas that had been mulled over and aged for centuries. As I shuttled between these historic institutions from one corner of India to the other, I began to understand why Pakistanis stubbornly held on to their national idea despite all the apparent failures. If Pakistan failed, it was more than simply a failure of a sixty-year-old state. It was a failure of centuries' worth of work done by the best minds of the land.

When it was time to return to Pakistan, I paid one last visit to Dr. Dey at the hospital in Delhi. It had taken three surgeries over the year to reconstruct my leg and I was finally feeling better. I asked Dr. Dey if there was need for any more surgery. Was I ready to return to Pakistan? As he examined my leg closely, poking at it with metal instruments, I told him that I was planning to cross the border between Lahore and Amritsar on foot. After a few moments, he announced that my leg could probably take the journey. "I would hire a porter," he said. With a friendly handshake and a wry smile, he told me that he hoped never to see me again.

A few days after I returned to Lahore, I drove to the Miyani Sahab graveyard near Chauburji with my parents to visit my grandparents' graves. They were all there now, all four of them, in one of the city's oldest graveyards. I had yet to visit Grandfather Akhlaque's final resting place so I felt a bit nervous as we approached the gates. We navigated the narrow dusty paths and I found my grandfather's grave freshly watered. There was no tombstone. There were still people alive who could recognize it, so what was the need for one? The healthy brown mound of earth was much smaller than I had imagined it would be. As I laid a garland of flowers at the head, my mother placed her flat palm on the side of the grave as if to signal to Grandfather Akhlaque that we were there. I lifted my palms and splayed them open as I said a prayer for my grandfather. At the end I spoke a few words to him, under my breath, maybe for the first time since he died. I thought maybe from this near distance he could finally hear me. Next to him, I said a prayer at my grandmother's grave and then walked a short distance to my Mufti grandparents' resting places.

As I was making my way toward the exit gates, I saw an elaborate domed shrine in the distance. It struck me as odd. The graveyard was badly running short of space, and I wanted to find out who had earned such a lavish plot of land. I walked over and a plump middle-aged bearded man, running prayer beads through his fingers, stood guard at the small entrance. "You have reached the eternal abode of Ilam Din," he announced in a gravelly voice. "This young man was not much older than you, when as a great warrior of Islam, he took the life of a Hindu man who defamed our dear Prophet." With that, he raised his palms to say a prayer. "Let us pray for him."

I joined my parents in the car. As we turned into the unruly Lahore traffic, my mother smiled and placed her hand on my head. "It's good to have you back home." It was the first time she had said this since I had returned from India. Now that I had visited the graves of the ancestors, she felt I had truly returned.

Six

ISLAMABAD, PAKISTAN'S CAPITAL, lies more than two hundred miles north of Lahore, on the northern edge of a tall table of land known as the Potwar Plateau. The plateau rises suddenly, more than a thousand feet from the plains of the Punjab, north of the River Jehlum, one of the five rivers of the Punjab. The plateau covers an area of nearly ten thousand square miles, roughly the size of the state of Vermont. Up along the northern rim of the Potwar, the Himalayan highlands begin charging upward toward the sky. Only a few hours north of the Pakistani capital are some of the highest mountains in the world, and the rough highlands of the Afghan frontier are to the northwest.

The Potwar Plateau is one of the most densely popu-lated regions in the world and a place as remarkable in its history as it is in its geography. Archaeologists have found fossilized tools here that they believe are a million years old, made by ancestors of modern humans in the early Stone

Age. A few miles outside the city limits of Islamabad are the remains of the ancient town of Taxila, which was the capital of the Gandhara civilization, a prosperous node in the historic Silk Road. Alexander the Great invaded Gandhara in the fourth century BCE, and the encounter with the Greek civilization produced some stunning Buddhist sculpture in the region. The city of Rawalpindi, which is adjacent to Islamabad, was developed only in the mid-nineteenth century into a major colonial military outpost of the British Indian Empire.

Islamabad was created when President Ayub Khan, the first military ruler of Pakistan, grabbed power in 1958. He was keen on undertaking major development projects like dams and industry, so he decided to initiate a brand-new capital for his country. Pakistan truly was in need of a city from where to run its government. Delhi had long been the city from where the shahanshah, the raja, or the sultan had chosen to rule, but when the line of partition was drawn right through the Punjab, that city was lost to India. Lahore was another historic capital city, especially for many Muslim empires of the past, but it was too close to the Indian border to be a safe choice for a modern Pakistani capital. After partition, Pakistan had hurriedly improvised government headquarters in the port city of Karachi, Pakistan's largest city, on the Arabian Sea. But Pakistan was a new nation, and a new nation, President Ayub decided, must have a new and special capital.

Picking a spot for the capital city for one of the most populous nations on earth was no simple task. President Ayub formed a commission made up of bureaucrats and

scientists and judges and geologists and of course members of the powerful military to study all the available options. Pakistan, in the late 1960s, was still made of two
equal halves. When it came to the most basic choice, between East Pakistan and West Pakistan, the commission
was quick to favor the west. It had always been dominant,
and the foreign relations committee justified the choice by
explaining that "geographically and historically the future
of Pakistan is linked with its Muslim neighbors in Central
and West Asia and the capital therefore should be located
in a region of West Pakistan which will promote a revival
of emotional link with its western neighbors." After many
months of work, the president was finally presented with
several options. There was land outside Karachi, for in-
stance. It was near the existing capital, but for a young in-
secure nation surrounded by enemies, a city on the coast
was not ideal. Quetta, an established city in the isolated
and sparsely populated southwestern province of Balochistan, was briefly considered but swiftly rejected because
it was remote and located far from the Indus, which was the
lifeline of the country. A small town called Fort Monroe, a
hill station on the western banks of the Indus almost exactly
in the center of the country, was a more attractive option.
But ultimately, the committee decided on a spot of land on
the Potwar Plateau.

The particular location, on the outskirts of the colonial
military outpost of Rawalpindi, was on the Grand Trunk
Road, the historic route that runs east to west across the
entire subcontinent. It was situated almost exactly halfway
between two historic capitals, Kabul in the west and Delhi

in the east, which were nearly eight hundred miles apart. The commission decided to begin right in the shadow of a spur of mountains in the lower Himalayas called the Margalla Hills. The evergreen Margallas would provide a picturesque backdrop to the city and become its impenetrable northern limit. Here, sitting atop a throne in the north of the country along the headwaters of the Indus, the capital would recline on the highest mountains on earth and look down south as the rest of the country unfolded along the Indus. On February 24, 1960, once the land was chosen, the president's cabinet agreed on a name. The new capital of Pakistan would be called "Islamabad": the City of Islam.

Surrounded by sprawling history, and with this extraordinary name, Islamabad was built from scratch with a searing focus on the future. Doxiadis Associates, an urban development firm owned by a Greek city planner, won the contract for planning and designing Islamabad. Constantine Doxiadis was an avant-garde practitioner in his field, famous for breaking new ground. He already had major projects under his belt in Greece, where he had initiated the field of ekistics, the study the natural human patterns of growth. Doxiadis had studied these patterns in order to create the ideal city of the future where inhabitants would settle in perfect harmony with their physical and sociocultural environments, and expand effortlessly to meet new needs, a utopian city that he called a dynametropolis. Islamabad was Doxiadis's attempt at just such a city, his most ambitious project to date. It was a city that could come to define his life's work. In building the capital for one of the most populous countries on earth, he would attempt to create what might be, from a design point of view, the world's most modern city.

The first team from Doxiadis Associates arrived in Rawalpindi in early November 1959 to meet the Pakistani commission and begin a field survey to collect data from the Potwar Plateau. The Greeks were made keenly aware that they were designing the city of Islam, and they paid close attention to invoking an Islamic aesthetic in the city's structure, from the macro city design to the very finest details. The designers borrowed geometric patterns from the great architectural wonders of Islam, from the Kaaba in Mecca to the carvings at the Taj Mahal constructed by the Mughals. The urban layout, the architecture, the Margalla Hills framing the city, the Indus River running past—all were entwined to weave the new fabric of Islamabad.

In 1962, the plans were finally complete and Constantine Doxiadis flew to Rawalpindi himself to present the proposal to the Pakistani president and his commission. The town would consist of three sections split by two major highways that formed a giant T on the map. A residential area was made up of a cluster of adjoining one-and-a-half-square-mile units called sectors connected by wide roads, which created a giant beehive structure. Each sector would have its own commercial district, mosques, schools, and hospitals. Another part of the city was the Margalla Hills National Park, which would hold the national stadiums, many museums, and an artificially dammed lake that would be a water source for the city and a favored picnic spot for denizens. The third part, running along the eastern edge of the city, was reserved for the business of government.

After a few hours of discussion, and after last-minute modifications, the master plan of Islamabad was finally approved. The city was now ready to come to life.

After the presentation, as celebratory drinks were served, one of Doxiadis's close associates, a man named Orestes Yakas who was in charge of running the operations in Pakistan, stared wistfully at the master plan that hung on the wall. General Yahya Khan, one of President Ayub's top generals, walked up to him. "Why so melancholic? This is a day of joy for all of us," he said, toasting his Greek collaborator. The Greek man must have had a keen sense of history. He was in a contemplative mood, and without taking his eyes off the giant map of the future city of Islamabad he replied, "Sir, this is the first time that I see the model of an important work in which I have participated, but I shall not be alive to see it in reality, after forty or fifty years." The city of Islam was ready to march into an uncertain future, populated by many new people.

I moved to Islamabad in the spring of 2007 to work as a journalist for an American newspaper. The work of writing crept up on me. It was in the weeks that I spent in bed in Delhi with my shattered leg that I started writing my first stories. It was part of my healing process and also a way of understanding the strange world I inhabited. I recorded the stories of people around me, the nurses, the cleaners, and other patients. I took notes on the conversations that I heard from across curtains and walls of the hospital. They were slices of people's lives and didn't always make much sense. When I set out to explore India, I started carrying a thick brown leather-bound notebook with me. I interviewed the people I met along the way in that enormous and diverse country. I tried to understand how people's stories fit into the larger puzzle of the world I was solving. I tried to record them honestly, faithfully. When I returned to Pakistan, it felt natural to keep recording the course of events.

But I was pulled away again, to another city that had long cast a spell on me from afar: New York City. I had heard that it was the perfect place to be a writer, and so I returned to America. I felt the city vibrate under my feet when I set foot in it. It was alive and it was as complex as any human being I had ever attempted to capture on the page. I began taking classes on writing and journalism at New York University and wrote about murders, and illegal exotic pets people were keeping in tiny apartments, and celebrities opening shoestores, and about retired forgotten Olympic boxers who wandered the streets. New York was also the place to show off your craft and be noticed. I began meeting editors of magazines and other writers. They all asked about Pakistan, and I always enjoyed telling stories about that place that was beginning to loom large in America's imagination of the world.

After a little more than a year, I moved back. Pakistan was now the rumbling epicenter of a raging global war on terror. The place was important to me, this much I had known, but now this faraway place had become important to all Americans, and my job was to explain how and why things happened the way they did in Pakistan. I found the work of a journalist fulfilling, and I also took writing seriously, for it is, as they say, the "first draft of history." The reporter's job gave me a front-row seat to fast-paced events that were brewing into a full-scale conflict. All the major players involved in shaping the country's course were a phone call away, and for the first time I closely observed the leaders, and the fighters, and the ordinary players of history.

Forty years after ground was broken, Islamabad was now a sprawling and scenic capital of one million people. The roads were immaculately built and the lush greenery of the Potwar region and the Margalla Hills provided a bright and cheerful natural landscape. Foreign investment was pouring in. High-rises were beginning to sprout in all parts of the city. The air was still cleaner than any other major city of Pakistan. When heading out of Islamabad, people would joke that they were "going to visit Pakistan." But compared to the centuries-old cities like Lahore and Karachi and Peshawar, Islamabad could feel awfully sterile. I hardly ever met anyone who was actually born there or even considered it home. It was a city of bureaucrats, businessmen, and bosses who passed through only long enough to get the job done and then abandoned it at the first signs of trouble. Any time a major holiday rolled around, Islamabad was deserted. It was the "city that mostly sleeps," they said, nestled quietly in the shade of the Margalla Hills, wrapped snugly in red tape.

When I arrived in Islamabad in the summer of 2007, all this was about to change. War was coming to the City of Islam. The man in charge was the military general Pervez Musharraf. Ever since America's war in Afghanistan began in 2001, Musharraf had seen himself as a man chosen by

history. More than just banal thoughts of ruling effec-
tively, after the War on Terror began, Musharraf developed grandiose conceptions of his place in the world. He
talked about lifting Pakistan to its "rightful place" in the
global order and as a leader of Muslim countries across the
world. He spoke about his role in healing the rift between
East and West. At the center of his grand scheme was a new
ideology, which served as his guiding principle in ruling
Pakistan. He called it "Enlightened Moderation." It was an
all-encompassing plan aimed at shaping the people of Pakistan and their national values, society, politics, economy,
education, culture, and religion.

Like all Pakistani leaders of the past, Musharraf's
scheme was also about Islam's place in the modern world.
In all its amorphous glory, this ideology was designed to
model a nation of "moderate" Muslims. It was everywhere:
on the city billboards depicting stylish models selling lin-
gerie and in the seven-star hotels under construction in
the heart of the capital. Lahore's first Porsche dealership
opened its doors in 2003, and after years of prohibition,
alcoholic drinks were casually being served in restaurants.
Enlightened Moderation was a freer media, a booming
telecommunications network, and cell phones for everyone. At the same time it was mass population displacement
in a dam-building project and the uprooting of fishing
towns to build mega-seaports. It meant the rolling back of
some of the most stringent Islamic penal laws that were put
on the books during the rule of General Zia in the eighties.

The project was helped along by an unprecedented
amount of wealth that was pouring into Pakistan at the time.

General Pervez Musharraf cut a friendly figure for his first appearance in front of Western journalists, days after he came to power in a coup in October 1999. (Source: Karen Davies)

Expatriate Pakistanis who had been ejected from America or left the West after the attacks of September 2001 returned with bloated dollar bank accounts, boosting property prices. After the beginning of the War on Terror, Pakistan also started receiving massive amounts of debt relief and aid from the United States, thanks to the terms negotiated by General Musharraf to guarantee his country's cooperation in Afghanistan. The rich were getting richer in Pakistan, but the poor were also getting less poor and more educated, at least according to the figures issued by the government. Seeing this growing middle class, multinational companies from all over the world came to cash in. Enlightened Moderation, Musharraf claimed in a typically megalomaniacal moment, was "bringing some order to this disorderly world."

Musharraf toured the world promoting his idea. I was in Washington, D.C., in June 2003 when I first saw him speak about this at the Mayflower Hotel to an auditorium full of fawning Beltway power players. "The sunshine of hope and justice will eradicate the germs of hate and self-destruction," he said as the crowd broke out into enthusiastic applause. "I urge all Americans to see their stake in the progress of Pakistan towards realizing the vision of its founding father, Muhammad Ali Jinnah," he said toward the end. He later penned an op-ed for the *Washington Post* laying out the details of the plan. Enlightened Moderation, he said, was "a win for all—for both the Muslim and non-Muslim worlds."

It was a well-timed pitch. After the attacks of September 2001, the policy circles in Washington had ordered the global Islamic religious and lived cultural experience into discrete, and arbitrary, blocs. There were "moderate Muslims," the thinking went, who could be potential partners of the West in its fight against the "extremists" and the "Islamic militants" or "Islamists." Musharraf's vision seemed very suitably "moderate." *The 9/11 Commission Report*, released in September 2004, said, "If Musharraf stands for Enlightened Moderation in a fight for his life and for the life of his country, the United States should be willing to make hard choices too, and make the difficult and long-term commitment to the future of Pakistan."

Governments of other Muslim countries backed it too, at least in public. Musharraf took his message to the Organization of Islamic Cooperation, and it adopted a resolution that said that Muslim countries would "avoid the policy of either confrontation or capitulation in dealing with the West." Instead, "We should stress polices of moderation and mutually beneficial cooperation through dialogue as reflected in President Musharraf's proposal of Enlightened Moderation."

In Pakistan, it was a different story. The country was slowly becoming a real and violent battleground in the War on Terror. After American forces moved into Iraq to overthrow the Arab leader Saddam Hussein in 2003, the American war in Afghanistan had begun to unravel. The American military blamed the horrible turn in the war in Afghanistan on the fact that the enemy, the Taliban, had crossed into Pakistan and was launching deadly attacks on American forces from inside a strip of autonomous borderland known commonly as the Federally Administered Tribal Areas. The American government began pressuring Musharraf to order the Pakistani military to attack the Taliban forces on the Pakistani side of the border.

This was no ordinary request. The tribal areas had joined the Pakistani federation in 1947 after an agreement that they would remain autonomous and independent forever. The Pashtun tribes who lived here were a rugged and proud people and no Pakistani military had ever operated in those areas and had little idea about the terrain. When armed militants, suspected to be part of the Taliban from Afghanistan, began killing off tribal leaders on the Pakistani side, in 2005, Musharraf finally saw an opening and decided to take action: he ordered the military forces into the tribal areas. The Pakistani military was sucked into the fighting in Afghanistan. While American forces battled the

Taliban in Afghanistan, the Pakistanis were now battling them and many of their own citizens on Pakistani territory to help America's military goals in Afghanistan.

For many Pakistanis this war in the tribal areas became indistinguishable from the rest of Musharraf's Enlightened Moderation. As a result, many Pakistanis began resenting and resisting the entire project. For those who opposed Musharraf's military alliance with America, Enlightened Moderation was an easy target. The Jamaat-e-Islami, the oldest and largest political Islamic party, called the program a "comprehensive and somber version of neo-colonialism." Dr. Ayman al-Zawahiri, the leader of Al-Qaeda, said in an interview conducted on the fourth anniversary of 9/11 that "today, the Pakistani army plays the same role that the British Indian army used to play in the aggression against the Muslims in India, and in quelling the Muslim uprisings in the British colonies." Musharraf, he said, "wants a Pakistan without Islam . . . They are inventing a new religion, which they composed for him in America. They call this fairy tale 'Enlightened Moderation.'"

By the time I arrived in Islamabad that summer, the lines had already been drawn. The latest phase of Pakistan's eternal project to define itself as a Muslim nation and a democratic Islamic state was no longer its own private struggle. As the world spoke of a clash of civilizations, Pakistan's experiment to bridge civilizations was now a central set piece in an international war. Pakistan was laid bare for the world to see. The country was sucked into a larger global war against terrorism, which had already shredded the society of a few countries in the world. Now it was only a question of who would fire the first shot in Islamabad, and at whom.

GROUND ZERO FOR THE WAR in Islamabad was an area no larger than a few hundred square yards, inside one of the oldest sectors of the city, G-6. On the surface it was a small dispute between Musharraf's government and the administration of a mosque over some construction on a small plot of land, but it would turn into a full-scale military battle. The battle of the Red Mosque would plunge Pakistan into an era of violence and change the country forever.

It started quietly one morning in the winter of 2007, when a hundred or so students from an all-women's madrassa on the grounds of the Red Mosque marched into their school library to occupy it. The seminary was a religiously conservative institution and the women, mostly in their teens and twenties, were draped in jet-black from head to toe, with only thin slits showing their eyes. To someone watching from the outside, these women would have seemed oppressed victims of a patriarchal Islamic order. But they were hardly that. They were all carrying tall bamboo staffs in their gloved hands as they marched and shouted slogans against the government of Pervez Musharraf. Far from seeking salvation, these female students from the madrassa were furious at the man behind Enlightened Moderation. They were out to protect their institution, their beliefs, and their worldview. It was clear from their orderly demonstration that they had been planning this occupation for many weeks.

The government had informed the mosque, months earlier, that the library adjacent to the women's school was built on land that the Red Mosque had encroached upon illegally, and that the city authorities would come and tear down the structure to reclaim it. The students were fighting back against the planned demolition, but in reality it was a much larger ideological battle. They issued a statement saying that they were also protesting the demolitions planned for half a dozen other mosques constructed illegally by Islamabad's municipal authorities.

The government ignored the occupation at first. The students would eventually tire and vacate the library, they believed. In another time and in another place, that might have been true. The demolition of a handful of mosque structures, in a country where every neighborhood and village had its own mosque, might not have become such a heated issue. Except this wasn't about physical structures. This wasn't even about the sanctity of religious locations. This was about Pervez Musharraf, his program of Enlightened Moderation, and his military assault on the tribal areas in alliance with America. This was about the general's revolutionary program to redefine the world's only Muslim nation and the original Islamic republic. The women occupying the library were rising up against it all. In many ways, the standoff at the Red Mosque was about the very meaning of the City of Islam.

The G-6 neighborhood is one of the most exquisitely situated sectors in the honeycomb residential structure of

Hundreds of female students from the Red Mosque armed themselves with bamboo staffs in preparation for battle against the state. (Source: B.K. Bangash/AP)

Islamabad. It is built on the vertex of the city where the Margalla Hills come closest to the national parkland. It was also the first sector to be populated. The initial inhabitants of Islamabad, who moved into the city in the mid-1960s, were mainly low-ranking government officials and city officials, young and middle-aged men from the middle rungs of state bureaucracy sent off to the newly constructed, dark and desolate capital city in the Himalayan foothills. Some came with their families, but most left them behind, reluctant to bring children up in the mountains where there were no good schools yet, and no proper street lighting, and where wild boars still roamed free, knocking over trash containers in the night.

What would the City of Islam be without a mosque? Construction of the capital's first mosque began in 1964.

Once it was completed, it was named Lal Masjid or the Red Mosque after the color of its exterior. It was a handsome mosque, not too lavish or too large, and smartly designed to let the sunlight through the large arching windows. It was capped by a white dome. The search for the right imam began while it was still being constructed, and it led to Abdullah Ghazi, a graduate of an Islamic seminary in Karachi. He was in his midthirties and hailed from a small and underdeveloped village in the southwest of the Punjab. In 1964, Abdullah moved to the brand-new capital with his wife and three daughters and two young sons to begin his duties as the first imam of the Red Mosque. Sitting there at his pulpit in the capital, the once simple man would over time become molded, with every convulsing turn of Pakistani politics, into a lightning rod.

Abdullah had strong educational pedigree. He was trained in a seminary that followed the religious tradition of Deoband, the sect of Islamic thought developed during British colonial rule, which was aimed at guarding the South Asian Islamic tradition against Western influence. Deobandis had been very influential in society and had set up many educational institutions. Still, Abdullah would have known that he was lucky to receive this assignment. Pakistan was an Islamic republic, but the state's judicial bureaucratic machine had been inherited nearly intact from the British colonists. The head of the state was the prime minister; common law in the British tradition was used in courts, where lawyers in black suits and ties addressed the judges as "M'lord." Pakistan's first prime minister, Liaquat Ali Khan, had said that the country was meant to be a laboratory of modern Islam, but in reality there were few opportunities in government service for a man like Abdullah Ghazi, trained in Islamic jurisprudence. Most other students who graduated with Abdullah, as muftis and qazis and other types of Islamic scholars, would have ended up leading prayers in their own local mosques and leading small ministries. Many of them would have lived off the charitable goodwill of their neighbors and followers.

Abdullah turned out to be a natural at his new job at the Red Mosque. He plugged himself snugly among the power players operating in Islamabad who would come to his mosque as well as the many national and international characters who passed through the capital in the sixties. Zulfiqar Bhutto helped overthrow the regime of Ayub Khan in 1969. While Bhutto did help design a new Islamic constitution for the country after the civil war of 1971, he was wary of religious leaders like Abdullah. When the political opposition led by the Jamaat-e-Islami began their campaign against Bhutto after his first term, Abdullah opened his doors to the most prominent religious leaders in the country, and the Red Mosque became something of a hub for anti-Bhutto political activity of the 1970s. That was the first time Abdullah was arrested. He was soon released after his followers at the mosque threatened to turn violent. This would become a pattern in the years that followed.

General Zia's overthrow of Bhutto was a boon to Abdullah's career. Zia was much more interested in strengthening religious leaders and created official bodies like the Council of Islamic Ideology and the Federal Shariat

Court, which were stacked with qualified qazis and religious scholars. These new institutions created more space for religiously trained jurists in the state's machinery, but a handful of institutions was still not enough to absorb the thousands of religious scholars being churned out by seminaries. So at the same time Zia also handed out cash grants to many autonomous Islamic institutions. In 1981, the Red Mosque was given a grant of more than seven million rupees, (equivalent to seven hundred thousand dollars) and Abdullah used the money to restructure and expand the Red Mosque and add a men's seminary to the complex.

General Zia had also initiated the construction of a new central mosque in Islamabad in the lap of the Margalla Hills. It was a magnificent project. The new mosque, capable of holding a hundred thousand people on its grounds, cost over one hundred million dollars. Its towering spires could be seen from every part of the city. With this new, larger mosque in place, Abdullah's Red Mosque melted into the quiet backdrop of the capital and acquired a new character at a time of great change. G-6 was by now a perfect mishmash of residential streets, large hotels, the city's largest shopping bazaar, and offices for many important government departments. The headquarters of the Directorate for Inter-Services Intelligence, or the ISI, the powerful Pakistani intelligence services, was also in G-6, and the ISI approached Abdullah in the early 1980s with a life-changing proposition.

The godless Soviets were waging war on the Muslim brothers in neighboring Afghanistan, they told Abdullah. Young Muslim men from all over the world would descend into Pakistan in the coming years to be trained in guerrilla warfare. They would learn to fight in the Afghan battle-fields, using money from friends in America and Saudi Arabia. In Islamabad, the intelligence services required a way station for these fighters, and so Abdullah agreed to make the Red Mosque an important stopover for many mujahideen leaders arriving in Pakistan. These included Osama bin Laden and Ayman al-Zawahiri on their way to battle the Soviets in Afghanistan.

The Soviets were finally beaten back in 1989, the CIA funds dried up, and General Zia's rule came to an abrupt end when his plane mysteriously exploded in the sky. When Benazir Bhutto became the new prime minister in 1988, Abdullah felt the wrath of the state as he had when her fa-ther, Zulfiqar Bhutto, had been in charge. Benazir ordered the arrest of Abdullah once again in 1990 but, like her fa-ther, she had to release him when his followers proved to be fiercely loyal and accepted no one else in his place. Then, a few years later, in another change of government, Abdul-lah found a religion-friendly leader in Nawaz Sharif. This time he used the big financial grants to construct a girls' school on the Red Mosque complex, the largest female Is-lamic boarding school in the country.

Abdullah had been a prominent fixture in Islamabad since the city was created and now was somewhat of an in-stitution. He was perhaps the only man in the city who had deftly survived every change of government, and his po-sition seemed unshakable. Abdullah, with his large tinted square glasses, thin features, and long gray beard, was a recognized, notorious operator in the capital of a country that had become a nuclear power in 1998. But he was a small-town man, after all. He had gotten too deep into this dangerous game with too many powerful people. In 1998, a few months after Bill Clinton launched missile attacks on Afghanistan to target a new militant group named Al-Qaeda, Abdullah was shot dead near his home on the grounds of the Red Mosque by people who were never seen or captured.

For the first time since it opened its doors to worshippers and students, the Red Mosque was in need of a new leader. In his will, Abdullah had nominated his older son, Abdul Aziz Ghazi, to take over the duties at the mosque, and the congregation accepted him in a heartbeat. Abdullah's youngest son, Abdul Rashid Ghazi, was appointed the vice imam. The Ghazi brothers had been at the job less than a year when the top military general Pervez Musharraf launched a coup against the elected government and became the new president of Pakistan, the new boss in Islamabad. The seeds of an ideological clash between the Ghazi brothers and Musharraf were there from the beginning. While the Ghazis' father was from the tradition of Deoband, Musharraf's father was a graduate of the more pro-Western seminary at Aligarh. Both fathers had been born as colonial subjects and studied at Muslim institutions, but they had radically different views on the relationship between Islam and the modern nation-state. It was quickly clear to the Ghazis that Musharraf would be more secular than any previous ruler in Pakistan's history.

After the attacks of September 11 in America, when Musharraf went on TV and announced his support for the

American war against the Taliban, he faced stiff opposition from many religious groups, including Abdul Aziz
Ghazi. As a child Abdul Aziz had seen the mujahideen pass
through his home in Islamabad during the Soviet war. He
had been taught that they were great heroes of Muslims.
How could Pakistan now side with America in attacking
these same people who were once so revered? Anyway, as
far as the Ghazi brothers could see, Islamabad was becoming a city that was not worthy of being called the City of
Islam.

"Our Muslim culture, which at one time sprouted with
knowledge and virtue and was a laboratory for the arts and
cultural production, has fallen victim to a collective sense of
inferiority, victimization, and helplessness," Abdul Rashid
proclaimed in a public letter a few months after the female
students took over the library. The younger brother was
not trained in the Islamic tradition. He had a master's degree in international relations from the best university in
the capital and this showed, as his speech was peppered with
English words. He was a good spokesperson and became the
public and political face of the mosque. "It is touching the
limits of decay, because of the absence of the implementation of an Islamic system," he continued, to explain the
mind-set in Pakistan. "Islam is perfectly capable of tackling
all of modernity's challenges," he concluded. Even though
Abdul Rashid saw things very differently from Musharraf,
that phrase sounded eerily like something Musharraf would
say in a speech about Enlightened Moderation.

The last straw for the brothers came in 2005, when Pervez Musharraf sent military forces into Pakistan's own tribal

areas to battle the rising Taliban spilling over from Afghanistan, on the recommendation of the American military. They finally saw an opening to confront the military ruler openly. A retired colonel in the Pakistan army visited the Red Mosque and asked its imam: Was it lawful for Pakistani soldiers to combat fellow Muslims on the orders of a ruler who is also Muslim? It was a complex scenario and a question of Islamic law that begged for a fatwa, a religious opinion. The question was answered in writing and the response discussed examples from a millennium of Islamic history and jurisprudence. The fatwa concluded that the soldiers in the Pakistani army should in fact disobey the commands of the government. In his capacity as a mufti, the older brother, along with more than fifty Islamic scholars and clerics from all over the country, signed the document that essentially instructed the army to mutiny against its commanders. With this fatwa, the Red Mosque became the first official dissenter to the Pakistani military's campaign in the War on Terror. The brothers were now in a position to inspire a rebellion. Musharraf ordered the removal of Abdul Aziz as imam of the Red Mosque, but he remained. His followers refused to pray behind anyone else.

So in 2006, when the mosque received a notice from the city authorities of Islamabad that the women's school library on the Red Mosque complex would be torn down to make space for a parking lot, the brothers were hardly surprised that Musharraf was sending in the wrecking crew. The library was a small part of the Red Mosque, no more than a few hundred square yards, but it is where decades, perhaps even centuries, of history were about to collide with thunderous clamor. And this time, the whole world would watch.

The winter fog lifted off the jagged green Margalla Hills as the spring of 2007 arrived. The library occupation had now grown into a full-blown movement and spilled onto the streets. The male students at the mosque had joined forces with the women and formed a group that people called the Red Mosque Brigade. They began vigilante moral-policing operations all over Islamabad. The women from the seminary would thuggishly swarm marketplaces with large sticks in their hands and rap other women on the arms if they deemed their short-sleeved dresses inappropriate. The male students busted prostitution rings, raided video stores that sold pornography, and burned mounds of CDs, and they also kidnapped police officials who got in the way. The brigade was no longer a mere nuisance; it was turning criminal.

Abdul Rashid, the younger brother, became the brigade's ringleader, but he never really looked the part of a militia commander. He was short and stout, with a bushy white beard and a gentle, plump, white smiling face. But lately he had taken to carrying an AK-47 over his shoulder. One June afternoon, the brigade kidnapped nine Chinese women from a notorious brothel that was frequented by government officials. They held the prostitutes and their madam inside the mosque compound and Abdul Rashid spoke to the press and answered questions in English. "The people of that area have been demanding the police and the police have not been doing anything," Ghazi said, sounding like nothing more than a concerned citizen. "So far as justifying this according to Islamic sharia," he explained the religious rationale of the actions, "Islam says that when you see some kind of wrongdoings, you stop it by hand. So, the students stop it." This is how they justified it: since the state was failing to do its job and run an orderly society, the Red Mosque would step in and help out.

On April 11, 2007, the older brother, Abdul Aziz, spelled this out explicitly. He announced that the Red Mosque was inaugurating a parallel judicial system. It was a "qazi court" system, he explained, where qazis trained in Islamic law would provide rulings on cases based on the law described in the Quran and the canon of Islamic law. To help interpret the law to reach just conclusions, the Red Mosque had appointed ten muftis to aid the qazis in their rulings. The brothers invited the people of G-6 and other neighborhoods of Islamabad to approach the qazi courts to settle any small disputes or claims, and promised "real justice" in the hands of the muftis and qazis. And so, on one regular day in Islamabad, the ancient judicial bureaucracy that my families had been part of centuries ago was resurrected inside the walls of a mosque at the barrel end of loaded automatic weapons.

What probably irked Musharraf more than anything else was that some people really did begin going to the qazi courts. The furious general accused the mosque leaders of setting up "a state within a state," and for the first time his tone turned threatening. If the group did not disband, he would not hesitate to use force, he said. The next month, the Red Mosque distributed guidelines with fifty bullet points to bring the entire country's bureaucracy in line with the laws of an "Islamic sharia." The release made a special plea to lawyers and the judiciary to become trained in the Islamic law to do their job rightfully, as real scholars and muftis and qazis would.

The first shots were fired on July 3, 2007, and it never was clear who fired first. For many hours, bullets whizzed back and forth between the mosque and the security guards stationed outside. Some students attacked a government office building and set fire to it, along with a few cars parked nearby. On the first day, nine people died, including four students at the mosque and a TV reporter. Officials esti-mated that 150 people were injured. G-6 was declared an emergency zone and sealed off by paramilitary troops. No one, not even reporters, could enter the area around the mosque after that. A curfew was announced and the mili-tary declared a shoot-to-kill policy for anyone breaking the curfew.

The next day, as the fighting continued, the govern-ment offered safe passage to all women who came out of the mosque complex and offered a chance to all men to surrender. Of the thousands inside, only one hundred or so took the opportunity. But as darkness fell that night, Abdul Aziz was unexpectedly captured as he attempted to escape the complex covered from head to toe in a woman's *niqab*. Musharraf saw an opportunity to win over some pub-lic opinion. Abdul Aziz was paraded on TV in the woman's costume and humiliated in an interview on national televi-sion. The interview was badly edited to make the man look even more pathetic and shameful than he already was. After Abdul Aziz's capture, more than a thousand students surrendered to the authorities. But Abdul Aziz had warned in the course of his on-air grilling that there were hundreds of hard-core holdouts who would stay until the bloody end.

With each passing day, the battle became fiercer and journalists from all over the world began descending on the city. The Marriott Hotel a mile away from the mosque was where all the journalists were living, but it felt insulated and controlled, a world away from the intense battle. I tried to make it inside the curfew zone every day but was turned back by the military guarding all entry points. At night, as I sat on the porch of my house in Islamabad, which was miles away from G-6, I could still hear mortar blasts in the distance and the *rat-a-tat* of automatic weapons. Islamabad had become a war zone.

Finally, on July 9, six days after the battle had started, I made it through. I simply did what I had been doing every day since the fighting began: I drove in the direction of the mosque, but this time when I was stopped at the first military checkpoint, I lied and said that I lived on a street in the distance and I needed to be with my family who were stranded. The soldier, who had the turret of his automatic weapon pointed at my head, looked me up and down and then waved me through without a word.

I had timed my entrance with a cease-fire that had been announced by both sides a few hours earlier to allow the residents of G-6 to step outside their homes to get basic essentials or to escape. I'm not sure what I was hoping to find, other than a visceral experience of a small slice of the battle. It was a grueling summer afternoon, and I saw a few men trickling out onto the streets in a nervous commotion. They scuttled in all directions, averting their gazes from the troops who stood at every crossing with their weapons loaded and pointed from behind piles of sandbags. I parked my car in a side street and followed a man down a narrow tree-lined alley and turned a corner to find a small tin-box store. It was overrun by a heap of men crowding the counter and demanding all at once bread, cigarettes, water, Coke, DVDs. Throwing myself into the pile, I emerged with a Coca-Cola in my hand and joined a group of men huddled in serious conversation.

One of the men worked for a government agency that printed national ID cards and another was an engineer who worked as a technician at the state television station. The women and children in nearly all their families had left when the battle started. The men had mostly stayed behind to protect their property.

"When will this stop?" the big round man from the ID office asked after some time of sharing war stories. It wasn't exactly a rhetorical question, but no one seemed to hazard a guess.

"What can they do?" another man asked. "Destroy the mosque?"

They all went silent. What had sparked this battle in the first place was the government's decision to knock down one of the buildings on the mosque complex. But now the stakes were much higher. There were hundreds of people inside the compound, and many of them were children. What to do about them? The army said they were hostages, but the leaders of the mosque declared on live television that everyone inside, even the children, were there by choice and carrying on for the righteous cause of jihad, or war to protect Islam.

"Such *zulm* this Musharraf is committing," one man sighed, taking a puff from a cigarette.

"And what about Ghazi?" another man shot back, referring to Abdul Rashid. "The real *zulm* is holding little kids hostage."

I must pause here to explain *zulm*. It is impossible to understand what was happening in Pakistan at that time without truly understanding this one word. *Zulm* is an Arabic word that literally suggests deviation from the middle, or sometimes to obscure or darken. It is taken from the Quran, and it specifically refers to any kind of injustice that occurs in the world. The word appears in the revelations to Muhammad dozens of times. *Zalimeen* are sinners who commit *zulm*, or injustice. Allah has not guided them, it is written—their eternal abode is fiery hell.

Zulm, it should be said, is a purely human quality. Allah says he is incapable of it. Allah is capable of many things— he is "the Dominator" or even "the Destroyer"—but he is never unjust. Instead, Allah is *al-'Adl*, "the Utterly Just," and *al-Muqsit*, "the Most Equitable." It is these divine qualities that are sometimes used to describe the opposite state of *zulm*, a balanced utopian social order of justice. Only when a just order is upset does *zulm* prevail. Or to imagine it another way, *zulm* is a harsh, parched desert, and only the path of sharia will lead you to the oasis of justice. It rumbled singularly beneath all the trouble that summer.

To some, what was being done to the people in the mosque was *zulm,* and to others it was the actions of the Red Mosque Brigade that were *zulm.* The Pakistani army's military campaign in the tribal areas was *zulm,* but so was the bombing of the girls' schools by Taliban militants in the same tribal belt. The U.S. military's operation in Afghanistan was *zulm,* and the suicide bombings by the Taliban that left heaps of dead human bodies were also *zulm.* The dishonesty and corruption of politicians, the torture inflicted by the police, the rule of General Musharraf—*zulm, zulm, zulm.*

Justice was the rallying cry for everyone fighting *zulm* that summer. The problem was, of course, that no one could agree on what was the real *zulm* or who were the real *zalimeen.* There were many different paths being offered, everyone claimed the right path, and no one knew which one it actually was.

The curfew was about to be enforced again, and the men were now speculating on the endgame. Would the younger Ghazi brother give up? Would Musharraf fold and allow safe passage to the holdouts? Or would they decide to fight it out like a war? No one even seemed sure which was the most desirable option. It's not all black-and-white when you're looking at it from inside.

"I just want the violence to end," the television technician said.

"Allah knows best."

They all scurried off into the separate alleys from where they had come.

When I returned home a few hours later, I turned on the television. The battle had started once again. I sat glued to my TV as the Pakistani army proceeded with Operation Sunrise, a final full-scale military assault to crush the holdouts at the mosque. It was the first time the Pakistani military had launched an assault on the residents of Islamabad. That night, in an awesome display of firepower, the army unleashed the might of its latest weaponry imported from America to fight the War on Terror.

After midnight, the younger brother, Abdul Rashid Ghazi, somehow managed to connect from a cell phone to a television station and spoke live to the news broadcaster. He said he was hiding in a corner of the mosque, and I could hear the loud explosions in the background as he spoke in a chillingly calm voice. He said he was cradling the body of his aged mother. She was bloodied and injured badly, and she was reciting holy verses as the life slipped out of her. He seemed possessed by the knowledge that he would die very soon too. "I think she has stopped breathing," Abdul Rashid said at one point in the interview. He stated it as a matter of fact. And then, after a few heartbeats, he burst into a brief final tirade. The vitriol came spilling out. "I want to give this last message to the world: this is blinded power. They are agents—agents of America— and they act absolutely like agents. They must be removed and there is no other option—" Then the phone line went dead.

The battle of the Red Mosque ended with mass graves in Islamabad. The government said 150 people died in six days of battle, but an undertaker, sweating and shivering, told me days after the operation had ended that the coffins were heavier than anything he had carried before. They were never opened, and he thought each was stuffed full of bodies of men, women, and children.

A few weeks later, the publishing house of the Red Mosque surreptitiously released a memoir written by Abdul Rashid Ghazi's widow, in which she recounted the entire tale that led to the final battle and to the death of her husband and countless others. It was titled *What We Went Through*. The back flap of the book contained this note: "Pay off the debt of history and your duty . . . If you have any informational material about the tragedy at the Red Mosque or the Hafsa School for girls, or the life and works of the great life of Abdul Rashid Ghazi or the martyred students, please send it immediately via mail or contact us by phone. The history of those who have inscribed history is now being written." The losers of the battle were compiling an alternate history. The supporters of the Red Mosque would record this battle as an epic saga, a great clash of *zulm* and justice. It would be shelved in some collections of the history of Pakistan and Islam to be read and judged at a later time, on the wrong or the right side of history. For right now, the battle had put the city of Islam in the middle of an international war.

"Musharraf is a strong ally in the war against these extremists. I like him and I appreciate him," President George Bush said a few days later. Osama bin Laden, on the other hand, released a videotaped message a few weeks after the battle in which he spoke to the people of Pakistan about what had happened in Islamabad. "It is obligatory

The battle at the Red Mosque ended in mass burials in Islamabad. (Source: AP)

upon the Muslims in Pakistan to carry out jihad and fight to remove Pervez, his government, his army, and those who help him," bin Laden said. "And it is obligatory upon them to pledge allegiance to an amir [caliph] of the believers who observes the rule of sharia rather than Pervez's polytheistic positive-law constitution."

But truth be told, not many in Pakistan spoke George Bush's language, English, and even fewer spoke Osama bin Laden's language, Arabic. What Pakistanis read were the words in Urdu of Abdul Rashid Ghazi. He had left his own will for his followers. I saw it plastered above the entrance to the broken mosque a few weeks later when I visited. It laid out the endgame of the new conflict in Pakistan:

We want the just system of Islam in our country. We are looking forward to seeing the implementation of sharia laws in the courts

of justice. We want the poor to have justice and bread. We want
an end to bribery, impurity, nepotism, injustice, and vulgarity.
The solution to all these problems is the implementation of Islam
and that is the only solution. This is the order of Allah and also a
demand of the constitution of Pakistan.

. . . Our movement began with the purest of intentions. We
consider it an honor and blessing to lose our lives while struggling
to demand the implementation of an Islamic law. By the grace of
Allah we believe that our blood will be the spark for a revolution.
The people of this world called us names: tools of secret agencies,
and insane. Today as rain fire pours down on us it is proven that
we fight in the way of Allah . . . Allah willing, the Islamic revolu-
tion is the destiny of this country.

8 July 2007

Two weeks later, the government reopened the Red
Mosque to the public, with a new imam to lead the prayer.
A suicide bomber hit Islamabad that day, killing eight people. I rushed to the blast site and snapped photos of traces
of steaming blood on the simmering roads. I interviewed an
eyewitness who spoke with wide-eyed horror and recounted
the *zulm* that he had seen. I wrote his words on my notepad, and later that evening I filed another dispatch about
the war for the newspaper. I signed off "by Shahan Mufti."
And for a brief second, I wondered, perhaps pointlessly,
if anyone back in America would notice my last name and
connect its meaning to the story of the Red Mosque. And
would they wonder where I fit into this war that was being
fought in the City of Islam?

Seven

IT BEGAN at the Red Mosque, and from its charred rubble
the violence uncoiled in all directions. The barbed wire that
lined the walls in G-6 crawled out of the heart of Islamabad
and slowly, purposefully, grew its knifed limbs around the
capital like the tentacles of an unstoppable and ferocious
creature. The barbed wire crawled into people's houses.
It wrapped its serrated length around the sloping domes
of other mosques and shrines, and it traversed the gates
to children's schools and to colleges. It lined the fronts of
ice cream shops and the entranceways to marketplaces and
parks. The barbed wire drew perimeters around the national parliament building and the president's residence,
embassies and police stations. It clung coldly to clunky
roadblocks that were plopped in the middle of roads leading in and out of "sensitive" neighborhoods. And soon the
shimmering knife-edge blades began to rust and turned
a red hue to match the color of the earth, surreptitiously

blending into the landscape. After a while, people stopped noticing the many battle lines the tangled barbed wire drew on the land, zigzagging across the map of the capital; it was as if they had always been there.

The Red Mosque had brought a sapling of the years-old war from the "unknown lands" of the tribal belt along the Afghan frontier and planted it right in the heart of the City of Islam. Out of the borders of the autonomous swathe of land in the northwest, the violence was now free to travel and descend the Potwar Plateau and spread down the Indus Valley. In the months and years to follow, it would enter Lahore in the Punjab and then on to Sindh, and farther down the river all the way to the one of the largest cities in the world, Karachi, a thousand miles away. The Pakistani military and intelligence services would fight militants; the militants would fight the Pakistani state and the Americans; the Americans would fight the militants; and the Pakistani military and intelligence would fight the Americans inside Pakistan. The war, which had been too far away for most Pakistanis even to imagine, now lurked around every corner, ruled over every waking moment, and haunted every night. It pushed an entire nation toward lunacy.

I would follow a trail of blood and witness the violence in all its many forms in every corner of Pakistan. This violence wasn't like a conventional war. This was no series of pitched battles in confined battlefields. It was a shadowy conflict—really many shadowy conflicts all at once—that unraveled in the streets, in refugee camps, in the courts and in the corridors of power, at dinner tables and in the blood and guts of a nation. It would rob many thousands of families of loved ones. The guilty were killed and innocents were killed too. The strange thing was that in this era of violence there was no way to tell the two apart most of the time. If someone was dead, it was because someone else probably wanted him or her dead for some sick, twisted reason. And to be truthful, no one fighting the war, not the Pakistani military, not the militants, and not the Americans, cared much about the difference anyway.

The battle of the Red Mosque marked sixty years since the birth of Pakistan as an independent nation-state. Make no mistake: there had been plenty of death and violence in Pakistan over six decades. The very birth of the country, with the partition of the subcontinent, was one of the bloodiest episodes of the twentieth century. Then there was the massacre of the Bengalis in East Pakistan carried out by the Pakistani army during the civil war of 1971. Years afterward, the military unleashed another vicious campaign against the Balochis in the southern province, bombing their villages and gunning down thousands of people when they staged a similar separatist uprising. Long before the War on Terror, there had been dysentery and malaria, and filthy drinking water that killed nearly one out of every sixteen babies born in Pakistan. Mothers died in childbirth, and unemployed fathers, unable to provide for their families, committed suicide. There were floods and earthquakes that almost invariably hurt the poorest the most. Many of these deaths were avoidable, yet they were allowed to occur year after year.

The desperation that came with this new era of violence was unlike any other war or misery of the past. This violence was fundamental; it was pivotal. When Muhammad Ali Jinnah's Muslim League helped attain the land for a democratic republic for a nation of Muslims in South Asia, Pakistan merged the historic tradition of Islam with the modern nation-state and created for the first time an Islamic democracy. Now, sixty years later in this era of great violence, Pakistan's founding ideal, its own constitution, was attacking itself. Pakistan had developed an auto-immune disorder, and this violence was eating away at the very membrane that was supposed to hold together a nation of Muslims in the first place. Islam was battling modernity; modernity was obliterating Islam; there was a clash of civilizations inside Pakistan.

Two days after the battle at the Red Mosque ended—the bodies had not yet been cleared and blood splatters were still on the walls—a renegade small-time local mullah named Fazlullah declared jihad against the Pakistani state from a small town in the northern mountains of Pakistan. Fazlullah, a man whom virtually no one had ever heard of before, led a band of a few dozen armed guerrilla soldiers. He operated an illegal FM radio channel to broadcast his religious and political sermons across a few towns in the picturesque Swat Valley, a few hours northwest of Islamabad, in the Hindu Kush mountains. Fazlullah had been planning and acting out a paltry revolt of his own for a few years now, but after the battle at the Red Mosque he decided to take up the mantle vacated by the Ghazi brothers. He was incensed and energized by the violence in Islamabad and vowed to extract revenge from the Pakistani military for the killing of the hundreds of students. Days after the battle at the mosque ended, some of his henchmen blew up a Pakistani military convoy traveling through the Swat Valley, killing many soldiers.

I had traveled through the Swat Valley with my family in the summer of 1996, months before I left for boarding school in America. Mingora, the largest city of the valley, was nearly a hundred miles north of Islamabad across the Indus. The area had one of the only developed skiing resorts in the country. It was one of the most idyllic mountain valleys of Pakistan's north, which is abundant with many of the world's highest mountain peaks. Up here, the vistas were endless and the snowcapped mountains were awesome. It was the farthest north I had ever been in Pakistan at that time, and I was amazed to see how magnificently large the terrain was only a few hours north of the capital. It was also here in the Swat Valley that, for the first time in my life, I cast an eye on the Indus from its western banks.

Up in the Hindu Kush mountains peering down at the Indus from a switchback on the steep mountainside, the river looked nothing like the languid run that I was used to seeing in the low-lying agricultural plains of the Punjab. In the mountains, the river charged down narrow ravines and spewed froth and foam. The Indus was so raucous that my brother had to shout over its roaring waves to have five of us huddle together to fit in the camera frame. I have a photograph from this trip in which I'm wearing an ill-fitting T-shirt over my lanky early teenage frame. My brother wore

a "CCCP" baseball cap—Cyrillic for "USSR"—that my father
had bought for him at a Moscow airport, during a work-
related trip. My sister had started covering her head with a
hijab. My mother was now a trainer of schoolteachers, and
she still looked young, but my father's mustache was turning gray. It was only a few years before he retired as the head
of the country's National Science Foundation. That trip
through the Swat Valley is forever etched into my memory.
It was the last trip we took together as a family, before we all
went off on our own paths. That is how I remember Pakistan
best, before the violence.

"Hindu Kush" means, oddly, "Slayer of Hindus" in
the Persian language. The mountains acquired this name
because it was over this range, marking the northwestern
border of the subcontinent, that waves of Central Asian
invaders began crossing a millennium ago to kill and conquer the "Hindu," the people who lived along the Indus
River, which the invaders knew as the "Hind." Muslim invaders from Central and Northern Asia like Mahmud from
Ghazna, Timur from Samarkand, and then his offspring,
the Mughals, all arrived on the Indus through passes in
these mountains. A millennium before them, Alexander
had led his Greek army to the Indus by crossing over the
highlands in the Swat Valley. The pitched battle on the Pir-
Sarai ridge, which overlooks the Indus River Valley, was the
most pivotal battle Alexander's army fought before crossing
the river. It lasted four full days and was written up by Alexander's historians as an epic. Alexander crossed the Indus
and entered the Punjab but stayed for only a few years. His
army was forced to retreat, and it carved an escape route

south along the Indus roughly following the contours of the present-day border between Pakistan and India.

Two thousand years after Alexander, the British became the first European invaders to approach the Hindu Kush. The maritime British Empire crept into the subcontinent from the seaports in the east and in the south. After capturing the Punjab and Sindh regions and formally declaring India a colony in 1857, the British tried to push the western frontier of the colony deeper across the Indus in the direction of the Hindu Kush. This became the era of the Great Game, a cold war between the British and tsarist Russian empires for control of Central Asia, which included all the lands of present-day Afghanistan. In 1893, after two testing wars with the local Pashtun on the Afghan frontier, the British agreed to draw a western border for their Indian colony with the king of the Afghans, who ruled over the largely Pashto-speaking population that lived in the lands between the Hindu Kush and the Persian Empire. The border, called the Durand Line, split some Pashto-speaking tribes, and it put the Swat Valley, along with the present-day tribal areas of Pakistan, on the British side of the border.

The British were never able to fully conquer these areas, though. Instead they signed pacts with local tribal leaders granting them autonomy in exchange for peace and loyalty. When the state of Pakistan was created in 1947, the new government led by Jinnah signed a similar pact with the Swat Valley and many tribal borderlands, continuing this state of semiautonomous rule. While most tribal areas continued to exist autonomously, the Swat region was special,

During a visit to the Swat Valley in 1999, I was stunned by the endless vistas the area offers. Several years after this photo was taken, the Pakistani government lost control of the region to the Pakistani Taliban, and I would try to enter once again as a journalist.

as it finally fully joined the Pakistani federation after the civil war in 1971. The absorption of Swat into the federation could have been a great first step in luring all the tribal areas to join the federation, but instead Swat became a cautionary tale for the rest of the autonomous regions. It became a tragic example of how poorly the Pakistani state was being run, and especially how badly it served its people's basic need for law, order, and justice.

In theory, the tools of the modern Islamic nation-state were suited to Swat. The region's own set of autonomous laws had been known as the *shariat*. It was a mix of ancient Pashtun tribal traditions and Islamic law as it had been practiced in these lands for centuries. While Pakistan's state laws also claimed to be Islamic, the Pakistani courts and police were largely run according to the laws of the nineteenth century, left on the books by the British colonists. When Pakistan's law came to Swat, it was not only inefficient but also appallingly corrupt. Court cases began piling up, and corrupt judges demanded bribes. The police forces were fickle and negligent. As the bureaucracy in Swat quickly decayed, the people grew more frustrated. They rebelled for the first time in 1993, when Benazir Bhutto served as prime minister in Islamabad. A group called the Movement for the Implementation of Muhammad's Law seized control of state buildings in Swat and demanded a return to the *shariat* of old. The government responded by sending in military forces to quash the movement, but it eventually negotiated a compromise.

More than a decade later, Fazlullah, the mullah with the illegal FM radio station, was claiming to lead a new band of armed followers demanding a return to the *shariat*. They called themselves the Pakistani Taliban Movement. It was an unmistakable reference to the Taliban, an armed political movement in neighboring Afghanistan, which ruled that country in the nineties and which now battled American forces. The Pakistani Taliban, Fazlullah said, would wage a similar jihad on the Pakistani state. In 2007, months before the Ghazi brothers established qazi courts in Islamabad, Fazlullah began setting up an independent administration and bureaucracy in dozens of villages and towns in the Swat Valley. The Pakistani Taliban introduced qazi courts. They too appointed qazis and muftis and charged them with providing justice to the people of the valley. These qazis and muftis, the Pakistani Taliban said, were filling in, to provide law and order and justice in Swat, where the state had failed. But who were these modern-day qazis and muftis? And how did they qualify to occupy these offices? It was difficult to tell. Fazlullah himself was believed to be illiterate and had presumably never studied a book of religion or history.

The qazi and the muftis of Swat, whoever they were, had their own vision of God's will, or sharia, and it was perverted. They handed out brutal sentences for the most minor crimes. The courts tried a girl who danced at weddings and sentenced her to death. Fazlullah's men executed her and dumped her body in the central square of her town. The voice on the radio said that "she deserved death for her immoral character." A schoolteacher refused to roll his pant legs above his ankles before prayer, as was the custom, and for this minor and routine infraction he too was shot dead. A former district council member publicly criticized Fazlullah's men for closing down a girls' school and she was dragged out of her home and shot in the head. Her corpse lay in the streets until it rotted.

As a journalist, I began traveling through the northwest of the country again after many years. The Pashtun people told me stories of obscene violence, and I felt jolted every time I heard the words "qazi" and "mufti." The muftis and the qazis of the past had worked through many epochs. Their roles developed in the early and medieval periods of Islam, when Muslim mathematicians were developing the Arabic numerals and the science of algebra. They were there in Spain when Muslim architects designed and constructed memorable structures like the Alhambra, and where Jews, Muslims, and Christians all lived remarkably peaceful and productive lives. They were there when the Mughals built the Taj Mahal and when Muslim astronomers were calculating the angle of the earth's tilt in Lahore, and medics were translating Greek medical manuals and inventing instruments for modern surgery.

Through all these periods, the muftis and qazis had passed on a system of law to their societies. They conducted philosophical acrobatics and lay the path, a sharia, to an imagined utopian society. But what was this sharia in Swat? Was this truly God's will on earth? Was this the system of law and justice that had developed in the Islamic civilizations that spanned three continents and fourteen centuries? Was this the legacy of my family names? I could not believe that my forefathers, who had once worked as muftis and qazis along the lands of the Indus, were in the same tradition as Fazlullah of Swat. This was something new. This was a resurrection of the past, perhaps, but it was mutated beyond recognition by violence and war.

IT WASN'T ONLY the muftis and qazis, the judges and jurists of Islam rising in the north who were in the spotlight. The courts of Islamabad were at the center of a much more heated battle that would change the course of politics in Pakistan over the next few years. In 2009 the president and army chief, Pervez Musharraf, had been in power for eight years already, and his detractors in the country's political parties were beginning to get agitated with his ironfisted rule. The general was becoming too powerful, and they were desperately trying to curtail his power. In 2006, Musharraf's opposition launched a legal assault on him in the Supreme Court, arguing that according to the country's constitution it was illegal for the ruler to concurrently serve as the chief of the army and also the president. For months, politicians had clamored for Musharraf to give up one of his offices, but Musharraf had ignored them. Now it was up to the courts to make him relinquish some of his power.

Musharraf was pitted against an unlikely rival, Iftikhar Chaudhry, the chief justice of Pakistan. Ever since Musharraf had appointed him as the country's top judge in 2006, Chaudhry had been using the court to embarrass Musharraf by investigating the corruption and crimes of his cronies. Chaudhry exposed the backroom deals that led to the sale of government-owned companies. He looked into the abduction of citizens by military intelligence agencies in the course of fighting the War on Terror. Now Musharraf feared that if a case challenging his dual role were brought to the court, Chaudhry and the other judges of the Supreme Court would rule against him again.

The judiciary in Pakistan had theoretically been independent since the constitution guaranteed independent courts. But in reality the judiciary had always been a lame sideshow to the powerful military and political elites. Dictators and politicians had pushed around the country's top judges for decades. Pakistan was plagued by inefficient and corrupt leaders and bureaucracy, and the impotent courts and law enforcement only made matters worse. So when Chaudhry began leading the charge against government corruption, he became something of a folk hero, a Robin Hood in a black robe.

While the Red Mosque standoff was festering in Islamabad in the spring of 2007, Musharraf made his move against Chaudhry. He called the judge to his military residence and strongly suggested that he resign from his post to avoid any public trouble. It was a barely veiled threat, but Chaudhry did what no judge in Pakistan had ever done before: he said no to a ruling military dictator. He refused to resign. And just like that, in the course of one conversation, the decades-old dynamic between the judiciary and the all-powerful military was upset. Musharraf fired the judge anyway, but by doing that he sparked a movement for "rule of law," the largest nonviolent social movement in the country's history.

Chaudhry, or "Chief" as his supporters began calling him, with his reticent air and one lazy eye, became the country's unexpected and great hope for a new and just order. "Chief, step forward. We are with you!" hordes of lawyers cried outside the court buildings, throwing flower petals at him. "Chief, your soldiers are countless." "Give one last shove, tear down these crumbling walls." In Islamabad and in cities all over the country, men and women of all economic and political backgrounds poured out into the streets. Families from educated and uneducated, middle- and high-income homes marched alongside lawyers and students and journalists and all the others who had long been on the peripheries of political life. People were emboldened by the sight of lawyers, men and women dressed in suits and ties, marching against the government in support of the judge.

The biggest political windfall from this social movement, though, came to Islamic parties. Justice is a potent concept in the history of Islam and Muslims. Since the time of Umar, the second caliph, who took the reins of the nascent Muslim Empire two years after Muhammad's death, qazis and the courts have been seen as vanguards of social justice, protecting people against *zulm* and all kinds of excesses by the more powerful and wealthy. Islamic history is littered with stories and parables of rulers being brought to justice by the ulema, the legal scholars in the judiciaries of the time. One story tells us that the caliph Umar was once himself summoned to the court of the qazi of the city of Medina from where he ruled. A citizen of the city had accused the great leader of Muslims of owing him a debt, and Umar was required to testify under oath. In the end, the story goes, the qazi ruled against the caliph and Umar had to pay his debt. These are the idyllic stories of Islamic

A lawyer protests against the regime of General Musharraf in front of the high court building in Lahore. (Source: Getty Images)

history. They are less about freedom than about equality and justice. Such is the utopian Islamic order.

One new political party, the Pakistan Movement for Justice, was formed in 1996 by Imran Khan, a former cricket player for the Pakistani national team. But he was no ordinary cricket player. He had captained the national side to their only World Cup victory in 1992, making them world champions for four glorious years. I had watched that World Cup as a young boy, and I was definitely not the only one in my school who dreamed of becoming a great cricket captain like Imran Khan one day. In a country where cricket might as well be a religion, Khan was a demigod. He was an athlete at the top of his game and ruggedly handsome for good measure. All the women wanted to be with him, all the men wanted to be him.

Khan was born in Lahore in 1952, a few years after Pakistan became an independent state. His family had long lived in the Punjab but he was ethnically a Pashtun; his maternal ancestors came from the Waziristan region in the autonomous tribal belt of Pakistan, which was becoming a center in the War on Terror. Khan attended Oxford University, where he studied alongside another Pakistani who would become a star politician: Benazir Bhutto. It was at Oxford that he began his cricket career. Khan's mother died of cancer in the eighties, so after retiring from the sport in 1992, Khan raised funds to build Pakistan's first cancer hospital in her memory. He called on his friends in the British aristocracy (he was a master of their favorite sport, after all) and he toured the length of the Indus in the back of a pickup truck where men threw their day's wages at him and women with nothing else to offer hurled their jewelry. He visited schools with his plea for funds, and I was one of hundreds of thousands of children who helped raise money for the cancer hospital in the midnineties. Khan eventually raised millions of dollars and the nonprofit hospital opened its doors to its first patients in 1994. True to Khan's promise, the hospital treated many of the poor at no cost. A few months after the inauguration of the hospital, Imran Khan came to my school to meet and individually thank all the kids who had raised money for the hospital. I remember that in the morning assembly I got to shake his hand. It was the first time I had seen him in person. I was fourteen and he seemed larger than life.

In 1995 Imran Khan, the former captain of the national cricket team, came to the school where Saadia was principal to raise funds to build a cancer hospital in Lahore.

When he formed the Pakistan Movement for Justice a year later, many described it as an Islamic party. Khan's party manifesto did promise to make Pakistan an "Islamic welfare" state, but beyond that there was little strictly Islamic about it. Most obviously, Khan did not cut the figure of an Islamic leader. In his cricketing days, he was a well-known playboy, spotted with a string of glitzy British socialites. Khan did later have a spiritual awakening under the guidance of a mystic in Lahore, but he still did not profess any special religious knowledge. He didn't even have a beard, which was fundamental if you wanted to be taken seriously as an Islamic politician. What he did have was a new party stubbornly calling for a system of social and economic justice. The party also insisted on a truly independent and powerful judiciary and in the context of the Islamic republic. This seemed enough to qualify him as an Islamic politician.

Khan's success in sports and philanthropy didn't translate well into politics. In the country's established power circles, packed with industrialists, landowners, and retired military strongmen, Khan was ridiculed for his earnest and stubborn political stands. His party never won more than one seat in the legislature despite contesting several elections. He was a joke. But when the powerful military president fired the country's populist chief judge in the shadow of an American war, it all seemed to click for Khan: justice was the new rallying cry for everyone. He began speaking about the need for a just society based on Islamic principles of equality. One day on live television he was asked what his idea of an Islamic state was. "The sharia is of the early Islamic caliphs," he said simply. "And what was the basis for that?" he asked rhetorically. "Justice and social welfare and an independent state that did not bow down to any power. This is the basis of a system of sharia." Imran suddenly became the new face of political Islam, and millions of people began flocking to him.

I met Khan for the second time in my life in the summer of 2007 at his party offices. He had just returned from a protest rally against the military president Musharraf and he was sweating profusely. He was now in his midfifties, but he still looked like an athlete after a workout, built like a tower with his broad shoulders. "What we have here is a revolution," he told me in English, his hands splayed out to stress the idea. "History will remember these days as the days of the justice revolution." Most people still did not take Khan very seriously in politics. Everyone knew that he would always talk big before the real game. But when he marched with everyone else in the streets, demanding the return of the judge to his place as symbol of justice, it appeared his slogan of "justice" was finally getting traction. The police in riot gear swept down on protesters all over the country, cracking open heads, rounding up people by the hundreds and throwing them in jail cells. But they kept chanting their simple common mantra: "Rule of law! Rule of law!"

All these political power plays and the social movement for the supremacy of the judiciary were unfolding under the dark shadow of the American war in Afghanistan. The Pakistani military assault on the Red Mosque, American bombing of Pakistan's tribal areas, and the rise of the Pakistani Taliban in the north and northwest all hung eerily in the background. The chief justice, the Taliban, the secular and the Islamic parties all had their common foe: President Musharraf and his backers in America. But the violence was an indiscriminate and senseless creature. There was no logic to it and there were no boundaries. The violence could hit anywhere, at any time, and target anyone. It was only a matter of time before it began to consume the political process.

In October 2008, I traveled to Karachi to report on what promised to be one of the largest gatherings of Pakistanis in more than a decade. Benazir Bhutto, the daughter of Zulfiqar Bhutto and the leader of the Pakistan People's Party, was returning after a decade. Benazir had been in self-imposed exile since 1997, when her political opponents chased her out of the country, laying charges of corruption against her and her family and threatening her with imprisonment. When Musharraf came to power in a coup in 1999, he added more charges against her for good measure, ensuring that she would not think of returning. But after the battle at the Red Mosque, and the legal attacks on Musharraf's rule, Benazir saw Musharraf's hold on power weakening, and she began to plot her return.

Musharraf had been America's most crucial partner in waging war in Afghanistan. For the most part, Musharraf had delivered on his promises of cooperation, but a few years into the war, the Bush administration had started to get frustrated with what it termed the military ruler's "double game." While he was helping the American military with supplies and intelligence cooperation, he was also providing safe haven to the Taliban and other militants who were battling American troops. But Washington had no better options and so it reluctantly went along with Musharraf, continuing to grant billions of dollars to Pakistan and trying its best to keep a close eye on Musharraf's strategic moves.

Benazir toured the American capital beginning in 2006, in an attempt to convince the Washington power players that she was a better option than Musharraf. She knew how to pitch herself. "A democratic Pakistan, free from the yoke of military dictatorship," she wrote in an op-ed in the *Washington Post* in March 2007, "would cease to be a breeding ground for international terrorism." This is what America wanted to hear. And Benazir knew that the Bush administration had enough influence over Musharraf to talk him into allowing her back in Pakistan.

Washington sympathized with Benazir, but it did not completely control Musharraf. Instead of pressuring the military ruler, they negotiated on Benazir's behalf. Through hushed backroom deals engineered by the American State Department, Benazir was finally able to get guarantees from Musharraf that would allow her to back in the country. Through intermediaries in Washington, Benazir and Musharraf agreed on a reconciliation formula: the military ruler would grant amnesty to Benazir, her family, and her party members from pending criminal charges, and in return Benazir would allow Musharraf to continue as president. It would work out nicely for both. Benazir would get a chance to try her hand at becoming prime minister once again, and Musharraf would get a powerful political player in the country who, for a change, was not bent on removing him from power.

Benazir had done this before. She had landed in the country in 1986 when General Zia ruled as dictator, vowing to bring him down. Then, a million people had turned out to greet her on the streets of Lahore. My mother had hung a portrait of her in our entranceway. And when President Zia's plane suddenly exploded in the sky, Benazir rose as the savior, the great hope for her country. But this time many people in Pakistan, especially those in the "rule of law" movement, saw the amnesty deal Benazir struck with

Musharraf as a corrupt charade, a horrible injustice. The lawyers called the deal unconstitutional. Imran Khan said it showed the collusion of an "avarice elite." It was *zulm*.

Benazir was now a different person. She was older, in her fifties, and she was tainted with two terms as prime minister, both times dogged by corruption charges. People were less sure about her. Was she doing all this to lead the country out of trouble and bring an end to the violence? Or was she simply leaning on America for another shot at power? Pakistan was also now a different country from the one Benazir had left a decade earlier. A decade of Musharraf's Enlightened Moderation and the American war in Afghanistan had changed Pakistan beyond recognition. There was a large educated middle class, the television and news media were freer than they had been under her democratic rule, and the major cities were drenched in violence. Benazir finally announced that she was ready to return soon after the siege of the Red Mosque ended. "I am returning to Pakistan on Oct. 18 to bring change to my country," she wrote in another *Washington Post* column in 2007. "When my flight lands in Pakistan next month, I know I will be greeted with joy by the people. I do not know what awaits me, personally or politically, once I leave the airport. I pray for the best and prepare for the worst."

I landed in Karachi the day before Benazir's flight arrived and found that Faisal Avenue, the city's main artery, was already lit up brightly. Karachi is the People's Party's base and the party workers went into overdrive prepping the coastal metropolis for her arrival. They wanted to give her a hero's welcome. Benazir's face, along with her father's, was plastered on huge banners and billboards covering every available square inch of town, on storefronts, billboards, bridges, and entrances to tunnels. On the morning of her arrival, when I walked to Faisal Avenue, it was already closed off to private vehicles. Hundreds of people were walking in the direction of the airport along miles of road. In the rush I saw a young teenage boy in tattered clothes lugging what appeared to be a large and heavy object the size of a small refrigerator on a trolley. I walked alongside him for a long time. No one stopped him or asked him what he was doing with such large cargo heading to a public rally. I began to get a bad feeling about this.

By afternoon, the crowds had grown dense and the energy was electric as I neared the airport. It was a carnival. Party anthems in all the different languages of Pakistan blared from speakers. Thousands of die-hard supporters of the People's Party packed the streets, waving flags and chanting slogans deifying Benazir and her father. One frail old man spoke to me adoringly of Zulfiqar Bhutto and how he had attended the older Bhutto's rallies as a young man in the seventies. A woman recalled being there in Lahore when Benazir returned from her exile in the eighties. In the midst of such fawning praise it was easy to forget that Benazir was returning as a deeply divisive figure and an ally of America. She was in the crosshairs from the moment her feet touched the ground.

It started to turn dark, but there was still no sign of Benazir on Faisal Avenue. So I began shouldering my way through the crowd. I finally reached the gate of the airport and spotted a large bus surrounded by swarms of people.

That was it. Hours after she had landed, Benazir's cara-
van had yet to exit the gates of the airport. I rushed up to
the bus and saw her sitting up top, surrounded by party
workers and a group of journalists and photographers. She
was waving wildly. Her cheeks seemed more filled out and
they were flushed, and her eyes smiled through her dark-
rimmed glasses. Garlands of flowers puffed around her
neck. She looked radiant.

Down below, near the wheels of the hulking bus, people were dancing, leading the way, and kicking up plumes
of dust with their shuffling legs. Some seemed like they
were in hysterical trances. I finally approached a young
boy. He was screaming Benazir's name out at the top of his
lungs by the wheels of the bus and I was curious. He was
not nearly old enough to remember Benazir when she was
last in the country a decade ago, let alone know the history of her father or the long history of the Bhutto family's
battles against military dictators in the country. "Why are
you here?" I asked him. He looked at me, quickly examining my collared shirt with my pen and notebook. Without
lowering his voice a notch, he shouted four syllables at me
in English: "Wel! Come! Be! Nazir!"

I had what I needed. The deadline to file my report
was midnight, so I began the slog upstream through the
crowds. I reached my hotel room at around 10:00 P.M. and
after furiously typing the report on my laptop, I closed my
eyes and lay my head on the pillow. I must have dozed off,
because I was jolted when I heard a deep thud and felt the
bed shake. It was just a minor jolt. A few moments passed,
as I lay there wondering if I had dreamed it. And then I

began hearing the sirens up and down Faisal Avenue. It was a bomb.

I picked up my notepad and pen and began speeding on foot to the Jinnah Hospital. I stopped outside the emergency room and saw bodies, sometimes just torsos being driven in on cars, ambulances, and rickshaw bikes. The gurneys were beginning to line up. Families soon started descending on the scene. I saw mothers fainting and fathers, sisters, and brothers wailing over dead bodies. The bodies they cried over were mangled and shredded. How did they even recognize them? One woman went into writhing fits on the ground, her face a sorry mess of sweat, tears, and spit, when she saw the body of her son, a heap of flesh and bones, arrive at the hospital. A TV cameraman shoved his lens mercilessly into the woman's face, broadcasting the pictures live across the country.

A group of men began chanting slogans against Musharraf, the police, and the army. "Musharraf is a Dog!" "Long live Bhutto." News was that Benazir had escaped the bombing with only minor injuries and was safely back in her home in Karachi. In a dark corner I spotted two young boys spray-painting graffiti on the hospital wall. One of them wrote in large block letters, WEL COME BENAZIR. The thick red paint trailed down from the letters like blood from a fresh wound.

Benazir Bhutto was assassinated in the city of Rawalpindi nine weeks later. I wasn't there that evening and learned of her death watching television in Islamabad, a few miles

A scene of carnage after the bomb blast ripped through the crowds gathered to greet Benazir Bhutto in Karachi in October 2007. (Source: Aamir Qureshi/AFP–Getty Images)

away. Benazir was at a public rally in the northern Punjabi city, which was also the headquarters for the Pakistani military. She was murdered after she finished her speech and as she was riding through the thick crowds in her Toyota Land Cruiser. She was waving at them, her head out of the vehicle's sunroof, when there were a couple of gunshots followed by a loud bomb blast. She was dead when she arrived at the hospital.

Benazir had walked right into her depressing demise. Soon after she returned to Pakistan, Musharraf had quit his post as army chief and declared himself president for another five years. Considering all the opposition he was facing, it was the only logical move left to make on the political chessboard. He had to lose some power to keep some. He then announced legislative elections for soon after the New Year. The Islamic parties, including Imran Khan's justice party, decided to boycott the elections, claiming that any elections held under Musharraf would be shams. Other parties, including the Pakistan People's Party, decided to go along and contest the election, and Benazir was now pit against Musharraf's loyalists and also against her old rival Nawaz Sharif. They would fight it out, just like the old days, to get a majority in the legislature and become prime minister again.

For all the excitement built up around her arrival in Karachi, Benazir's election campaign had devolved into a tediously dry affair. Pakistan was being swept by powerful crosscurrents of history and was at the crossroads of an international war. The country's very national ideal was being put to the ultimate test. Yet Benazir's speeches sounded painfully hollow. In her last speech in Rawalpindi, for example, she held up her party's election manifesto, a slick, glossy publication, and clutching it in her hand promised to implement its contents—"bread, cloth, and shelter" for all—receiving unenthusiastic applause. This was the slogan her father had coined four decades ago in what was, quite literally, a different country. It had helped him win that election in 1971, but now, when Benazir repeated it, it seemed stale and unfit for today's challenges.

The news channels did not even bother showing her last speech in full. But the last moments of her life, captured by television cameras, were played over and over again. They showed the silhouette of a man pointing a gun at her from the crowd and firing two shots. Then a powerful bomb goes off in a blinding white flash. Officials cleaned up the crime scene within hours and a minister appeared on television to announce the official cause of death: Benazir had died after hitting her head on the sunroof. The assassination was hours old and was already a farce. In major cities, Benazir's party loyalists and angry mobs destroyed property and burned cars and shops in furious riots. Within hours, the blame game had started. The government of Musharraf pointed a finger at the Pakistani Taliban. Benazir's party members blamed Musharraf for her death. And in quieter corners, some accused Benazir's own husband as the one responsible. In the fog of war, as always, nothing was clear.

Benazir became a martyr for democracy, and Pakistanis came out to vote in record numbers in the elections after her death. The People's Party won convincingly, and one of Benazir's close loyalists became the new prime minister. Less than a year later, in the fall of 2008, Musharraf finally quit as president. He didn't stand a chance after Benazir's assassination. Her party, along with all the others in the new legislature, doubled their efforts to throw Musharraf out. The president finally caved when they threatened him with impeachment. In one last hour-long speech on national television, Musharraf blasted the conspiratorial plots by his enemies. The man had truly believed that his ideology of Enlightened Moderation would deliver Pakistan into the next century. He truly believed that he had cracked the code to the Pakistani experiment in Islam and democracy and that he would lead the rest of the Muslim world with his example. But he was not the first to think this and he was not the first to fail in making his dream a reality. Choking on his own words, he concluded his address indignantly, raising his hands toward the sky: "Pakistan's fate is now in Allah's hands." He soon flew out of the country and into exile in England. Benazir's widower, Asif Zardari, became the new president. He was notorious for being one of the most corrupt people in Pakistan.

Through it all, the movement for "rule of law" kept up the pressure in the streets. The protest rallies demanding the reinstatement of Chief Justice Chaudhry continued. A dictator had fallen, a legend had been killed, but as far as the rule of law movement was concerned, it was as if nothing had changed. The judge was still being kept from taking his place in the Supreme Court, the Pakistani military still continued to battle against its own population in the tribal areas, the militants kept their guerrilla war going in the cities, and the CIA kept bombing Pakistan with its robotic drone aircrafts. The only change seemed to be that the ironfisted military ruler was replaced by an incompetent and corrupt civilian president. Something had to give.

It did. On the night of March 16, 2009, my phone rang incessantly. There was a buzz in Islamabad. A million-man march, which had started in Lahore a few days before, was now almost at the gates of the capital. The judge's supporters in the hundreds of thousands had announced plans to stage a sit-in outside the parliament building in an attempt to grind the capital to a halt. Rumors running on the phone lines were that the government was finally ready to reinstate the chief justice. I arrived at the judge's residence close to midnight and waded into a sea of supporters. In one corner of the yard, a group of college students and human rights activists sang nationalist folk songs accompanied by a beat-up electric guitar. Lawyers still dressed in black suits and ties in the middle of the night were already celebrating in anticipation, dancing the bhangra on top of parked vans to the throbbing beat of large dhol drums being played nearby. Families with young children stood at the peripheries of the jubilant crowds and joined in the sporadic cries of "Long Live Pakistan!" There were dozens of TV cameras everywhere.

Droves of workers from the Islamic parties marched through with their flags. The Movement for Justice workers carried their green-and-red banners. Amid the folk songs and the pop tunes blaring out of lawyers' parked cars, they chanted "*Allahu Akbar*," Allah is the Greatest. And then the official announcement came before dawn. The prime minister appeared on television and announced that the chief justice was restored to his position. The chief justice's spokesman, who was conducting media interviews in the grounds outside, shouted into a microphone, "This is not the end, this is the beginning of a revolution." As he spoke, all the disparate voices outside—the young musicians, the lawyers, the human rights activists, the journalists, and the Islamic party workers—began chanting outside the judge's home in one voice: "Rule of law! Rule of law!"

ALL WAS STILL NOT WELL. Two years after they had taken control, the men with the black turbans, the Pakistani Taliban, still ruled in Swat in 2009, more brazenly than ever before. For all the brutality of the Taliban regime in the valley, the system had been accepted. The people had no choice but to start using the new qazi courts and move on with life. They approached the courts cautiously, hoping for justice, but often were disappointed. Still, the courts were actually functioning, or at least getting through cases. In that sense it was a vast improvement on the nonfunctional Pakistani state courts they had replaced. The arbitrary and violent sharia law they were using was another matter altogether.

In 2009, the new Pakistani government abdicated judicial authority in the Swat Valley. They began hammering out a deal with the Taliban in Swat that would allow them to legally run their independent qazi courts to implement their so-called shariat. The parliament introduced the Nizam-e-Adl bill, or the System of Justice bill. It was based on an agreement between the government and the Taliban, in which the state would recognize the Taliban's judicial system in the valley as an autonomous and official system of law. Nearly all the major political parties in the parliament in Islamabad voted for the bill and it became the new law. The Islamic republic officially ceded its authority in the valley, and the Taliban's qazi courts were now officially sanctioned.

That same summer of 2009, I was in Islamabad when Barack Obama, the new president of the United States, visited Cairo to deliver a message to the Muslims of the world.

He was hosted by Cairo University and Al-Azhar, one of the oldest Islamic educational institutions in the world, known for training countless muftis, qazis, and other Islamic scholars over its thousand-year history. Obama presented his rationale for speaking to the Muslims of the world: "We meet at a time of tension between the United States and Muslims around the world." These tensions, he said, are "rooted in historical forces that go beyond any current policy debate." He was in Cairo to "seek a new beginning between the United States and Muslims around the world," and he concluded that, despite all differences, "the people of the world can live together in peace."

But when it came to Pakistan, Obama wanted to "disrupt, dismantle, and defeat" Al-Qaeda. This, he believed, would make America safer. He revved the engines of war more than those whom he replaced and sent tens of thousands of additional American troops into Afghanistan. In Pakistan, he ordered an unprecedented wave of attacks by drones, robotic warplanes, which began to kill countless people in the northwest, leaving piles of dead bodies, hundreds and thousands of them. Once in a while, Pakistan would respond by secretly hitting American targets inside Afghanistan, or by choking off America's main military supply route that ran through Pakistan. And as this escalated, here's the dirty secret no one in Washington or Islamabad would admit to: America was now battling Pakistan for control of Afghanistan.

The American government was also livid about the Pakistani government's deal with the local Taliban in Swat. "I think the Pakistani government is basically abdicating to the Taliban and to the extremists," Hillary Clinton, secretary of state for the new American administration, said in a press conference in April 2009. President Obama's special envoy to Pakistan and Afghanistan, Richard Holbrooke, said that the "people who are running Swat now are murderers, thugs, and militants, and they pose a danger not only to Pakistan but to the U.S. as well." The Pakistani government was indebted to the Americans. It was the American State Department that had helped Benazir get back into Pakistani politics in the first place. The Americans felt they had enough leverage over the new government to change the course of events. The government began dragging its feet on implementing the deal, the Taliban called off the cease-fire in the summer, and the Nizam-e-Adl law officially broke down.

The Pakistani army now launched a full-scale military assault on the Swat Valley. Ground troops attacked Taliban positions and the air force sent in attack helicopters. Swat became a war zone. Nearly two million Pakistanis were driven out of their homes and became refugees in their own country. It was the largest displacement of people in the history of Pakistan, and for some it brought back the memories of the great partition. The Americans now breathed easier. America's top military brass met with the new Pakistani military chief, Ashfaq Kiyani, to affirm their support. Richard Holbrooke flew to Islamabad to meet with the army chief in person. "The purpose of my meeting today was to express our support and appreciation of Pakistan-U.S. military cooperation," Holbrooke said in a press conference.

I tried to make it into Swat by road to see for myself what the war in the north looked like, but I was turned back a few miles from the first town in the valley. The battlefield was closed off to journalists, the military police told me. Thwarted, I traveled instead to meet with refugees who had been evacuated from the valley and had moved into the camps in the northwest border regions. I arrived at a refugee camp near the city of Nowshera one morning in June. It was an open field, a sea of UNHCR, Red Cross, and Red Crescent tents stretching far into the horizon. Children played in the dirt, their faces caked in mud, their nostrils infested with flies. One of the organizers at the camp told me about a pregnant woman whom he carted around on a wheelbarrow to get her to the faraway first aid tent for delivery. I spoke to one man who was trying desperately to construct a makeshift wall out of loose rock outside his tent. He said that the women were too modest to step outside in plain view of everyone else, but they were roasting sitting inside. As we were speaking, a security guard arrived and told the man to tear down his wall because that wasn't allowed in the camp. The old man protested and started to scream loudly, but it was no use. He finally tore it down, sobbing.

It was lunchtime when a fistfight broke out between two men over a vat of clean drinking water, and another security guard jumped in to break it up. As one of the men was dragged away, I saw him frothing at the mouth, livid. And why wouldn't he be? Until weeks ago, almost all these people were living in their homes in towns of the Swat Valley. They were far from wealthy folk, but they were hardworking and living basically comfortable lives in the tourist resorts of the north. But now they were refugees in their country's civil war.

As the crowd from the fight dispersed, I saw a man, my age perhaps, leaning back on a supply truck plastered with a banner displaying the face of Benazir Bhutto, the martyr. He was smoking a cigarette and dejectedly watching the fight from a distance. I walked up to him. Let's call him Ahmed. He'd been here twenty-five days, he said, the worst twenty-five days of his life. He had a bachelor's degree in engineering. He worked as an electrician, repairing small household appliances in the town of Saidu Sharif in the valley. The army had dropped leaflets over their house a few days before they started bombing. The leaflets warned them to leave immediately by whatever means possible. I asked him about all that had happened in the valley in the past year that had led to this horrible fate for the people. So he told me this story about his family.

For as long as Ahmed could remember, one of his uncles had been caught in a land dispute. The uncle's case file was buried at the bottom of some bureaucratic pile of red tape in the district offices. You needed cash; you needed favors to get things done in the courts, he explained. His family had neither money nor influence so the uncle moved in with his family at their home. The uncle had a small electric shop, and that's where Ahmed ended up working as a repairman.

One afternoon, while the uncle had stepped out, one of the customers at the store got into a big fight with Ahmed and started throwing things around and knocking over the microwaves and toaster ovens he had just fixed. That's when the police walked in. The customer ran away and instead they took Ahmed to the station. Just like that, no questions asked. At the station they threatened to beat the life out of him unless he paid up. "Hey, doesn't he look like the guy who's wanted for murder?" one policeman snarled at the other. "Yeah, he does kind of look like that. Maybe we should throw him in the hole for a few weeks and let him think about all his dirty crimes." They chuckled. "Let him drink his own piss." Ahmed's father worked as a clerk at a small city office and the family had lived paycheck to paycheck for his entire life. The father certainly didn't have the clout to come and get him out of jail. They'd lock his father up just as quickly if he came anywhere near the station. Ahmed finally gave up every penny he'd made that year and was allowed to walk out of jail a few days later.

When the men with the black turbans and wild-looking beards and long matted hair started riding through town in the night, Ahmed was worried at first, but they didn't bother him too much. Secretly, he was kind of looking forward to someone shaking things up in the town. The old system was worthless. There was no law. He was almost excited for somebody to give the crooked cops and lazy judges a taste of their own medicine. At first, the Taliban didn't use much force to take over the valley. They played on people's independent spirits. They offered them a change they could believe in. They promised to get the courts running again, establish law enforcement that served the people, and straighten out the police once and for all. When the Taliban's qazi courts began running, the backlog of cases really did start shrinking. Things felt like they could begin moving forward. His uncle got a date for a hearing after all these years about his land case. At this point his uncle couldn't care less if he lost the land or got to keep it. It was a chance at conclusion, no matter how perverted.

But it was wishful thinking that the Taliban was there to help. The black turbans were thugs after all. They promised sharia but they were ignorant and barbaric. These guys had never seen the inside of a school in their lives. They'd never so much as worked through a math problem or read and understood a chapter of the Quran. They knew nothing but violence and revenge. They were *zalimeen*. They went after the soft targets firsts: the musicians, the artists, the video stores. They chased tons of people like that out of town. Then they focused on politicians who dared to organize any opposition. The qazi courts turned into witch hunts. They accused their opponents of petty crimes and started hacking bodies into pieces and stringing up carcasses from lampposts in the middle of the night. You'd wake up to a stinking corpse hanging outside your window, waiting for the sanitation workers to get to it. But there were no sanitation workers left. And the Taliban kept attacking the army outposts. All they wanted was a fight. It was war after all.

All Ahmed had ever wanted was to save up enough money to get out of that town. He could go to Karachi, Islamabad, Dubai, anywhere. They need electricians in those big cities. Big appliances, big jobs. But now he was here, in a refugee camp. Why? Because Pakistan had gone to war with itself. Why doesn't the government just set up qazi courts all over the country, become a country of Islamic law? And if the qazi courts don't work, if this Islamic law is simply a mirage, then why not let this whole Islamic system go? Why can't we just have one system in which everyone has faith? Why can't we just have one law?

He needed another cigarette, he told me abruptly. He would go to find one in the camp. He walked back into the mass of people scurrying aimlessly around the refugee camp, without homes and without hope.

Eight

HOW DID I get here? Religion and nation were laid out before me in an expansive, mangled, and debauched land-scape of war. I had walked through this rubble and exam-ined it up close, and at so many turns I found my family stories strewn among the violence. It made my guts churn. I had returned from America, after those wretched attacks of 2001, to discover if and how this clash of civilizations was to unfold. As I had suspected, I found that the clash between Islam and the West was occurring right inside Pakistan. But I did not expect to find myself right in the middle of it. These words, "mufti" and "qazi," had always been part of my own story, but now they were at the center of the battle for a nation.

For some in the country, my family history and the idea and images of Islamic justice that they inspired were worth fighting for. But the call for Islamic law had also become a tool of war in the hands of people who wanted only power and to kill and destroy whatever stood in their way of getting it. My family names rose in the battle cries of these militants, and echoed with every gunshot fired. With every bomb blast in every city of Pakistan, I felt the ground shake beneath my feet.

In this battle between the Western and Islamic imaginations of law and justice in Pakistan, any remaining veneer of law or justice began to rot. How do people live without an agreed system of justice? They all create their own. There were everyday stories of extraordinary brutality by the most ordinary people. In Karachi, three robbers were caught and stopped by a neighborhood mob in the middle of the day. Instead of handing them over to the police, the people from the neighborhood began beating them until the robbers' joints became unhinged. Their limp bodies were dragged into the streets and piled up. For a few moments, people watched and yelled at the moaning beings. Then someone stepped forward and began to pour gasoline on the pile. Someone else threw a match onto it, and they all screamed defiantly, insanely, as the men burned alive.

In Toba Tek Singh, a village in the center of the Punjab, a few villagers cornered and killed eight men they accused of being criminals. They beat them with clubs and then threw heavy stones at them to crush and flatten their skulls. In Sialkot, a mob attacked two brothers as they rode through the town on their motorbikes. People had found it suspicious that they carried such a large cargo and decided to attack them, believing they were criminals. They too were beaten with sticks and punched and kicked to death, then hanged, as dozens of people—men, women, children—gathered to watch. This time the entire episode was captured on a cell phone camera and put on the television screens for the whole nation to watch. It was unbelievable to many. What had happened to people's humanity? I will spare you the hideous details but for this one: the video clearly showed two police officers watching the entire lynching, unmoved, from a safe distance.

Violence is insanity and sickness. It wasn't only taking lives of humans and turning others into monsters; it was poisoning the soul of a nation. It began to consume and replace culture. Bombs went off at stadiums, at art shows, at concerts and restaurants, at schools and theaters. The violence began to strangle the life out of anything good. One beautiful bright spring day in 2009 in Lahore, a few men armed with grenades and machine guns crawled into the heart of the city and laid siege to a convoy carrying cricket players visiting from Sri Lanka. It all happened in a few minutes in the middle of the day at the busiest intersection of the city. And just like that, the country that treasured the sport lost it. No one would come to play in Pakistan again.

The violence ate away at Islam too. Being a Muslim became a crime. It didn't matter what kind of Muslim you were, because someone would find it objectionable and carry out divine justice with his or her own hands. Sunni supremist mobs would drag Shia Muslims off buses and leave their dead bodies on the roadside, and the bodies piled up. And Sunnis killed other Sunnis too. In July 2010, two men were caught on closed-circuit cameras bolting into Data Darbar, the thousand-year-old shrine of a Sufi saint in the inner city of Lahore. The saint was one of the earliest Muslim preachers to arrive in the lands a thousand years ago. The men had explosives wrapped around their bodies, which they detonated deep inside the complex. Fifty people died, including the suicide bombers, and hundreds ended up in hospital beds. The crime scene investigators discovered that the attackers had packed their explosives with tiny ball bearings. They were not satisfied with just killing; they wanted to shred the humans who had gathered in the shrine. And what did many others do in response to this bombing? They called for more blood. They wanted the military to find the homes of the attackers and flatten their neighbors and families.

Violence inspired more violence, until the violence became a coherent whole. Each episode of violence built on the previous episode of violence and legitimized the next episode of violence. The violence was one reinforced, self-sustaining whole. I, for one, could no longer separate the good violence from the bad violence. It was death, darkness, and decay.

In Pakistan the experiment to bridge Islamic and Western civilization was being shredded one bomb, one bullet, and one ball bearing at a time. Most other countries in the world had now decided that sharia, the Islamic idea of law and justice, was a backward and dangerous path. It *was* the worst-case scenario, what ought to be avoided at all cost. The choice was between modernity and Islam; there was no third way. For Pakistan, accepting this would be accepting that the nation was built on nothing because Pakistan was supposed to be that third way. But even if Pakistanis were all to accept it now, was there even a way to extract Islam from the nation? Was there a way to pick out Islam, one brick at a time, from Pakistan's palace of stories?

And I was faced with another question that seemed more pressing to me: Could I extract Islam from my own life story? I wanted to find out how Islam had become a part of the story in the first place. I decided to leave the battlefield behind and journey into my family's past. I drowned out the explosions and ripping gunshots of war fired across invisible battle lines and set out to find the tales of family. Islam was engraved into my name. This story ran through my veins. Only by dissecting my own past would I learn how Islam was injected into my bloodstream in the first place. And perhaps if I could answer this question about my own past, I might be able to answer the bigger questions of the nation.

I never thought I would have to report and investigate a family yarn. My father had always told me about our Rajput heritage. These were tales of the great warriors who had defended the Indus against centuries of assaults by Muslim invaders. The Rajputs had later become Muslims themselves ranked high in the bureaucracy as muftis. And on my mother's side, I was told I was Faruqi, descended from Umar, the second caliph of Islam and a man from deep inside Muhammad's trusted inner circle. I never thought I would have to take the scalpel of objective historical analysis to these tales. The truths revealed from mother and father to son and daughter are part of a person's fabric. Who is mad enough to unravel such truths by tugging needlessly at the loose ends? But these were desperate times, times of war and violence. If a family yarn was all I had to decipher the world around me, I decided to pull on the loose end one day and hold my breath as it all unraveled.

I sat down next to my uncle Afaq one day after lunch as he lazily reclined on a comfy couch in the living room watching a cricket match on TV. "This thing about being descendants of the first Muslims," I said. "Is this stuff really true?" He was my mother's younger brother and Grandfather Akhlaque's oldest son. It was the first time I had spoken to him frankly on the subject, or spoken about it all. And the way I had phrased the question, it sounded as though I was casting doubt on a belief held in the family for countless generations.

"What do you mean?" he asked, unperturbed. "Of course it is." Then he thought about my question for a few moments, peeled his eyes away from the television set, and asked me with a serious look, "Did you not ever see the family tree?"

I had not. "Have you?" I asked him.

He dialed down the volume with the remote control. "I hadn't seen it for the longest time," he began. "I had some memory of Father showing it to me when I was younger but I didn't think much about it. When your grandfather passed away, I was cleaning out his things from his closet when I found this old scroll inside." The scroll, he explained, traced the family to its earliest origins. "I remember I showed it to a few people a few days after your grandfather's death. But I think you were in India at that time, weren't you?" I remembered sitting in my apartment in Delhi that morning speaking to my mother on the phone as the sun trickled through the window. I had felt so far away from everything.

Where did the scroll come from? I asked. How many generations back does the family tree go? How many copies are there? Could I see it? We walked into his bedroom and he closed the door behind us, then reached into his closet. He is a meticulous man, very organized and neat, just like my grandfather. Uncle Afaq reached into the back of the closet and carefully extracted a piece of antiquated paper, folded over a few times. He held it with both hands like a delicately balanced tray and walked it over to the bed. It appeared old and frail, as if it could crumble in his hands at any moment. The yellowing paper was blotched with blue and black spots, stained by its own ink from being folded over. It looked as if it had taken a beating from itself over the years.

He placed the yellow paper on the bed and slowly and deliberately unfolded the document on the mattress. It began to reveal an expansive map of hundreds of names inscribed in beautiful, painstaking Persian and Urdu script. Chains of unbroken lines connected one name to another and moved on to the next. Some names carried long notations next to them and some others had only a few lines or none at all. Fully opened, the family tree covered almost a quarter of the full-size bed.

At the very top, it begins with an Arabic prayer from the Quran, which is the way every story ever told in the Islamic tradition has begun.

In the name of Allah, the most beneficent, the most merciful.

And then this title underneath:

A Copy of the Genealogical Tree of a Quraishi–Faruqi Family,
Renowned Qazis of Sodhra and Environs

Toward the top is a row of four names, presented emphatically in large, bold strokes of a calligrapher's pen. The largest of these names, the largest on the whole scroll, is in the middle of the row: "The Master, the Messenger, Respected Muhammad, Prophet of Allah, Blessings upon him and his Family." To the left of the Prophet's name is the name of Ali, his cousin and son-in-law. To the right of Muhammad is Uthman, the third caliph of Islam who shared a great-great-grandfather with Muhammad. And to the far right and far left of the row of names are two more men, Abu Bakr and Umar, the first and second caliphs of Islam. All their names are specially decorated, made to look as if they are engraved into ornate plaques, in a most intricate and elegant script.

It was from the plaque that reads, "The Leader of the Faithful, Umar, May Allah Be Pleased with Him," that a thin black line begins to grow downward through dozens of generations. There is no notation next to Umar's name, probably because he needs no introduction to anyone in the family reading the scroll. Umar was one of the most defining figures around the Islamic Prophet in the Arabian Peninsula in the seventh century. He was from Muhammad's tribe and was known around the Prophet's city of Mecca as a stern, ill-tempered, strong-willed man and a highly skilled warrior. Muhammad had made many

enemies with his new message of submission to the will of
one all-knowing, unseen God, and Umar was one of his
detractors. Historians write that Umar left his house one
day to murder Muhammad, but on the way, after a series
of extraordinary events, he became a believer. When he
got to Muhammad's home, he bowed down to the Islamic
Prophet and pledged his allegiance and became a Muslim.

Less than two years after Muhammad died, Umar became
the second caliph, or leader of Muslims. Under Umar's leg-
endary military leadership, Muslim forces moved far into
Africa, reaching Tunis, within a hundred miles off the coast
of Sicily. In the north, Muslims occupied the western end of
the Mediterranean Sea, and to the east Umar's armies ran
through the Persian Sassanids and approached the banks of
the Indus in what is today the south of Pakistan. Umar appointed governors and qazis to form the bureaucracy of this
vast empire and began implementing Muhammad's teaching as the law of the land. In the decade that Umar ruled,
the Islamic community turned from a religious group held
together by the memory of one great prophet into a vast empire run according to Islam's own unique set of rules, which
Muslims believed to be passed directly from God to man.

The thin black line from Umar's name turns sharply toward the middle of the page to a name in the next generation:
Abdullah, his son. And then the line traces through nearly
two dozen generations, flowing down the length of the scroll.
It runs through some historic names, and my uncle pointed
to a few: Ibrahim ibn Adham, the great-great-grandson of
Umar and one of the great Islamic mystic saints from the
kingdom of Balkh in present-day Central Asia; Farrukh

Shah Kabuli, another ten generations down, ruled Kabul as king; Fariduddin, the revered Sufi saint known as Baba Farid, who preached Islam through the subcontinent in the thirteenth century. It is a thousand years of history splashed onto the page that tracks the slow spread of Islam, eastward from the holy lands in Mecca and Medina toward the Indus.

"Where is the rest?"

My uncle lifted the scroll and flipped it over. "It's fragile," he said as he straightened out the edges. Unlike the front, where the names were listed along the length of the scroll, from top to bottom and one or two in each row, this reverse side was oriented in landscape. The names spread out in width rather than in depth. At the very top is the name: Qazi Muhammad Yusuf, the Grand Old Qazi, and from him three lines lead to three sons and from each of these sons three different family lines. It is a sprawling network of men descended from the one man and travels through more than a dozen generations, over the period of what I guessed was a few hundred years. On this side, I do not recognize any of the names. That is, until Uncle Afaq finally points to a name along the long bottom edge, toward the middle: Akhlaq Hosain. My grandfather was one of the last generations to be noted on the family tree. There is no notation next to his name and he is listed next to his brother, Ashfaq Hosain, who had died when my grandfather was young. A few boxes to the right of my grandfather is Yusuf, the nephew my grandfather adopted and who became my mother's dear adopted brother. He was the same brother who had taken Saadia to Islamabad before her wedding to meet with President Ayub, and where she had cried for the old ruler.

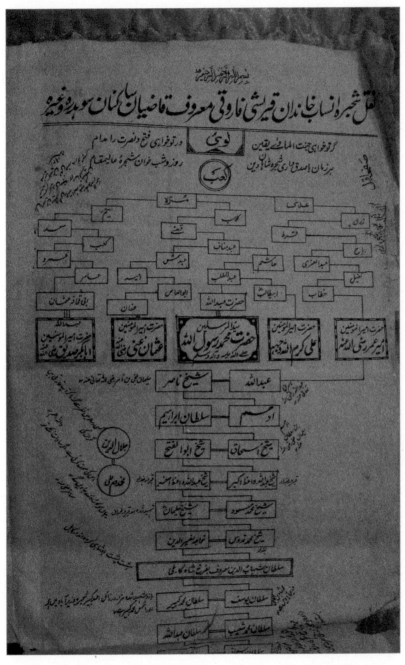

The top half of the scroll with the Qazi family tree. The largest and most prominently displayed name in the middle is the Islamic prophet Muhammad's. My maternal family line grows from Muhammad's favored general and advisor, Umar, whose name is to the far right in that same row.

"I'll give you some time with this," my uncle said as he left the room and closed the door behind him. I pulled over a low stool and began to pore over the document. I carefully flipped the scroll over again and began reading a full paragraph of notations in Urdu at the bottom of the front side, halfway through the generational map. It was an author's note written by a man who identified himself as "Musafir Azizuddin." From the notation I understood that this man, whose nom de plume "Musafir" translates to "traveler," was born in the mid-nineteenth century and he was "75 or 76 years of age" at the time of the writing of the scroll. There were a few lines about his early life. At the age of thirteen, he had traveled to the town of Abbottabad in the north to meet an older relative. "After a few months of my residence there, I was offered a job as a scribe for having a very stable hand at writing," he wrote, adding "at that time this skill was valued greatly."

It was around the year 1885, while traveling through the north of the Punjab to visit the family, that the scribe was riffling through some old papers of a long-deceased relative when his eye fell on something that looked like a family tree. Intrigued, "I traced a copy of the tree." It seems to have sat around for many years. The scribe said that he lived "in exile from his home" for nearly his entire life. He began investigating the family's roots only when he returned to the Punjab decades later "as a retired pensioner." He began "investigating conditions and exploring grave sites with the help and knowledge of family in the area." He didn't have an easy time of it. Only a precious few elders were still alive to help him sort through the many names on the family tree. The scribe did his best, but he was not satisfied. "I could have done better," he wrote toward the end of the note. I notice that the copy of the document in my hand was published in the city of Multan, in southern Punjab, in 1931.

I flipped through the scroll over and over without any sense of the time passing. My eyes traced the precarious and faded, but unbroken, line up and down through more than forty generations that connected my grandfather, Akhlaque Qazi, to Umar, the second caliph of Muslims and the Prophet Muhammad's close confidant. The paper was tattered at the edges and the lines on the page were frail and fading, but they were still visible to me, as real as the veins I can see in the back of my hand. I am a descendant of Umar on my mother's side. This is something I had known for as long as I could remember; there was nothing new here. But for the first time, as I read this family tree, something stirred inside me. When I saw the fact written and published on this scroll, as real as the news reports I wrote that were published nearly every day, I began to see things differently. I saw, with my very own eyes, my blood mix in with the earliest moments of Islam and travel through the many great sagas of its history. I had never imagined that a family tree actually existed. But when my eyes landed on the inscriptions on the scroll, the words finally registered and caused my heart to pump faster. I felt drops of sweat on my brow. I also noticed something I had missed in my first reading. Right at the top, just under the opening prayer, is a brief quatrain in Persian written in miniature hand:

If it is the everlasting garden of refuge you desire,
Always and forever remember the greatness of religion.
If it is success and recognition in this world you want,
Morning and night recite the greatness of ancestors.

My uncle Afaq walked in, and I bolted upright as if woken from a dream. He carefully examined my expression and waited for me to speak this time.

"Is this real?" I finally said, and I was struck by the logical desperation of the words as I uttered them.

Uncle Afaq responded with the only truth that there ever could be: "You read it with your own eyes, didn't you?"

A FEW MONTHS LATER, Uncle Afaq's son Taimur and I drove northward from Lahore toward Sodhra, the birthplace of my grandfather and the birthplace of Azizuddin, the scribe. Taimur and I were both grandsons of Akhlaque, and we were nearly the same age. When I first moved to Pakistan as a little boy, Taimur and I were inseparable. We were a team. We schemed together, and we even went into business together as teenagers. When I asked Taimur if he wanted to come along to Sodhra, he didn't think twice. It was just another chance for a long drive, another adventure.

We crossed the bridge over the River Ravi, out of Lahore, and headed toward the Chenab River, the next Indus tributary that runs along the southern edge of the Potwar Plateau. Sodhra is almost seventy miles north of Lahore along the

Grand Trunk Road, the five-hundred-year-old road that runs across the width of the Asian subcontinent. It is a highway now that cuts right through the many towns and cities in this heart of the Punjab. In the towns, we would slow down to a crawl, driving carefully through marketplaces where shopkeepers lounged on the street sides watching the traffic go by. We would have to brake suddenly to avoid the schoolchildren in uniform crossing the street with reckless abandon, or the odd stray donkey cart laden with fruits breaking free of its owner's grip. Between towns we would accelerate again through the endless green farms as the pastureland whizzed past us in a verdant blur. Some of the fields were inundated for the rice sowing, but in others, men and women were still at work clearing the wheat harvest.

The Punjab is half the size of Spain, with a population twice as large as Spain's packed into it. It is one of the most densely irrigated and agriculturally productive regions in the world. After the British arrived here in the middle of the nineteenth century, the Punjab became strategically vital. Beyond the Punjab lay the lands of the Pashtuns of the Afghan kingdom and the sphere of influence of the tsarist Russian Empire. To fortify their claim over this frontier region, the British developed modern towns and populated them with subjects of the empire. The Punjab was only one small part of the subcontinent, but from this land of five rivers the colonial army also began recruiting a majority of its local fighters, making it a major center for one of the mightiest armies in the world at the time. Today, the area remains the largest recruiting ground for the Pakistani army, which has the sixth-largest ground force in the world.

The environs of Sodhra, though, were never known for their militaristic streak. This was a small town of people like my grandfather, who had more mundane desires in life. Before I left Lahore, I was curious to learn anything I could about Sodhra and was able to find this bit about the town in an old British colonial document published in 1884. It made me excited for what I might find out about the family there.

> Sodhra is an ancient town five miles to the east of Wazirabad and lies on the Chenab River. It was founded by Ayaz, a favourite of [the Muslim emperor] Mahmud of Ghazni, and takes its name from having once had 100 gates (soh-dara). After Ayaz's time it fell into decay, but was re-founded under Shah Jahan by the Mughal governor Nawaz Ali Mardan, who constructed a splendid garden, dug a canal from the river and called the place Ibrahimgarh after his son . . . Under the Mughals, Sodhra was a flourishing city and the headquarters of a district with a revenue of one hundred and twenty thousand. There are many ruins of Mughal architecture to be seen . . . There are many influential Khatris of Chopra who are in the service of the British government or of the Jammu State. There are also several respectable Kazi [sic] families many of whom are in government service.

Two hours later we reached the town of Wazirabad on the banks of the Chenab. We left the Grand Trunk Road and took an offshoot that runs east along the river. This road was quieter and the lighter traffic moved lazily in single lanes in each direction. The unbroken stretches of farmland, which we had been watching from a distance, now enveloped us, sprawling in all directions, and the air began to smell heavy like wet earth. The road was still well paved and it was sheltered by a thick canopy of the large leafy trees that rustled in the thick wind. The road signs disappeared. Sturdy bullocks plodded lazily, pulling wooden carts along the sides of the road carrying towering bales of hay. It was as if time itself had slowed down since we got off the highway. Very soon, we were lost.

Taimur pulled over onto the side of the road, and we saw an old man approaching, slowly following a hulking bullock, smoking a cigarette pegged in his fist between his pinkie and ring finger. He wore a white turban, tied hurriedly around his head. I stuck my head out the rolled-down window and said, "We're looking for Sodhra." He was amused to see what were clearly two city boys out here, far from the highway. He decided to make the most of it. "Which Sodhra you boys looking for?" He offered a broken-toothed smile as he walked over to the car and sucked his fist for another long drag from his cigarette.

"There's more than one Sodhra?"

"Well, there might as well be. Who you looking for? You have business with the Maliks, the Alavis, the Qazis?"

"The Qazis!" We both jumped at the word. "The Qazis."

"Are you Qazi?" he asked, suddenly straightening to measure us through the car window, still adamant about not giving a straight answer.

"I am Taimur Qazi," my cousin volunteered first, then added as might be appropriate "son of Afaq Qazi . . . of Lahore." He glanced uneasily at me.

"I'm his cousin," I explained, "his aunt's son, actually. I'm Mufti . . . Shahan Mufti . . . of Lahore."

"Well, there aren't many Mufti areas around here." He smiled and turned to Taimur. "The Qazis' area is up this road you already passed. You want to turn around and take a right at the tube well," he said, pointing at a water irrigation pump that Taimur glanced at in his rearview mirror. "Then keep going straight up the hill until you come to the Press Club. Then just tell people you're Qazi," he concluded. "They'll take care of you." We thanked him and he stood and watched us make the U-turn.

We followed his directions and turned right at the tube well and began driving up a narrow graded hill. Soon brick houses were lining up in rows on either side. We were approaching the town of Sodhra. As we drove into the marketplace, the road kept getting narrower and more crowded. Above us, where there had been a green canopy of leaves on the main road was now a dense web of crisscrossing telephone lines and electrical cables. The charm of the old historic town could only peek through the tangle of semiurban ugliness. By the time we were ready to park near the Press Club at the top of the hill, the road was so narrow that the thick rush of shoppers in the marketplace had to step out of the way to let our car pass through.

Somehow word of our arrival had traveled up the hill faster than we did. As we stepped out of the car into the bustling marketplace, a man approached us. "You're looking for the Qazi *mohallah*?" he asked with a broad smile. He was wearing a blue *shalwar kameez* and he eagerly shook our hands and led us down an alley off the main street. It was only just broad enough to allow two people to walk past each other without brushing shoulders. Constructed of brick and cement, tall boundary walls for the houses ran along each side of the alley, cutting off all direct sunlight. The walls were painted with advertisements for cell phones and calling plans. As we meandered through the neat alley, our guide pointed to the nameplates on the gates of the houses we passed. He ran through all the names of the many different Qazi families who lived in the houses. "He owns a natural gas business," "You must have heard of their family in the south," "Their son fell in love with a dancing girl." Taimur and I exchanged a quick look. We didn't recognize any of the names.

The labyrinthine alleys finally led us to a dead end where three metal gates opened into three interconnected but separate houses. "These are all your family's," he told us, gesturing grandly and pointing us to the door on the left. We entered an old *haveli*-style house through the metal door. It was a traditional construction suited to multigenerational family living, the kind of house hardly ever constructed in the big cities anymore. It was built in two levels around a large square courtyard. A dozen or more doors opened on each level on all sides of the courtyard, leading to different rooms. We were invited upstairs into a room where a man with graying hair and wearing glasses sat on a couch reading an English newspaper. He was in his fifties, perhaps, and he got up to greet us with a smile.

"Taimur!" he said, embracing my cousin. "Afaq called and told us you'd be coming!" And then he turned to me. "You're Saadia's son," he said, examining my face closely before embracing me as well. He apologized that the power was out and for the oppressive heat inside. "Come sit down."

He pointed us to the old but comfortable sofa. "The power should be back on soon." It soon became obvious that as first-time visitors to Sodhra, Taimur and I had not pieced any of this together. Who lived in this house? Who was our host? We all worked on figuring out how we were related, and as we did, we drew mental maps of the sprawling family tree that I had seen. His name was Irfan, and he was visiting from his regular home in Toronto, Canada. He asked us what had brought us to the ancestral town, and I told him that I had recently seen the family tree and I was interested in finding out about our family's old roots.

Over the next few hours, we talked about our many Qazi relatives and ancestors. He told me of the Grand Old Qazi, who was the last person in the family to serve in the office of qazi, during the Mughal Empire. The image of his official stamp, he told me, survives to this day. The British officially abolished the position soon after they claimed the subcontinent as a colony. In 1864, the British parliament in London passed Act XI, which declared it "unnecessary to continue the office of Hindoo and Mohammaden law officers" in the colony. For the first time in perhaps a thousand years in the Punjab, the sovereign power in the land had no need for the muftis and qazis in the state apparatus anymore. "Qazi" has been no more than a surname ever since.

He had many other stories to tell. He brimmed with harmless gossip about distant relatives living in far corners of the country and followed it up with heavy historical tales of ancestors like the one about Ibrahim ibn Adham, who was the king of the Central Asian kingdom of Balkh a thousand years ago and who left his throne and wandered into the forest one day never to return. There were fantastical stories about spirits being summoned to reveal truths and others more sober about people dying at a young age from preventable diseases. Legend mixed with history and memory, and Irfan told them all with the same genuine conviction.

"Who was the first person to come here to Sodhra?" I asked him. He took a deep breath. "You are asking me about Sheikh Abul Fateh. He's here," he said, and I assumed he meant that he was also buried in Sodhra, "but that is a long story. I think it will be good for you to visit the ancestral graveyards while you're here and that will answer some of your questions. But there's plenty of time for all that. Come, let me show you the place where your grandfather was born." We walked across the alley through another door and into another *haveli*. We met more Qazi relatives and walked around examining the house. There was nothing there that belonged to my grandfather, or anything that even suggested he had ever lived here. But what choice did we have but to believe my family's tales? Taimur and I examined everything closely, as if it were an elaborate exhibit in a museum.

It was sweltering hot when Taimur and I set out to find the ancestral graveyard. Before we left the house, I was given a small thick notebook by a relative in the *haveli*. It was filled with handwritten pages written in Urdu by the scribe Azizuddin. It was a compendium volume to the

scroll and contained more detailed biographical entries
on nearly all the names that appeared in the family tree.
"You'll find answers to many of your questions in here,"
I was told.

Our car bucked and tossed as we drove along the muddy
unpaved roads on the outskirts of Sodhra, and suddenly we
spotted the waist-high walls of the cemetery that Irfan had
described to us. We parked the car in a nearby empty lot and
entered the cemetery through a short metal-wire gate. The
plot of land was no larger than a few hundred square yards.
The grass was patchy and dry in some spots, and a giant
gnarly banyan tree grew in one corner, shading nearly half
the graveyard with its enchanting canopy of leaves. A lone
baby goat with a rope tied loosely around its neck grazed
among the dozen or more grave mounds and headstones
that speckled the plot, in various states of repair.

Directly next to the thick tree trunk was the largest and
most elaborate grave on the plot. The arched marble headstone was a few feet tall and appeared to have been recently
reinforced with cement. An unreal-looking lush patch of
grass surrounded the grave. It was beautiful and inviting,
and both Taimur and I were drawn directly toward it. We
stood on each side of the gravestone to read the epitaph:

In the name of Allah most beneficent, most merciful
There is no God but God and Muhammad is his Prophet
Hazrat Sheikh Abul Fateh Faruqi
The great ancestor of the family of Qureshi Faruqi
Sodhra, Wazirabad
Date of death 1358 CE, or 825 of the Great Migration

This was the man Irfan had spoken of: the first descendant of the caliph Umar to arrive in Sodhra. I found a flat
rock under the tree and opened my notebook in the shade
to the table of contents and began scanning the names
listed. I found Sheikh Abul Fateh almost exactly halfway
between my grandfather and Umar. When I turned to page
twenty-six, I noticed that Shiekh Abul Fateh's was also the
longest entry of the entire book:

His father was still alive when the Most Respected Sheikh Abul
Fateh took on the noble path of meditation, and he would remain
deeply involved in it, day and night. In the environs of Baghdad
he was eminently respected, considered a master of his time. He
had constructed for himself a house for solitary prayer in the desert
near Baghdad, and that is where he spent most of his days. There
was an assigned time for visitors and only then would the needy
and the loyal followers begin arriving. After worship and prayer,
he would see off each one personally. Some of his most loyal fol-
lowers would stay over to serve him. He was a great worker of
miracles, a true saint.

After the great emperor Timur of Samarqand had captured
the kingdoms of Balkh and Bukhara [in Central Asia], he turned
his gaze to Baghdad. He came to the city and conquered it. He ar-
rived at the shrine for the revered saint Sheikh Abdul Qadir Jilani
(May Allah be pleased with him) to pay his respects, and after-
ward he met with some of the most respected families of Baghdad.
He told the gathering: "This city, in fact this whole country, is
radiant with the blessings of the saint Abdul Qadir Jilani. It is
renowned in this world and in the heavens. Is there any living man
who embodies these blessings of this city?" The people gathered

said that here there is one elder by the name of Abul Fateh, who is
the descendant of the second caliph of Islam, Umar bin al-Khat-
tab. Even though he spends his time in the wilderness, his sons live
here in the city.

The Emperor Timur sent his vizier [chief officer] to meet
[with Abul Fateh] and instructed him to inform the saint that the
Emperor Timur wished to grant him an audience. The vizier ap-
peared before Abul Fateh and delivered the message as instructed.
But Abul Fateh said nothing in response. The loyal followers of the
mystic saint present at the spot informed the vizier that this was the
time when Abul Fateh would speak to no one. He might try again
the next day during hours of daylight.

The next day the Emperor Timur sent his vizier to the saint
once again. After delivering greetings and offering some prayers,
the vizier recounted the emperor's message. Abul Fateh gave the
vizier his own message to deliver to the emperor: tell him that
he may be the Shah of the world but he is not greater than the
King of Kings whom we all must return to one day. The vizier
returned to the emperor and delivered the message from the
saint. The Emperor Timur said: "Go again and remind the saint
that Allah instructs in the noble Quran: 'O you who believe:
obey Allah and obey the Messenger and those in authority among
you.'

"Allah has passed on the kingship on this earth to the em-
peror. And now I am the almighty on this land. Therefore, it is
obligatory on the sheikh that he deliver himself in my court so that
we may indulge in sagacious and enlightening conversation. Does
the saint truly follow Allah's way or not?"

The vizier returned once again to the saint and delivered
the emperor's message in its entirety. But Abul Fateh had great

mastery of knowledge. He countered that the Emperor Timur is not a just man. He is a lover of worldly pleasures and he has committed grave zulm. In greed of empire, he has laid destruction on Allah's creation. He is delivering great injury to this world. A true representative of God is one who not for one breath negates the orders [of Allah]. How will all this bravado and worldly influence serve him on the day when he stands for his judgment?

The vizier returned to the emperor and conveyed the message from the saint. The Emperor Timur fell silent. And then he spoke. "Without a doubt the saint is a pure man of God. He depends on no one in this world. Surely he is of the sufis. A person of such spiritual standing has no need for anyone." And with this, the Emperor Timur set out to present himself in the audience of the great saint, Abul Fateh.

When the Emperor Timur neared the abode of the saint, he dismounted from his steed. He kissed the saint's hands. For some time he humbly conversed with Abul Fateh. Once he felt familiar with the saint's character, he fell for him completely. Swells of respect and love burst forth from the emperor's heart.

After staying a few days in Baghdad, it was time for Emperor Timur to embark toward the lands of the Indus. He presented himself to the saint once and again with this request: "I have plans for tourism and travel in Hindustan [the lands of the Indus]. May I request that you, along with your honorable sons, join me in these travels?"

At first, Abul Fateh refused. Then later, after some thought, he reluctantly agreed. It was in the year 802 of the Great Migration [1400 CE] when by the grace of Allah, and accompanied by his sons, Abul Fateh traveled with Emperor Timur, and became a denizen of the lands of the Indus.

The story went on to explain that when it came time for Timur to leave the Indus and return to his homeland to the north to quell a rising rebellion, he offered Abul Fateh a chance to return to Baghdad. But Abul Fateh chose to stay along the Indus. Abul Fateh's three sons were appointed qazis of Delhi, Lahore, and Kashmir. The great saint chose to live most often with his eldest son in Sodhra, near Lahore. The date of his death according to the Islamic calendar is listed as the eleventh day in the month of Rajab in the year 825 of the Great Migration, or 1425 CE. "Abul Fateh's offspring now live in Sodhra," the story concludes. "Among his progeny there are many renowned and wise elders, people of knowledge and miracles, living examples of righteousness. Most of them served in the rank of qazi, for which reason his offspring are commonly known as Qazi."

I looked up from the handwritten inscriptions on the page and stared at the elaborate grave site of the man whose story I had just read. The story written by the scribe explained the importance—perhaps even the existence—of this grave site in his hometown, Sodhra. The man in the grave, the scribe wrote, had been carried onto the banks of the Indus River against his best judgment by forces of history too powerful to resist even for a man of God like himself. And then, when the opportunity was offered to him to return to the place of his birth, he chose to end it here on the banks of a stream of the Indus. Here was a man who had chosen this land for eternity. Here is where Islam chose the land and the land embraced Islam.

I looked over at Taimur in the distance. He was strolling around inspecting the other gravestones. He was sharply

With the family scroll in one hand, my cousin Taimur checks his BlackBerry messages while standing by the grave of the legend Abul Fateh under the banyan tree.

dressed, as always, a handsome goatee, hair slicked back. I wondered whether he knew that the great Central Asian king he was named for had played such a pivotal role in the Qazi family's story. Emperor Timur, from whom grew the prodigious line of Mughals, one of the great Muslim empires, had single-handedly ripped a lofty bloodline from its home along the Tigris River in the fertile crescent of the Middle East and transplanted it to the Indus on the subcontinent one thousand years ago. So the story goes.

Taimur had paused at a particular gravestone. "Shahan," he called out, "what was grandfather's brother's name?" he asked.

"Ashfaq, I think," I said as I walked over toward him.

"I think this is him," he said, pointing to a gravestone only a few yards away from the grave of the legend Abul Fateh. The headstone was smaller but carried a more elaborate epitaph.

The resting place of Ashfaq Hussain Qazi M.A. B.T.
"This flower, for its beauty, could be appreciated not
It bloomed, no doubt, but blossom it could not."
1939

I remembered that my grandfather would sometimes talk about his deceased elder brother. He was the one who had a master of arts in English and a bachelor's degree in teaching from Punjab University. He had died, suddenly, in his thirties. "That's him," I said. We both held our palms flat out in front of our chests to say a prayer for him. Next to him was the grave of his wife, and we prayed at her grave site too, even though neither Taimur nor I had ever known anything about her. We spent hours under the sun in the quiet graveyard. The lonesome goat that was grazing earlier had wandered off, but we still crouched over graves examining the fading gravestones, deciphering the epitaphs and inscriptions, connecting them to page numbers in the scribe's book. In and around the legend of Abul Fateh, the family had laid their dead, burying the real with the remembered and the imagined, making it all history, indistinguishable.

As we walked to the gate to leave, once again we faced the large grave of Sheikh Abul Fateh under the banyan tree. The headstone was pristine, no more than a few years old. Behind the grave I found a stack of older headstones, and I understood that someone in the family kept a careful eye out for the upkeep of the graveyard, including replacing the headstone with fresh marble every few years. The banyan tree too, I learned from the book, had been the work of the family. The scribe wrote that his maternal aunt planted it in 1880 "to provide shade to the great man's grave." It was handsomely trimmed and had grown over a century and a half into a sturdy landmark of its own, calling attention to the graveyard on the rocky road near the outskirts of Sodhra. Before we left, we said a prayer at this grave too. It was family, after all.

Had the scribe imagined his history, and the history of his family? Had he invented it? It was a question that had nagged at me since I had seen the scroll. But my doubts were eased as I read the scribe's words in the book while sitting in the graveyard. It was not that I had been convinced of the truth of the stories or that I had been confronted with some irrefutable evidence. Far from it: if there was any evidence at all, it was buried deep in the ground and long gone. But my peace with this history had more to do with reading the words the scribe had written in the story. If there were any shadow of doubt in the mind of the scribe about the family tale, then it would surely appear somewhere in the text. As a journalist, I knew this to be true. I hunted in vain for this speck of doubt in the hundreds of pages of writing. The man truly did believe every word he committed to the page. This history was sealed with belief so strong, so overwhelming, that I was finally able to see it clearly: the faith trumped reality itself. Had it all happened exactly the way the scribe recorded it? It did not matter. What mattered was that the scribe believed that it happened. And his offspring believed the record he had written for them. That, more than any fact, is what makes history.

The scribe had done a great service to his family. There was a time when the centuries of history that tenuously linked the scribe to the caliph Umar through Abul Fateh had been nearly lost. The scribe writes that during his youth the graveyard had fallen into disrepair, the family tree was forgotten in piles of paper, and the men and women were no longer doing the hard work of remembering their past. But then it was resurrected, not only on paper but also in the land. Books and scrolls were written and graveyards were repaired, and over several generations this faith in history was reinforced so thoroughly that today the historical connections are more explicit than perhaps they ever were before. The scribe's work was not just to record what had passed. It was as much about nurturing a tale that others could hold on to. "I pray to God," he wrote in his book, "that in the future generations we have family who takes on responsibility of the upkeep of the graves."

As we drove back to Lahore, for the first time I began to see the signs that this faith was not my family's alone. It populated the entire landscape. We drove beneath a large arch in one small town and saw that it was named Iraqi Gate, built in 1931 in memory of one Malik Ghulam Muhammad of Iraq. From the road, we saw an elaborate shrine in the distance and we parked on the roadside and walked over to explore it. It was the grave site of one Syed Lal Shah covered in shimmering green cloth with golden trim and bright yellow and red garlands. His epitaph read that he had "arrived from the Arab lands" and had converted a local Hindu woman to Islam and married her. There was no date for his death. We passed a small community that called itself Mufti Colony. At each place we met people praying at the shrines, tending to the graves, using them as portals to a spiritual realm, and a past that they cherished and needed. And these shrines, left as signposts in the land by generations past, also pointed everyone on the land in the direction of a shared history, which led back to Islam.

It isn't just the name of a religion or the name of a system of law or even a code of life. Here, Islam is what lay

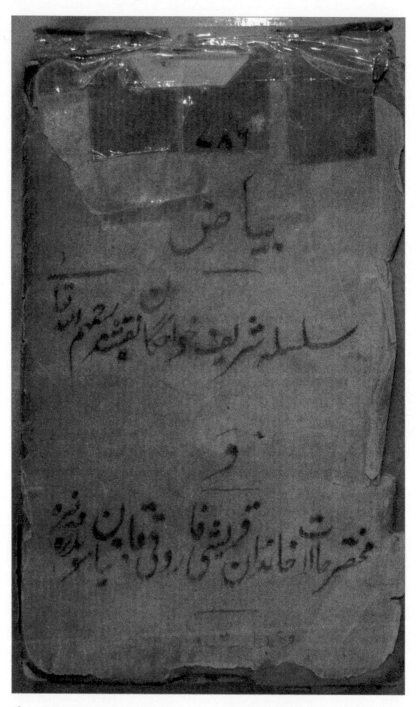

The scribe's handwritten reporter–style notebook, with biographical sketches of all the people whose names appear in the genealogical tree.

strewn in the landscape. Islam is centuries-old richly decorated shrines, and Islam is family stories. Islam was what tied people's guts and blood to the land. Islam was a faith that created a nation. How could Islam be extracted from this? Why would Islam be extracted from here? Islam had been here for centuries. It had gone through empire, colonialism, monarchy, crisis, blossom and decline, war and peace. And it was still here now in Pakistan. Islam would stay.

Nine

THE MONSOON WAS ALWAYS my favorite season to be in the Punjab. The deadly heat of the summer prickles the skin and flattens the spirit. The land of the subcontinent begins to bake under the orblike sun, creating a vast stream of low pressure that pulls in the moisture-laden air from the Indian Ocean. The winds rush northward, with great speed, until they hit the Himalaya Mountains. The icy cold wall deflects the air up toward the sky, where it condenses and forms thick clouds. These clouds of the southwestern monsoon then begin their slow, purposeful journey back toward the sea where they originated, leaving heavy rain along their sodden path.

The monsoon comes as a savior. There are moments during the dry summer when you might begin to doubt nature's plan and wonder if the heat will ever end. Then the brilliance of the monsoon begins to reveal itself. It flirts at first, rumbling deeply in the distance before casting a cool shadow over the land. It's the sort of weather that makes you lose yourself. Lovers rendezvous in quiet and parched grasslands and stare at the horizon, waiting. When the monsoon begins pouring down in heaving sheets of rain, men forget their umbrellas at home on purpose. Women, momentarily forgetful of their modesty, wander out in their flimsy summer garments. The plump raindrops, perfectly matched to the temperature of the human body, beat on the skin, replacing the sticky layer of the summer's sweat. The first drops of rain kick up plumes of dust from the earth, unlocking scents that have been trapped inside the land for many months. Everything is transformed. The cruel summer is forgotten. Nature is forgiven for its torment.

But in the summer of 2010, the monsoon was different. It was too early, too quick, too ferocious. I was in Islamabad and I watched, mesmerized, from the window of my house as it began to rain in the fleeting days of July. It rained for four days and four nights and did not let up for a moment. The drains, dug so efficiently on the sides of the roads, began to clog up with leaves, and the water transformed into churning rapids in the streets. At first, it was exciting to sweep away the pools of water from the landing leading out to the gate from the front door. But then the news of terrible floods started coming in from the north. The monsoon had dumped more water into the river system in one week than it usually does over several months. The summer sun had also melted an exceptional amount of ice in the Himalayas from some of the mightiest glaciers in the world. The headwaters of the Indus became bloated. The river began charging down its course, through the length of Pakistan.

The floods of 2010 were the worst ever recorded in the Indus River's long history. Pakistan's total irrigated land area, all of which stems from the Indus, is the fourth largest in the world. Only behemoths like India, China, and the United States have more tracts of irrigated land. The floods inundated one-fifth of Pakistan, an area twice the size of Austria. It was devastating. The World Bank put the damage at nearly ten billion dollars. The average GDP per capita in Pakistan is only a little over one thousand dollars. Natural disaster wrought financial havoc. Pakistan, which had been one of the world's leading food producers for many decades, was put on the list of the twenty-nine countries in the world "requiring external assistance for food." On August 14, Pakistan's sixty-fourth Independence Day, the prime minister announced stunning figures: twenty million people were affected, of which four million were left homeless. Thousands died immediately. It was the single deadliest event in the country since the partition.

The floods spared no one. They hit every province of Pakistan. The Taliban strongholds in the northwest were inundated. The floods wracked Rawalpindi, the headquarters of the army. Even Islamabad, the most modern city and the seat of the government, was flooded. The floods descended the Potwar Plateau and into the Punjab plains and turned millions of people into refugees. Farther south, the river submerged Sindh, the province along the southern coast, and even Baluchistan in the southwest, the country's poorest province, most distant from the Indus River and only tenuously linked to the federation.

In the middle of the country's bloodiest war, the skies over Pakistan had torn open and fed the river, which had swollen with rage and viciously burst from its banks. It was as if nature was striking the nation of Muslims living on its banks, reminding them of their fragile human reality. Pakistanis might not have been tied together by any language or by any race. They might not have shared a common culture, and perhaps they had never even seen their shared religion of Islam in the same way. But the floods reminded everyone that the river touched everyone's lives. For millions of years, the Indus had given life and sustenance, and it had also taken life away. And now the winds and the mountains and the rivers had conspired once again to change the course of history. As always it was the Indus, more than anything else, that was ready to play its role in forging a new shape of the land and a new future for its people.

A few weeks after the rains ended, I received a phone call from Lahore. Uncle Afaq had discovered a few more records, nearly a century old, some of which seemed to be personal letters written by the scribe, Azizuddin. It was exciting news to me. As much as the trip to Sodhra and the book of biographies written by the scribe had helped me understand my family and the nation's identity, I had learned little about the scribe himself. I thought afterward about his conspicuous absence from the family records. He had been born in Sodhra and he had written a thousand years of history as it unfolded in the small Punjabi town. Everyone in the town knew of his stories and believed them to be true. But not during my visits to all the grave sites, and not during the meals with extended family members or while wandering through the *havelis* or exploring the markets had I seen a trace of the scribe himself. There was no house that belonged to Azizuddin, not even a grave site with his name on it or those of any of his direct descendants.

After my trip to Sodhra, I had found that I was more closely related to the scribe than I had first realized. Azizuddin was the grandfather of Yusuf, my grandfather Akhlaque's adopted son. It was Yusuf's untimely death that had led my parents to question their continued stay in America and eventually made them decide to move back to Pakistan. I had long recognized that Yusuf's life and death had played an important role in the story of my own life. Now that I knew that he was the scribe's grandson, it made me feel in a strange way closer to my maternal family's history.

I had learned a little about Azizuddin from the scroll on which he had written the family tree. Azizuddin had written in his author's note that he was "75 or 76 years of age" around 1931. I calculated that he was born in 1856 or 1857, in the midst of the subcontinent's bloody rebellion against the rule of the East India Company, after which the subcontinent formally became a British colony. The scribe had come into the world just in time to live during the first real clash between the law and bureaucracy of Western civilization and that of the Islamic civilization. In the scroll he wrote

The scribe's son, Abdul Rahman, photographed at his son Yusuf's wedding. He stands to the groom's right, and my grandfather Akhlaque, who adopted Yusuf when he was a young boy, stands to the groom's left.

that at the "age of 13 years I traveled to Abbottabad." This would have been the late 1860s, a few years after the British officially abolished the posts of qazi and mufti from the bureaucracy. Azizuddin had grown into a young man carrying the name Qazi, which was a hallowed surname, a vestige of a political past that no longer existed. Instead, he had relied on a natural skill to get work: "I was offered a job as a scribe for having a very stable hand at writing."

Azizuddin returned to Sodhra decades later, in his old age, and threw himself into the project of tracing his ancestry and recording the history of his family's past. As Azizuddin neared his life's end, he became consumed with answering one very ordinary and profound question: Where do I come from? In his last years the scribe finally started to build himself a new palace of stories. He lovingly laid the foundations and built his fortress up around him, brick by brick, until he was completely enveloped in his own stories. From inside this palace, Azizuddin could tell the world who he was and where he came from. But what made him write down everything? What had happened in those many decades after he left his home that he would return to feverishly record the story of his family and trace its roots to the earliest moments of Islam?

The new stash of papers in Lahore wasn't immediately helpful in answering these questions. It was a scattered puzzle of history. There were some letters which, I recognized from their elegant, professional-looking Urdu script, were written by the scribe himself that discussed family matters interwoven with history and legend. They were addressed to different family members, including a few to my great-grandfather Mushtaq, Akhlaque's father. All the letters were signed by "Musafir Azizuddin" and they all were written from a place named Qaziabad. There were also elaborate maps and sketches of what appeared to be large landholdings, with specific dimensions of plots neatly labeled along the straight lines on the paper. And there were also a few documents in English, mostly on the letterhead of the British Indian Army, from the years after First World War. These were addressed to a certain Kazi Abdul Rahman.

I took the papers to my aunt Tasneem, the wife of the scribe's grandson Yusuf and the mother of my cousin Erum. Although she was not a direct descendant of the scribe's, she was the closest I could get to his family line. I visited her at her home, a comfortable apartment in the busy and charming Shadman neighborhood of Lahore, almost halfway between the walled Old City and the Punjab University campus in the south. Now in her sixties, Tasneem was a kind and gentle old woman with a sharp wit. Over tea and biscuits, we examined the sheaf of papers and Tasneem helped me piece together the life of her late husband's grandfather, Azizuddin.

He was fluent in Persian and Urdu, she told me, and family lore is that he had always been greatly interested in history. He could provide a couplet of classical poetry on demand for any occasion, and he had a great passion for calligraphy. Azizuddin was married at an early age, and over the course of his life he fathered ten children. Only four of them survived to old age, and only one of those four children was a son. Abdul Rahman was the jewel of Azizuddin's eye, and he grew up to become one of the most handsome men in the family. But what Abdul Rahman had in charm and good looks he lacked in any real employment prospects. He was lazy and careless, and in his wayward path he fell for a dancing girl.

When Abdul Rahman flunked out of school, the scribe enlisted his son in the British Indian Army. The discipline of the army would be good for him, the scribe believed. It was a line of work that many Muslims in the Punjab, locked out of other employment prospects, took on at that time.

But only a few months after Abdul Rahman had joined the military, there was news of an assassination in Sarajevo. The Great War began. Owing to his decent command of spoken English, young Abdul Rahman worked through the war in the British Indian Army's administrative offices. Surprisingly, he was a success. One letter written by a British officer named C. G. Oxley Brennan reported that Abdul Rahman "worked in the office of the Assistant Recruiting Office Gujranwala for some time, much to the satisfaction of the officer in charge. From my own observation I knew him to be exceptionally energetic."

Abdul Rahman returned to the Punjab after the end of the war in 1919. He married a respectable woman and began to plan his future. He told his father that his British superiors had given him a few options. He could stay on in the army, they said, and he would have a good chance of getting promoted through the ranks. Or, they said, he could retire. In that case he would draw a lifetime monthly pension. It would be enough for him to live comfortably for the rest of his days and support his own family and his aging father. Finally, there was the third option: land.

The British Empire had become the largest empire ever to have ruled. It controlled nearly a quarter of the landmass of the globe. The British crowed that the sun never set on the British Empire. Even after the tragedies of the Great War, land was one asset the British were not short on, especially not on the subcontinent, its largest colony. The British army offered the scribe's son an estate of approximately one hundred acres in the southern Punjab region known as Ganji Bar. The land was freshly irrigated

25 - 2 - 1921.

Kazi Abdul Rahman has been working as Head Clerk of the A.R.O's office & I have had frequent opportunities to deal with him.

I have always found him smart obedient & well up in his work. He is quite a Capable hand found & I trust he will be proving satisfactory in any other position as a Clerk. He is leaving his present post on account of

A letter admiring the work the scribe's son did during the First World War for the British army, written by a British officer in 1921.

and prime for harvesting. Abdul Rahman could build his
home there and become the lord of his very own estate.
He could harvest the crops of his choosing, but he would
be required to deliver a set portion of the crop to the empire. Occasionally he would also be required to provide the
British army with some useful livestock, for war or sport.
But other than that, the wealth from the land would be his
to keep, for as many generations as he could imagine.

Of all the new institutions that the British brought along
with them to the subcontinent—the courts, the police, the
tax collection system, the queen—none would eventually
be more fateful than the institution of private property.
Under the rule of the Mughal Empire, it was the emperor
who owned all the land. He would sometimes bestow *jagirs*
to his favored subjects, who would then work on making the
lands productive and collect revenue from them. But in the
end the land belonged to the emperor alone. The British
inverted this human relationship with the land. From the
colonial perspective, the Mughal system was inefficient. The
colonists were interested in extracting as much wealth from
the land as was possible with the least effort. The colony was
nearly the size of all of Europe and it would be impossible
to keep ownership of all of the land. So the British introduced private property, parceling out plots of land to local
subjects in return for tax revenue, raw material, livestock,
food, and most important, a lifetime of loyalty. It was the
perfect way to keep the colony under control.

The scribe and his son had never dreamed of such an
offer. How could one possibly own a piece of land? They
mulled their options. A pension paycheck for the rest of

316

Abdul Rahman's life would guarantee easy and comfortable days, at least as long as the colonists remained. There was no doubt he would be able to support his aged father with it. Working and living off the surplus of a hundred acres of land, on the other hand, was a riskier and more complex proposition. They heard that the soil was very good, though, and who knows the possibilities that land might open up down the line? In the end he decided to take a gamble: Abdul Rahman accepted the land grant. And so the scribe and his son became the first Qazis ever to own a piece of God's land on this earth.

Everything changed. Abdul Rahman and his father the scribe hauled in dozens of peasants and their families from surrounding villages, who all settled on the land and built a new village colony along one edge of the estate. Some of the poor folk became farmers, others became workers and transporters, and all became completely dependent on the Qazi landlords for their livelihood. Abdul Rahman planted sugarcane and cotton crops and started experimenting with different trees that were laden with colorful fruit. Within a few years, Abdul Rahman's British patrons named him the *lambardar* of the surrounding district. He became the local representative of the queen in his area, the colonists' point man for this small speck of the empire. Within a few years, father and son had become a snugly fitting cog in the machine of colonial enterprise, built to extract wealth from the vast subcontinent.

Ever since Azizuddin the scribe was born during the war with the British East India Company, he had watched as his family's place in the world demolished brick by brick.

First, the Muslim Empire fell. Then his family's Muslim profession, qazi, was discarded by the British in favor of a new colonial bureaucracy. Urdu and Persian, written in the Arabic script and spoken and read by other Muslims to the west, were the languages of the scribe's pen. But even these started to melt away as other local languages and English began replacing them. Now, in the twilight of his life, Azizuddin finally gained something from the colonists. He had gotten his own land. He accepted this important part of the Western tradition.

As his son worked the lands and began building his agricultural fiefdom, the scribe embarked on his own deeply subversive mission. He would collect the rubble of all he had lost in his life and devise a scheme to sow his losses and hopes into the land that the British had given to him. His family history might have been bathed in symbols of Islamic and Muslim civilization, but it was also his very own, deeply personal history. Azizuddin would shape his land and write a new history for himself and for his land. By doing so, he thought, he would lay the path for a new future, a future where Muslims like himself would once again own all the land. This would be his redemption and the redemption of everyone he considered to be his own family, his nation. Once father and son had settled in, they named their new estate "Qaziabad," the Land of the Qazi. But this was just the beginning. There was a lot more work to be done.

I asked Tasneem if she could take me to the agricultural lands in Qaziabad. She was now the matriarch of her family and she had been managing the lands ever since the death of Yusuf, the lord of Qaziabad. I wanted to venture out there to see the scribe's last home on the land. I hoped that from inside the house he had built for himself on the estate I might be able to see how he would have seen the world around him. From the agricultural lands, I hoped, I might catch a clear vista of his life. And if I was lucky, I might even catch a brief glimpse into the future of Islam in this land.

WE DROVE SOUTH from Lahore toward Qaziabad. The village was more than a hundred miles downstream along the Ravi, near the spot where its tributary joins the Indus close the city of Multan. As we drove, Tasneem pointed through the car window at all the different crops being grown and harvested on each side of the road. The landscape of this region, where the five rivers of the Indus system converge, is surprisingly similar to what I was used to seeing in the north of the Punjab. Wide-open, unending stretches of farmland divided into smaller private plots unfolded in all directions. Water buffalo sloshed lazily in artificial ponds, swatting birds off their backs with flicks of their tails. Men and women worked the fields here, and the tones of the women's clothes turned brighter and more radiant with every passing mile.

South Punjab had not always looked like this. When the British arrived here in the mid-nineteenth century, much of it was densely forested swampland. Until it was arable, it was useless to the British. In the nineteenth century, European colonists started to view agriculture as a lucrative source of wealth creation in their colonies. It was better than the more traditional sources like mining for precious metals like gold or stones like diamonds, or finding ancient treasure. Those were all finite enterprises, while agriculture was only as limited as the land itself. In the south of the Punjab, the British undertook one of the most extensive transformations of land ever seen on the subcontinent. They drained the swamps, cleared the forests, and reclaimed the land, building a far-reaching network of ground irrigation canals linking the Indus River waters to the newly created plains.

The colonists handed out parcels of this newly productive land as grants to their favored subjects, and the Punjab became a source of great wealth for the British Empire and also for some locals like Azizuddin and his son Abdul Rahman. After a few decades of migration onto the land by enterprising locals, this engineering miracle yielded the largest surface land irrigation system in the world. By the beginning of the twentieth century, the Punjab had become not only a densely populated area but also one of the most agriculturally productive ones on earth.

The region around Qaziabad sits at the confluence of history like few other spots on the subcontinent. Miles away from Qaziabad, along the banks of the Ravi, British archaeologists discovered the ruins of the ancient site of Harappa in the late nineteenth century. Harappa was one of the most important cities of the Indus Valley Civilization that thrived five thousand years ago along the river. Thousands of years later, the armies of Alexander the Great also passed through the south of the Punjab while traversing the Indus, and they planted many cities along the way. The great Hindu Rajput kingdoms made this region home, and the earliest Arab Muslim armies arrived only a few decades after Muhammad's death. That the first seeds of an Islamic civilization in South Asia were also planted right here is evidenced by the countless ancient shrines of Muslim saints, which are spiritual portals of divine blessing for the people who live on the land today.

Was it the millennia of history trapped in the land of the Punjab that made Azizuddin obsessed with answering questions about his own possible past? More likely it was simply the richness of the land that did it. Azizuddin would have felt a sense of independence and power that can come only with owning a piece of land for oneself. It was this amazing new sensation that made the scribe concerned with deciphering the course of history that had landed him here in Qaziabad. The richness of the land had made him hungry to explore his own glorious past—whether or not it really existed. Azizuddin had to find this past for himself in order to find his place in the present. And it was equally necessary for molding his future. He began digging deep.

Among the Urdu letters that I examined with Tasneem, there was one addressed to my great-grandfather in Lahore:

> My dearest, most respected brother,
>
> I had, for the longest time, due to lack of any real emerging evidence, sidelined my project of tracing our ancestral lineage and family tree. Now, with the grace of God and with the newfound cooperation of the younger generation, the matter is looking to revive . . . If, in our family tree, we are able to trace a well-known

*king of the past of great renown, and if we are able to get some
written records from his court from the history books, it would
be an unrivaled aid in understanding the [historical] conditions
of the Qazis, which has become a matter of great necessity today.
Perhaps the library in Lahore will have treasured material on
this subject or perhaps the pages sitting in Wazirabad might shed
some light on this matter. I have heard that there do exist some
pages in Wazirabad. When you get a chance, please do try to find
those and witness them with your eyes. It will be the heaviest of
evidence for us.*

*Many prayers,
Musafir Azizuddin
Qaziabad
[1927]*

After six hours on the southbound highway, many family tales, and scores of farming lessons, Tasneem and I
were almost at Qaziabad. We turned off the main highway
and onto a smaller road in the direction of the town of
Burewala. Another turn, and we were on a gravelly unpaved
road devoid of any road signs, passing through endless
tracts of agricultural land. There were no more cars here.
The marketplaces disappeared and only the odd brick house
stood out among its mud and thatch counterparts. The only
sturdy structures were a few mosques. We were at the place
where Islam had first become part of our family, the land,
and the nation.

It was getting dark as we entered Qaziabad, but Aunt
Tasneem insisted that we take a small detour. Before we
settle in for the night at the farmhouse, she said, we should

go pray at Azizuddin's grave. It was only a few miles away, she explained, not far from the fields. "I know it's inconvenient, I'm sorry," she said shyly, glancing at the red horizon for signs of the dying sun. "But once, a couple of years ago, I decided to go straight to the house without paying my respects at the grave first. And you know what happened? We got a punctured tire even before we had reached the house." Azizuddin, she said, wasn't happy at all. "He gets upset when family doesn't come greet him first."

I woke up on a charpoy rope bed in Qaziabad at the crack of dawn. When was the last time I had been woken up by a rooster's "prayer call" at sunrise? There was no heating at the farmhouse and it was a cold night, but the heavy blanket had kept me toasty as I slept on the open veranda. The building was a minimalist structure with one large square room with four rope beds lined up in a row and another smaller room with three beds lined against three walls. There was only one shared bathroom on the other side of the courtyard, whose floor was littered with twigs and grass. It was all far from lavish.

From underneath my blanket I could hear the sound of the water buffalo outside being lead in the direction of the foggy grazing fields. The metal bells tied around their thick necks rang sweetly. Heavy metal pots banged over open fires in the not-so-distant village, while the women called at each other in shrill tones, laying plans for the day ahead. It wasn't fully light yet, but the entire village was already at work. We had just finished a breakfast of fresh cow milk and carrot puree when a peasant woman from the village walked into Tasneem's modest living quarters and announced that the horse groomer had arrived, with a horse in tow.

I followed Tasneem out the gates of the farmhouse and inspected the majestic gray-white animal. There were already a half dozen children surrounding the horse. The children were covered in dirt, some without shoes on their feet. The horse looked more taken care of than any of them. I joined them in petting its muzzle and shoulders. The groomer, holding the reins tightly, pointed out the muscular legs and the healthy mane to Tasneem. "It's in fantastic condition, let me tell you, ma'am," he said too eagerly. Tasneem frowned as she examined what seemed like a healing wound on its sturdy-looking back. When she asked him about it, he ignored her completely. "There is no way this will get rejected," he said, now pleading.

Tasneem explained that in exchange for allowing her to hold an extra twenty-five acres of land, the government of Pakistan demands that she deliver a horse or cattle raised on her land. It's a way for the government to gain from privately held property, and also a way of exerting influence by rewarding some landowners and punishing others. One way to avoid angering anyone in the upper echelons of the bureaucracy, or getting slapped with unexpected land taxes, is to keep a steady stream of healthy livestock going to the government and military. Horses, mules, and even some bulls are useful for battle in the mountainous terrain in the north, and some of the best horses are sometimes recruited for polo, a favorite sport of the air force and army officers. But that's not all. She also told me about the many levels of the bureaucracy that grew out from the land and how she had to grease the entire chain that led up to the top. In its essence, the estate appeared to be operating under a similar arrangement that the scribe and his son had established with their colonial masters a century ago.

The government-appointed land record keeper for the area, the *patwari*, was perhaps the most dangerous, Tasneem said. He had free rein to alter land records at will. If he was crossed, he was fully capable of "losing" all the concerned land records and redrawing them from memory. Of course he could alter the borders as he wished and in the process hand over little bits to neighboring owners who had been more coopertive. *Patwari*, she explained, are officials who have been notoriously corrupted by the power they have over the contours of the land, but there was also the long list of provincial government officers who sat in cities like Lahore and Multan and even Islamabad and who had to be kept equally happy in order to keep the lands running smoothly. It sounded like an exhausting and draining exercise.

While colonialism had come and gone, and while an Islamic republic was erected and run from a pristine capital in the hills, here in the agricultural lands of the Punjab the antiquated system of patronage had survived and mutated. In some ways the land system had become even more viciously extractive, more corrupt as it passed from colonial masters to the modern rulers who were required to keep up the pretense of being democracies in service to their own people. "We're three years behind on delivering a breeding horse," Tasneem explained, as a wrinkle appeared in her brow while she still examined the wound on the horse. They had sent a horse to the military five years ago but it had suddenly died months after it was delivered. Now they finally had this mare ready, but she seemed in less than ideal condition. "I think it looks fine," she said with a sigh, concluding her meeting with the breeder. "Just try to keep her like this until the colonel comes to collect her next week." The agitated horse groomer shooed the children away and they scattered like timid livestock.

The morning sun turned warm as we lounged on charpoy beds in the open veranda. A stream of village folk—peasants and farmers, men with their wives and children—began arriving at the farmhouse to pay their respects to the matriarch Tasneem. She was an absentee landlord and passed through the village only every few months, so this was a rare opportunity for all the villagers to come and plead with her for help. They were all dependent on her revenues from the land, which were dwindling. Each family brought astounding tales of their hopelessly poor lives. One young couple brought in their newborn child, emaciated and no larger than a housecat. It barely seemed conscious, and I could not imagine how it would survive a cold winter. A much older woman demanded Tasneem's attention and complained that she had lost all sensation below her waist. Her husband had died years earlier, and her sons had abandoned her and left her all alone. Another family mourned the loss of their toddler son, who had died of diarrhea in the summer.

Everyone came begging for money and help, and Tasneem could only mumble vague encouragement and empty promises. The system of the land was built to extract wealth toward the top. The welfare of these folks at the bottom was never really a concern that was built into the system of the colonists, or of the state that inherited it all. Tasneem recognized the rotten system she is a part of. "I feel helpless when I come to Qaziabad," she told me in between the depressing meetings with the peasants. "But how much can one woman do?" It wasn't her fault. The agricultural system, she said, was specifically designed to keep the system of hierarchy intact. The people at the bottom had no chance.

We arrived at the croplands as the sun was high in the sky and a cool wind blew across the expansive fields. Haq Nawaz, the land manager, had a large family, and they had prepared a meal of mustard greens and corn bread for us. He had two adult sons, each of whom was married and had a couple of toddlers of his own. They were a healthier-looking lot compared to the peasants who lived in the village. They had built a house on a decent-sized plot of land along the side of the road that overlooked acres of farmland. They did not do any farming themselves but were trusted by Tasneem to manage the lands while she was away. They were responsible for overseeing the work of the dozens of farmers who toiled on the land. While the farmers were free agents and paid wages, Haq Nawaz and his sons were given a share of the crop by Tasneem, which they were free to use for their own purposes or sell for a profit.

After the delicious lunch, I asked Haq Nawaz if he might show me around the lands. He was a scrawny old man with a squawking voice. His teeth were nearly demolished by a lifetime of smoking Capstan cigarettes. He had thick white stubble on his face and wore a mangled pair of prescription glasses. He was vulgar and tactless, and I took an instant liking to his refreshingly rebellious manners. His no-good sons were ripping him off, he announced to Tasneem as she stepped in the door and while the two sons in question stood beside him. Those greedy grabby farmers are spending way too much time drinking booze and far too little working the crops, he complained over lunch, when one farmer passed through to deliver some fresh milk. I found it strange that he was so candid. While he wasn't wealthy, he was still clearly embedded decently high into the lower chain of extraction. But he acted like a man who had nothing left to lose.

We went for a walk around the estate. "This isn't what it used to be like," Haq Nawaz announced out in the fields, after wrestling with a sugarcane stalk until it snapped. He offered a piece of it to me to sample, and I chewed on it and sucked on its sweet nectar. He lit his third cigarette of the hour and explained that his family, like Tasneem's, had been on this land for three generations. His grandfather had started working the fields with Azizuddin and his son when they had first arrived almost a hundred years ago. He said he remembered his grandfather working the fields alongside some of my ancestors. "It was a different time back then, you know, sir? Those owners back then, they lived off the land. They used to care for the land. They used to care for the people on the land. There was a bloody mission to it all." He shook his head disapprovingly. "Now they're out in Lahore. They never see us. We never see them. How do they expect me to manage the lands like this? How long do you expect these farmers are going to keep in line? How long before they start robbing it blind?"

The land ownership system, feudal in nature, is at the root of many of Pakistan's problems. Many people have recognized for decades how unsustainable the system is in a modern nation-state. Since its creation six decades ago, Pakistan has tried to reform its land ownership laws on three separate occasions, and to chip away at the system of control that has survived since the colonial era. Each time the maximum landholding limit was shrunk to encourage large landowners to sell off their immense tracts of land in smaller parcels to allow small farmers to emerge from poverty. But each time the big landowners used chicanery, deceit, and imaginary paper trails to evade giving up any land or the power and wealth that come with it. The extractive system is simply too intoxicating for the powerful. It is also through this patronage system that "democratic" groups get their votes during elections.

It's telling that it has mostly been Pakistan's military rulers who have even made any of these attempts at land reform. The elected politicians have never been interested in land reform because the land has been the source of all political power at any level in the Punjab and in much of the rest of the country. The canal and agricultural system is at the root of the political structures that have been ruling the country since it became a state in 1947. The estate at Qaziabad is a tiny speck compared to some of the larger landholdings in the country. The true disparity between the haves and have-nots becomes starker on the larger feudal estates. The more prominent landowners, many of whom

A farmer stands atop a water canal in the fields of Qaziabad.

similarly gained land grants from the British colonists, are now prime ministers, presidents, ministers, and advisers, and overwhelmingly pack all levels of the bureaucracy. They are some of the most powerful people in the country today. They are the true winners in the modern state and they have made sure that the corrupt and broken system of land ownership and patronage remains untouched.

But things are changing on the ground now. "It's all rotting, I tell you, sir. It's bloody rotting," Haq Nawaz said as he spat another streak of yellow mucus onto the field. The floods, he said, didn't come as a complete surprise to him. The monsoons had been getting continuously shorter and more intense for a decade now. I had read that the giant glaciers in the Himalayas were melting faster. The Indus was simply no longer the same river that had flowed through this land a century ago. After the floods, some people hoped that it was finally time to start afresh. But the Pakistani state used billions of dollars from international donor states to restore the land irrigation structure to exactly the way it was before. It made no sense, of course. It was guaranteed that the same old structure would lead to repeated floods year after year. Millions of people would suffer again and again. But when land has become a source of such power and political influence for a few, they are willing to do anything and everything to resist change—even at the risk of destroying themselves and everyone else in the process.

Over the few hours I walked the fields with Haq Nawaz, he pointed out countless small and ominous signs that the postcolonial land system was finally coming undone at the grass roots. The skies, the ocean, the mountains, and the river were working in mysterious and unprecedented ways, he said. The land itself was changing, disrupting the way power had been set in place for centuries. The floods laid bare the physical and the moral decay that had been building in the modern state for decades. How long before this rot travels to the larger landholdings? And how long after that would the decay work its way up the chain to the highest levels of power? Perhaps it already had. Perhaps the chaos and violence in the bigger cities really did take root out here in the shifting earth of these troubled agricultural lands.

Later, as Haq Nawaz tutored me on how to extract a cotton flower from its bud, I wondered if he had heard of the justice movement supported by Islamic parties in the cities that vowed to remove the decayed "Western" and "colonial" order. I wondered what he would make of the populist judge who wore a suit and tie in Islamabad and who promised to defend the rights of the oppressed in all of Pakistan. I had seen flags of political parties up until the main highway near Qaziabad, but they had disappeared where the paved roads ended. Surely he must have heard of the Taliban and the other militant groups entrenched in the mountains in the north fighting the "westernized" Pakistani state. Before I could ask him anything, Haq Nawaz, true to form, spoke first. "The things I'm hearing the peasants say, oh sir, let me spare you those words. It would make your hair stand on end," he raged as he stamped a cigarette butt into the earth. This place was ripe for change.

AZIZUDDIN THE SCRIBE had arrived at these lands a century ago with great hopes. In these tracts of land he saw a way to restore the greatness of his clan, albeit in a completely new way. They used to be qazis once upon a time, when it had mattered, but now, in a new political reality after the Western encounter, he reinvented himself as a landowner. This was an enterprising line of work where wealth was created and could grow exponentially. It was modern work. His future generations would live comfortably, he thought, and they would remember him and his son as the pioneers who developed the land and claimed it for posterity.

Azizuddin's thoughts were about more than just his immediate family. His project was about the betterment of a whole community of people. Even if the scribe did not recognize the word at that time, he was concerned with the fate of a nation. Owning land, like nothing else before, opened up the scribe to the world of possibilities that lay ahead for man in modern times. He knew that to look forward, you also must look back. When you own your own land, he learned, you could control the past and transform the future.

He was convinced that his family and his nation must never forget about what held them together in its distant past: Islam. They must always remember their shared experience of being Muslims. Only then would they stick together and lay claim to the land and enjoy its blessings like he did. For this reason the scribe began his genealogical project. The process of tracing his bloodline to the origins of Islam was no easy job for Azizuddin. It took the final decade of his life. He had spent years writing letters to relatives, recovering and examining old family papers, sending money to maintain the graves of the ancestors in Sodhra. In the end, Azizuddin was confident that he was able to trace his bloodline to the caliph Umar ibn al-Khattab. Umar was from Muhammad's clan and was the early Islamic Empire's greatest ruler, the man who had laid some of the foundations of an Islamic bureaucracy a millennium and a half ago. It was under Umar's rule that the first Muslim armies arrived on the lands of present-day Pakistan. By tracing his bloodline to Umar, the scribe managed to capture, in one linear path, a story that traversed through a millennium and a half of history and neatly wed together family, Islam, and nation. In the story of his genealogy, the scribe recovered the essence of all that had been lost during his first clash with Western civilization—the colonial encounter. He wasn't alone. Countless other Muslim families took on similar projects, recording memory and history for their own reasons.

Once he had traced this genealogy, Azizuddin began to write his book. Through the ink of his pen he injected this entire recovered history into the blood that ran through his veins. His story may have been partly imagined, partly true, but by writing it down he transformed it into history. In December 1933, a few months after the word "Pakistan" was first published in a short pamphlet by a Muslim activist studying far away at Cambridge University in England, the scribe wrote a brief note from Qaziabad to a family member in Lahore:

> Today, with the grace of Allah and the strength of the dear Prophet Muhammad I have been able to complete the family tree. I am now done with my life's work. The final papers came to me in time of sickness in October 1933. I was so afraid that life would not give me enough time to finish what I had started. But after all, I am done. Praise the lord! Praise the lord! Praise the lord! The family history is complete.
>
> > Musafir Azizuddin
> > Sunday, 3 December 1933
> > Qaziabad

It was a project of faith. Azizuddin had faith that the history he had uncovered, however tenuous it seemed, was indeed the truth. He had faith in the history recorded and written by the historians before him. It was also the scribe's faith that made him believe that by laying this foundation for a new palace of stories, he was not only salvaging the Islamic civilization but also laying the foundations for a future Islamic resurrection. He had faith that tying his blood to the founding moments of Islam would truly prove to be the salvation for his people. He had faith that the Muslim could embrace modernity without losing himself. The system of Islam would be resurrected one day in the future.

This was not the end of his project. Not yet. He had captured only his lost history on paper. Only once it became part of the soil of the earth would the lost civilization of Islam be fully preserved. There was one last important step: the scribe needed to mix his blood in the ground. Reading his words a century later, it is clear that he knew the importance of his own death. In one letter, written after the untimely death of a child in the family, the scribe ponders the nature of life, death, blood, and land:

> *They say that at the time of conception, by the order of Allah, an angel handles and deposits into the mother's womb the soil of that place where the human is destined to die one day. And this soil then becomes part of the human. When his death nears, Allah, the merciful, creates such specific conditions that the person has no choice but to somehow travel to the place where it must all come to an end.*
>
> > *Musafir Azizuddin*
> > *13 February 1934*
> > *Qaziabad*

The memory of where you must go to die at the end of your life is mixed in with your body and soul in the moments of conception. Life, memory, blood, and soil all congeal into a single clinging mass that guides you, with its gravitational force, through life. Azizuddin had arrived in Qaziabad via a long, circuitous path, along which some phenomenal forces of history tossed him around. It was his destiny to settle in Qaziabad. He was now nearly seventy years old. Azizuddin's hand was beginning to quake as he wrote. The steady and bold looping strokes of the scribe's pen were no longer visible on the page. Instead, the pen had become harried and unsettled, the strokes had become halted. Maybe his muscles were no longer capable of holding the pen steady. But more likely, his hand was disturbed because he felt the angel of death lurking nearby. A few days before he died, the scribe wrote this final note:

My Most Respected,

The dear brother from Lahore has promised to come and visit me here. He is awaiting some companionship for the journey. Let's see when it is in our destiny to meet him. I will, Allah willing, tell him to send you a copy of the completed family tree, or alternately ask him to bring it to you himself. Please let me know where is the best place to deliver this document to you. Inform me of this, while consider-ing time is of the essence. God forbid that this copy of yours sits and languishes here. Please keep me informed of your health and life every so often. Because a letter exchanged is truly half a personal union.

Musafir Azizuddin
25 April 1936
Qaziabad

His body was buried on the edge of the agricultural lands in Qaziabad near the roadside a few days later. The arched gravestone added an undeniable feature on the land, a landmark in time and space. In his old age he had became a spiritual healer in his own small village, and now the local peasants began visiting his grave to pray to God. He was the descendant from the Islamic Prophet's clan and in his death he became a portal to God for the faithful. Now deep inside the earth, his history was safe and eternal. It would be part of whatever new would ever grow out of the ground, centuries later. Islam was preserved, forever, in the earth.

For the longest time I wondered for whom this last letter was meant. I was curious to know the identity of this person the scribe seemed to be waiting for in his last days in this world. Who had promised to come see him in Qaziabad? After I returned to Lahore, I spent days asking close and distant relatives. I did realize that the family tree he referred to in his last letter was in all likelihood the same one that ended up in my hands through Grandfather Akhlaque and my uncle in Lahore. The words of the scribe had unexpectedly pulled me into the scribe's lands. But I was never able to find out whom that letter was for.

And as I read the letter over and over again, I decided that it was probably written to no one. The scribe had written it as a timeless note for posterity. It was meant for whoever in the family, however many generations down the line, received it. It had fallen into my hands, the work of a faithful scribe, and it is like this that I met him, on a piece of paper—it was, as the scribe said in his last words, half a personal union, anyway.

IN ISLAMIC TRADITION, like the other Abrahamic religions of Judaism and Christianity, the faithful believe that God sent the flood during the time of Noah to cleanse the earth of its sins. It was a way to start over again when the way of the world had gone irreparably wrong. The floods of 2010 in Pakistan felt like that. After six long decades, the state that had been built as a refuge for the nation of Muslims had failed to deliver for most of its people. The work of dogged visionaries and hard-nosed politicians had, decades ago, succeeded in bringing together millions of Muslims of different races, languages, and cultures as a nation, but then the promise of a modern democratic Islamic political society had sputtered and stalled one too many times. Pakistan was supposed to be the world's most advanced laboratory of Islam and democracy, but the experiment of mixing the tradition of Islam with a modern nation-state had not found the right balance. At times, it appeared a disaster.

The historic floods would become a defining moment in Pakistan's political history. They wrecked much of the irrigation infrastructure that made these agricultural lands possible and, in turn, the structures of political power that were built on the land. They scuttled the strong remnants of Pakistan's postcolonial system. As many had predicted, the floods struck again in the summer monsoon of 2011. This time they hit the southern province of Sindh, and once again they killed thousands and left millions of people homeless, hopeless. And once again, little was done to change the system of landholdings and irrigation. It would take more than repeated floods to alter what had been in place for centuries.

In October 2011, months after I returned from Qaziabad, Imran Khan, the leader of the Movement for Justice, called a public protest rally in a large park outside the walled Old City of Lahore. Khan chose a poignant spot to hold this rally, where many eras of history overlapped within a one-mile radius. The stage was set under the Minar-e-Pakistan, the Minaret of Pakistan, the national monument built where Muhammad Ali Jinnah, the leader of the Muslim League, had delivered an address demanding a separate state for Muslims in 1940. Adjacent to the park is the Lahore Fort, an immense construction built by the Mughal emperor Akbar four hundred years earlier. On the grounds of Lahore Fort is a mosque, in the courtyard of which lies the poet Muhammad Iqbal in his grave, a national monument in its own right. Qutbuddin Aibak, one of the earliest Muslim Central Asian kings to rule Lahore, was buried in the Old City eight hundred years before. His grave shares the sinewy streets of Old Lahore with even older temples and countless other layers of history that make this city.

Khan promised that this gathering would be one for the books. Everyone waited to see what kind of crowd would come out to greet him. The last time the Movement for Justice had contested elections, a decade earlier, a year after the War on Terror began, it had won only 1 out of 342 parliamentary seats. In total, it received less than 1 percent of the popular vote. But the last decade had changed Pakistan completely. It had brought war to its people, changed their relationship with Islam and their constitution, and plunged the state into an existential crisis. Now it was time to see if it had also made a dent in the entrenched political machinery of the state.

He took the stage that night of the rally to the deafening roars of hundreds of thousands of people. It was the largest crowd witnessed in the country in many decades. The size was a powerful statement in itself, but it was the makeup of the crowd that was most surprising. The wealthy elite of the city who drove Japanese and German cars bopped their shoulders to the loud and throbbing sound track of bhangra music alongside the farmers, migrant laborers, and others who had been held hostage by the system for decades. They jostled alongside young families with toddlers, the workers of Islamic parties, and the supporters of the Supreme Court chief justice. They had all come together to demand justice and were all chanting "Long live Pakistan!" It was like the perfectly timed monsoon after a terribly hot summer.

Imran Khan promised the crowd that from this very spot the people were "beginning a new Pakistan." He blasted the prevailing order. "What is the greatest problem facing Pakistan?" he asked rhetorically. "Corruption!" It was the root of all the evil, he said, and also the reason "we are today enslaved by America." He swore to bring the "big crocodiles" of the corrupt Pakistani political order to

Hundreds of thousands of people gathered in the walled Old City of Lahore for the rally led by the Movement for Justice in October 2011. (Source: Arif Ali/Getty Images)

justice. No power in the world "will stop this flood," he bellowed at the riled-up crowd. "Whoever stands in its way will be swept away."

America was no silent observer to this. Months earlier, American forces had captured and killed Osama bin Laden at a compound in the northern city of Abbottabad. A CIA contractor had shot and killed two Pakistanis in broad daylight in Lahore weeks before. The politics of the War on Terror played an integral role in shaping this newest experiment in Islam and democracy. America was the neocolonial entity in opposition to which Pakistan could define itself anew. But in Lahore, Khan had left an opening. "O Americans!" he cried out. "I want to give a message to the Americans: When the Movement for Justice comes to power, we will extend friendship to all nations of this

earth. We will befriend you as well. But we will not be enslaved by you!" The crowd erupted.

The people of Pakistan, he said, had been bled dry by the
vicious triad of "police," "local courts," and "*patwaris*," the
land record keepers. He promised to clean the lower courts
by freeing the judiciary from political influence. He promised to "depoliticize the police" by letting people elect their
police chiefs "like they do in America," with sheriffs. And
he promised to "get rid of the *patwari* altogether," replacing them with computers that can keep more accurate land
records and cannot be bribed. Computerized land records,
functioning courts, and elected sheriffs—this was the new vision of Islamic rule in Pakistan, an "Islamic welfare state."

"At critical moments in their history," Muhammad
Iqbal, the poet-philosopher, the dreamer of Muslim nationalism, had told an audience of Muslims in 1930, "it
is Islam that has saved Muslims and not vice versa." The
Muslim nation continued to believe that Islam was the savior. And much like what Iqbal had described in 1930—an
amorphous amalgamation of Islam and the European idea
of nationalism—what Imran Khan described also sounded
like a vision of economic development and social order
that emulated the West but was firmly Islamic in its essence.

Over the next several months, Khan toured Pakistan. He soon became the most popular politician in the
country. He promised to change the land—the way people
lived on it, and even the way they related to it. He promised "revolution." Newspapers and magazines all around
the world ran long news stories about Khan, wondering
whether he would really become the next leader of the

world's only Islamic republic with a nuclear bomb. They debated whether he was truly capable of bringing a revolution to Pakistan. What would it all mean for the rest of the world? Some championed him while others feared him. But it was clear that there was little anyone on the outside could do but to watch and wait.

Khan was hardly the only one gathering such crowds in Pakistan. In the months that followed, other leaders pulled massive crowds in other cities up and down the Indus. They each offered their own formula for Islamic democracy. Some called for elections, others for bloody revolution, and others for revolution through elections. All the while, the violence continued to consume people and places. Was this the beginning of a new Islamic democracy? Or was it the final stage of a long experiment? After Jinnah and Iqbal's two-nation theory, Zulfiqar Bhutto's Islamic Socialism, Zia's System of the Islamic Prophet, and Pervez Musharraf's Enlightened Moderation, the future was uncertain in the laboratory of Islam.

In all likelihood, there were still more successes and more failures to come. This was not the beginning or the end of a story. This was simply another layer in the palace of stories that the nation of Muslims had been building for itself along the Indus for centuries. Khan was only the newest Pakistani leader to promise a mix of Islam and democracy to find the right balance. It was impossible to know how his vision would develop, or if it would ever get a chance to develop at all.

The only thing that anyone knew for certain was that people would continue to live their lives as they always had.

Islam was never about religion in Pakistan anyway. Islam was about the history of people. And millions of ordinary people who have orbited the peripheries of power were choosing to believe once again, because they had no other choice but to believe. Some families would undoubtedly choose to leave, escape the newest political reality; others would remain, unable or unwilling to rip themselves from the soil that had soaked up the blood of generations. And still others might find reasons to return to the land that has been calling them for many years, to be near the place where people are more familiar—each one an architect of his existence, all authors of a nation.

Homecoming

I LANDED IN TOKYO'S NARITA AIRPORT in the last days
of 2011. It was my first time in Japan, and I had come
to meet a woman whom I had fallen for many years ago
in New York. I had met her at a friend's dinner party
in Brooklyn. She wore a pink sweater and I could not
quite place her appearance, so I asked her, "Where are
you from?" Her father is Japanese, she told me, and her
mother is Welsh. She had grown up in Japan before she
moved to the United States for boarding school. I told
her that I was from Pakistan. And later on the inevitable
question came up: "Why is Pakistan such a mess?" I told
her that was a good question, but I steered the conversation to the future. I was hoping to write in New York, I
told her. I wanted to become a journalist, a recorder of
history as it happened. We spoke about Japan too, and
then a friend said something about delicious fish tacos

in Queens. At the end of the night we made plans to go together to find them sometime.

We were speaking one cool evening by the ocean, many years later, about family. And we both agreed: family is the most important thing. So I was here in Tokyo to see her and finally meet her parents. When I arrived at the front door with my suitcase that cold evening, her mother greeted me with a warm hug, and her father, to my surprise, also hugged me. I was in a place as foreign as I had ever been, but the inside of the house felt strangely comfortable. They told me over dinner one evening that they had met in Japan and then lived in a university town in the United States after they got married. I told them that I was born in an American university town, and we were happy at discovering that connection. It was comforting to know that despite our apparent differences we all have stories that overlap. It also makes it easier to see how we all view the world from our own unique places.

Her father was born near the city of Nagano, west of Tokyo, a few months before America dropped the atomic bombs on Hiroshima and Nagasaki. The years after the war were very difficult. Historians estimate that more than two million Japanese died because of that terrible war that lasted many years. Her mother was born to a working-class family from the north of Wales. Some of the worst bombing by the Luftwaffe had ended a year before she was born, but life remained difficult throughout the war. When she had first moved to Japan, she told me, some people mistook her for an American, and she was once refused service by a Japanese restaurant owner in Tokyo. War leaves deep scars, but they eventually heal.

On New Year's Day, we all walked to the nearby temple. It was the second-oldest temple in Japan, built nearly fourteen centuries ago, not long after Muhammad had died in the city of Medina. The long alleyways that led to the temple were lined with stalls selling hot foods and colorful trinkets. It was the year of the dragon, the water dragon, specifically, and striking dragon sculptures were displayed all around. The water dragon indicated a year of new beginnings and mixed blessings. The passageways were packed with people. Some of them were the faithful, while others were simply following tradition, but they had all come together here to celebrate the New Year. The air was a mix of all sorts of tastes, full of sounds that I did not yet recognize. Still, it felt right that I was there, even if I did not share the faith or the tradition.

On our way out, we all lined up at the kiosk by the exit to have our fortunes read. I was handed a long wooden box and I shook out a thin wooden stick from a hole at one end. The number on the stick was then matched to a small white printed scroll. The fortune was written in archaic Japanese, and her father announced it carefully. It was not the best of fortunes, and so I decided to give it another try. This time it turned out better. It was a blessing and a good fortune for the coming year. He was genuinely happy to read it to me. I slipped the good fortune into my pocket to keep, and we tied the other scrolls up on a tree branch as we left. Thousands of other fortunes, some good, some not so good, clung to the branches like cherry blossoms and they rustled in the cool wind. I asked her to be my wife. And we agreed to become family.

Months later, we arrived in Lahore to celebrate our union with the Mufti and Qazi families. The family networks were extensive, and we arranged for everyone to gather for dinner in the bustling and trendy restaurant district. We had been to Pakistan together once before, so we had experienced the quiet rumbling war together already. But a few days before we arrived, the violence hit a terrible new low. All of Pakistan had been stunned with the news of a young girl named Malala Yousafzai. She was fourteen years old and lived in the Swat Valley, where the Taliban had ruled briefly a few years ago. During the short-lived Taliban rule, Malala had written a diary describing daily life under the Taliban. Her diary was published and circulated all over the country, and in the months and years after Taliban rule ended, it was read by many people around the world. A few days before we landed, a young man who claimed to be from the Pakistani Taliban stopped the school bus carrying Malala back home from school, climbed on board, and shot the girl at point-blank range in the head. Incredibly, she survived. As Malala recovered from brain injuries in a hospital in England, the all too predictable deceitful dynamic of war began to rear its ugly head again.

The Taliban, by sending an assassin after her, was hoping to send a signal to the world. "Malala was targeted because of her leading role in preaching secularism and so-called Enlightened Moderation," read a statement released by the Taliban to journalists. It accused her of being an "American spy" and an "enemy of sharia." Faced with common outrage over their inhuman act, the militants released another full statement justifying the attempted assassination with examples from Islamic history and from Muhammad's life. They tried to prove that shooting a little girl was in line with sharia, or the will of Allah. To counter this, fifty prominent muftis in Pakistan issued their own fatwa, blasting the assassination attempt as illegal by any standard of law, especially Islamic law. The man who had attempted the assassination should be tried for attempted murder, they argued.

Not far behind were the conspiracy theories. They always come quickly in a country gripped by fear and paranoia. The assassination attempt on Malala was engineered by "unseen" political forces who wanted to arouse public opinion to escalate the war in Pakistan's northwest, some argued. Others said that she had not been shot at all, that the entire episode was a "drama" scripted by America and "Western forces" to distract from America's brutal aerial war.

President Obama said the attack on Malala was "reprehensible, disgusting, and tragic." The secretary-general of the United Nations, Ban Ki-moon, was "outraged." The perpetrators of the "heinous and cowardly act" must be "swiftly brought to justice," he said. Even the most cowardly and despicable cheerleaders of violence jumped to defend Malala. More sickening than the images of a girl unconscious in a hospital bed from a head wound were the images of political opportunists inside and outside Pakistan who co-opted her misfortune to further their own military and political goals.

In the final analysis, Malala was not simply the victim of the Taliban. Malala was not unduly brainwashed by Enlightened Moderation. Malala was neither secular nor religious. She was not a spy and she was not a hero. Malala was a child. She was another victim of senseless war and of violence. Everyone who fought the war on any side, cheered for war, or pushed for just one more day of violent retribution shared the responsibility for what happened to Malala Yousafzai.

At the dinner in Lahore, I joyously introduced my wife to my family. For a few hours that night the war completely disappeared and was replaced by love. They all embraced her as one of our own. The Muftis and Qazis who had gathered here to celebrate were not the same ones who had come to Saadia and Shahzad's wedding in this city in the middle of another war decades ago. These Muftis and Qazis were mostly my cousins, members of a younger generation, but we all shared some vague notion of history. We were bound together by the same old bloodlines and beliefs.

After some days, we boarded the plane to leave. "Let's go home," she said to me as we held hands in the departure lounge. We were somewhere over the ocean, suspended in the air, relatively free from the forces of land when I felt the need to write. She was fast asleep next to me. I pulled out a pen from my breast pocket and began to sketch our names in calligraphic style on a paper napkin laid out on the tray in front of me. I wrote them close together, next to one another. Then, above each name I wrote the names of our parents. And then I stopped. I had forgotten her grandparents' names. I thought of waking her up to ask her, but instead I just stared at what I had on the napkin already. All our parents were born in the 1940s, in different places across the world, all tied together by the great violence and war of that era. Did I need to go farther back than this? This could be the beginning of the new family tree. This is the beginning of the story that I hope to leave behind.

I began imagining: future generations that come from us will read this family tree. They will see that it begins in war and they will read of the suffering that war brings. They will live in a time when violence will be an abhorrent, unacceptable human urge. They will find it unbelievable that war once existed so commonly between civilized people. They will look back at the crimes of our past and wonder: how could we ever believe in the things we believed in? Maybe they will accept us regardless. We lived in a time when things were different, when people believed in violence out of fear, ignorance, and desperation. They will forgive us, our future generations.

May peace be upon them.

Acknowledgments

This book would have been impossible to complete without the help of my extended family, Qazi and Mufti. I would like to specially thank the following people: Afaq Qazi, for providing me with many opportunities to examine the original copy of the family tree and for paving the way on more reporting trails than I could possibly remember; Asdaq Qazi for access to some valuable family history; Taimur Afaq, for driving me around Lahore and all over the Punjab, sometimes through the most horrible traffic, always with great eagerness and excitement; Tasneem Yusuf, for her incredible hospitality in Chak 84/12-L. Some valuable and enlightening family documents and photographs were passed on to me by Raja Farook and the late Qazi Iqbal Hussain Faruqi.

Ian Barrow at Middlebury College first took me on a journey into the murky history of South Asia, as we traveled together on a fellowship from the American Institute of Bangladesh Studies. The Fulbright program allowed me to spend a year in India, which was the best way to understand the partition of South Asia. Bill McKibben and Christopher Shaw at the Middlebury Fellowships in Environmental Journalism were extremely generous in their support, which allowed me to travel and spend time studying the land- and water-management systems of the Punjab. They, along with the crew in Bread Loaf and Esalen, helped me sort through my material upon my return. The dean's office at the University of Richmond also supported a trip to Pakistan to research parts of this book.

Judith Gurewich brought a vigor and passion to this project that I could never have dreamed of from an editor—her faith in this book kept me going through the most arduous of passages. Sulay Hernandez was the perfect reader of my work and her essential feedback helped carry this project through to the end. Larry Weissman, my agent, was there for me at important times, not the least of which was when he first decided to take a gamble on an adventurous proposal. Totoro was always eager to help by typing up passages on the keyboard with his paws whenever I left the office for more than a brief moment.

This book would not have been were it not for my parents' unending love. I have no words to describe the debt I owe to them—they, after all, taught me to see for myself. My brother Shehryar's creative energy is contagious and for that I am thankful. My sister, Afia, has always pushed me to look beyond the obvious, and she also urged me to think of the children. My wife, Mimi, first saw this book when it was nothing more than an elaborate scrawl on a whiteboard pinned to a wall in the smallest apartment in Brooklyn. Since then, she has been by my side, supporting me every moment as I constructed this story from the ground up. I am forever thankful to her.

Principal Figures

BENAZIR BHUTTO: The daughter of Zulfiqar Bhutto who led the Pakistan People's Party after her father's death and was prime minister of Pakistan from 1988 to 1990 and again from 1993 to 1996.

ZULFIQAR BHUTTO: The founder of the Pakistan People's Party and the father of Benazir Bhutto.

IFTIKHAR CHAUDHRY: The chief justice of the Supreme Court of Pakistan from 2007 to 2013.

ABDUL AZIZ GHAZI: The imam of the Red Mosque; son of Abdullah and brother of Abdul Rashid.

ABDUL RASHID GHAZI: The coleader and principal spokesman for the Red Mosque in Islamabad; son of Abdullah and brother of Abdul Aziz.

ABDULLAH GHAZI: The first imam and leader of the Red Mosque.

MUHAMMAD IQBAL: The poet-philosopher who first articulated the idea of a separate state for the nation of Muslims in South Asia.

MUHAMMAD ALI JINNAH: The founding father of Pakistan; as the president of the Muslim League, he was a leader of the movement for independence from British colonial rule in the subcontinent.

AYUB KHAN: The first military leader to take the reins of power in Pakistan, he ruled as president from 1958 to 1969.

IMRAN KHAN: The former captain of Pakistan's national cricket side; the founder of the Pakistan Tehreek-e-Insaf (Pakistan Movement for Justice).

SYED AHMAD KHAN: The founder of the Aligarh Muslim University, created in 1875 to educate Muslims living under British colonial rule through a course of study that infused Western philosophy and sciences with traditional Islamic education.

ABUL ALA MAUDUDI: The founder of the Jamaat-e-Islami, the largest and oldest Islamic political party operating in Pakistan.

PERVEZ MUSHARRAF: Through a military coup in 1999, he became the last Pakistani general to take power, ruling first as chief executive and then as president until 2008.

MUHAMMAD QASIM NANOTVI: The founder of Darul Uloom, a seminary established in 1866 in the town of Deoband in present-day northern India. The theological tradition that took root in Deoband was hostile to colonial rule in South Asia, and later spread across the region. Today it is the inspiration for some anti-Western Islamic movements.

NAWAZ SHARIF: The founder of the Pakistan Muslim League and Benazir Bhutto's main political rival through the late 1980s and much of the 1990s.

ZIA-UL-HAQ: Pakistan's second military ruler who ruled as president from 1978 to 1988.